World Culture

To Jennifer and Lisbeth

World Culture

Origins and Consequences

Frank J. Lechner and John Boli

Blackwell
Publishing

BLACKWELL PUBLISHING
350 Main Street, Malden, MA 02148-5020, USA
9600 Garsington Road, Oxford OX4 2DQ, UK
550 Swanston Street, Carlton, Victoria 3053, Australia

First published 2005 by Blackwell Publishing Ltd

1   2005

Library of Congress Cataloging-in-Publication Data

Lechner, Frank.
    World culture : origins and consequences / Frank J. Lechner and John Boli.
       p.   cm.
    Includes bibliographical references and index.
    ISBN 0-631-22676-1 (hardback : alk. paper) – ISBN 0-631-22677-X (pbk. :
alk. paper)   1. Culture. I. Boli, John, 1948– II. Title.

    HM621.L43 2005
    306–dc22

                                                              2004023326

ISBN-13: 978-0-631-22676-5 (hardback : alk. paper) – ISBN-13: 0-631-22677-2
(pbk. : alk. paper)

A catalogue record for this title is available from the British Library.

Set in 10 on 13 pt Sabon
by SNP Best-set Typesetter Ltd, Hong Kong
Printed and bound in the United Kingdom
by TJ International, Padstow, Cornwall

The publisher's policy is to use permanent paper from mills that operate a sustainable
forestry policy, and which has been manufactured from pulp processed using acid-free and
elementary chlorine-free practices. Furthermore, the publisher ensures that the text paper
and cover board used have met acceptable environmental accreditation standards.

For further information on
Blackwell Publishing, visit our website:
www.blackwellpublishing.com

Contents

Tables

Acknowledgments

Many colleagues contributed to this book with ideas, comments, and conversations. We especially want to thank Terry Boswell, John Meyer, Roland Robertson, Jan Aart Scholte, and a Blackwell reviewer.

We are also grateful for the excellent assistance of many talented graduate students. Rob Constantine, Michael Elliott, Velina Petrova, and Anna Rubtsova helped to make this a better book. We thank the graduate students in our courses on globalization, social change, and sociological theory for helping us push our thinking forward.

Throughout this project, Ken Provencher at Blackwell Publishing provided his strong support and good judgment. It was a pleasure to work with him.

We dedicate this book to our wives, Jennifer Webster and Lisbeth Boli, with deepest thanks for their love and support.

Abbreviations

ECOSOC	Economic and Social Council
FAO	Food and Agriculture Organization
ICC	International Criminal Court
ICGC	International Central Gospel Church
IGO	intergovernmental organization
IMF	International Monetary Fund
INGO	international nongovernmental organization
IOC	International Olympic Committee
ISO	International Organization for Standardization
ITU	International Telecommunication Union
MNCs	multinational companies
NAFTA	North American Free Trade Agreement
SWIFT	Society for Worldwide Interbank Financial Telecommunication
TNCs	transnational corporations
UNAIDS	Joint United Nations Programme on HIV/AIDS
UNCED	United Nations Conference on Environment and Development
UNCHE	United Nations Conference on the Human Environment
UNCTAD	United Nations Conference on Trade and Development
WIPO	World Intellectual Property Organization
WSF	World Social Forum
WTO	World Trade Organization

Chapter 1

Introduction: The Olympic Games and the Meaning of World Culture

The Olympic Games and World Culture

The first modern Olympiad, held in Athens in 1896, hardly lived up to the grand vision of its organizers. Though they seemed an "indescribable spectacle" to some participants, those Games were a decidedly modest affair (MacAloon 1981: Ch. 7). Several dozen athletes from just a few countries competed in events, both classical and newfangled, before a Greek audience whose enthusiasm found no resonance abroad. The American delegation, one of the largest, consisted of college athletes from Princeton and Harvard and arrived barely in time, not knowing that Greece followed the Julian rather than the Gregorian calendar. The opening and closing ceremonies derived some dignity from the participation of King George of Greece, who had supported staging the event for political reasons, but they involved no further pageantry. The winner in discus throwing had not practiced much (he was an English tourist who had signed up for tennis on the spur of the moment) and the famed winner of the marathon was a peasant rather than a trained athlete – amateurs all, in more than one sense. Newspaper coverage was limited – a few articles in major French and English newspapers, a small number of pieces in the *New York Times* – and far less prominent than that for domestic events. Though satisfied that his brainchild had come to life, even Baron Pierre de Coubertin, the moving force behind the "restoration" of the Olympic Games, appears to have felt some disappointment, not least because the Greeks seemed eager to turn his vision of an international sports festival into a Greek event, always to be held on Greek soil (ibid.: 241ff.). When the Games were over, the Olympic movement's future was still in doubt. Subsequent Olympiads at Paris and St. Louis, disorganized appendages to the world expositions held in those cities, did little to solidify its fortunes. And yet, from these inauspicious beginnings, the Olympics grew to become a grand spectacle, the largest regularly staged event in the world (Rothenbuhler 1989).

Both the surprising success of the Olympic Games as a quintessential global event and their actual content as ritual performance tell us much about world culture. Claiming the attention of a global audience, the Games have helped to foster a shared awareness of living in one world society. Run according to now-familiar rules, they show how people around the globe increasingly organize their common life on the basis of shared knowledge and principles. As the focus of athletic ambition for individuals and nations alike, they express widely shared values. The experience of both participants and audience shows how the world now has a repertoire of symbolic forms that enable, in fact impel, people to become conscious of the world as a single place and act in accordance with that consciousness. In this sense, the Olympic Games embody world culture. To some, that may sound unduly grandiose. After all, critics have derided the Games as the plaything of right-wing aristocrats, an arena for the mindless pursuit of national glory, and a hypocritical display of crass commercialism. Writing in Atlanta, the city that hosted the 1996 Olympics to distinctly mixed reviews, we sympathize with such interpretations. Yet as an event and institution embodying a certain kind of global consciousness, knowledge, and values, the Olympic Games also illustrate important features of world culture.

Although it is risky to interpret the late nineteenth-century founding of the modern Olympics with the benefit of hindsight, that history does have some bearing on the movement's later success as a global event. When Pierre de Coubertin first conceived of the idea of reviving the Olympic Games, he sought support among his friends in aristocratic circles. Members of an elite that cultivated ties across national boundaries, not beholden to any government, they endorsed his plans and several served as members of the fledgling International Olympic Committee (IOC). Not all senior figures in the early movement were aristocrats, to be sure, but the aristocrats' role left its imprint. From the beginning, the IOC would be run as a secretive, independent organization, professedly above partisanship of any sort, which capitalized on the connections of its elite leadership. While this may now seem the quaint legacy of a world long lost, in some respects the early IOC was very much a modern creation. It was, in fact, only one of many voluntary international organizations devoted to a humanitarian vision founded in the late nineteenth century. Its classic predecessor, of course, is the International Committee of the Red Cross, but several hundred other organizations had become active as well. Coubertin's initiative, modest though its initial accomplishments were, was part of a welter of similar activities in numerous fields, on both sides of the Atlantic, in which private citizens articulated high-minded ideals – in other words, it contributed to "idealistic internationalism" (Hoberman 1995). The Olympics thus represent movements that, important in their own right, together also set a precedent for their flourishing after the Second World War.

Coubertin envisioned the Games as distinctly international events. They would be staged in different countries every four years; they would bring together athletes from many different nations. In recognizing the importance of national loyalties and requiring that athletes represent nations – another fateful legacy of the early days – Coubertin's thinking obviously reflected the realities of the age. But he was no nationalist. Even before working on the Olympic revival, he had opposed French sports organizations devoted mainly to French glory. Notwithstanding his own experience, he also did not think of himself as a cosmopolitan. What the world needed, he thought, was not the cosmopolitanism of those who have no country, but rather the internationalism of "those who love their country above all, who seek to draw to it the friendship of foreigners by professing for the countries of those foreigners an intelligent and enlightened sympathy" (quoted in MacAloon 1981: 265–6). Accordingly, the Games would promote encounters in which, as Coubertin's biographer summarizes it, "real cultural differences were discovered and celebrated," leading foreigners to "true experiences of common humanity" (ibid.: 267). Apart from their Greek heritage, the Olympics would favor no country or culture but remain neutral, devoted only to their own cause, a secular religion capable of binding humanity as a whole. In this way, the Games would also aid the cause of peace among nations. The Olympics, then, arose as a hopeful expression of "pan-human" unity at a time when the nation-state seemed inexorably on the rise (ibid.: 142). Balancing national sentiment against universal aspiration, the Olympic vision thus displayed a close affinity with the chief Western ideological currents of its day. The essential "contest" in the constitution of the Olympics (Hoberman 1995: 15) still expresses larger cultural forces that swirl around it.

This vision was not just an exercise in political philosophy; it also enshrined sports as moral activity, amateur athleticism as virtue. Coubertin had long been interested in Thomas Arnold's use of sports as part of moral education in his public school at Rugby. In such English schools, Coubertin thought, sports helps to form character and devotion to the public good. Physical activity produces "a happy equilibrium in the moral domain"; in sport, liberty "is complete" and courage exalted; it aids morality by "pacifying the senses and calming the imagination" (MacAloon 1981: 81).

Considering athletics essential to overall intellectual development, he had actively promoted physical education in France. The Olympics were Coubertin's effort to elevate his moral vision of the athlete to a higher level. While this particular vision did not command any great consensus at the time, Coubertin did tap into the rapidly expanding interest in organized sports in Europe and America. The rules of several games were being worked out, contests proliferated, participation across social classes increased, and sports performances were beginning to find an audience. International organizations were established for 16 sports before the First World War, including the International Skating Union in 1892 and football's FIFA in 1904 (Van Bottenburg 2001: 5). Prized in most sports was masculine physical prowess displayed through athletic competition. With his Olympic project, Coubertin thus helped to channel an emerging transnational trend. Over time, it fostered, and in turn benefited from, the continuing diffusion of sports as a rationally organized, systematically pursued activity, which ultimately crystallized into a "global sporting system" (ibid.: 2, Ch. 6).

The Olympics' nineteenth-century movement heritage, their tension-ridden version of internationalism, and their role in the rationalization of one segment of popular culture all connect the Games to the larger story of world culture we tell in this book. World culture as we know it today took organized form in the nineteenth century and nongovernmental organizations contributed much to it. World culture, as we stress throughout this book, is not all of a piece, but rather shot through with tension and contradiction, notably between forms of particularism and universalism. World culture has become ever more rationalized, in part the work of specialists running specialized institutions according to formal rules. The Olympics are nicely illustrative in these respects, but without their enormous expansion in scale and reach they would hardly justify the attention we have given to their origins. That expansion took several forms.

The Games themselves became vastly more elaborate. At the very first Olympiad, events like swimming and tennis were already added to the ancient disciplines it was presumed to revive. Over time, from the early introduction of judo to the later inclusion of beach volleyball and table tennis, more and more sports became part of the Games. Inclusion in the Olympics became the goal of many international sports communities, for it constituted a stamp of global acceptance. To qualify, sports had to satisfy IOC demands, leading to similarity in the way they were organized. At a minimum, every self-respecting sport needed its own international organization. At the same time, the sheer diversity of sports made the Games a much more varied spectacle. Thus, while sports were being standardized, the Olympics were also allowing different forms to flourish on a global stage.

The Games also expanded dramatically in size. After the Second World War, they attracted representatives from both the communist bloc and newly independent countries, ultimately making the Olympics a globally inclusive event; in parallel, new countries also gained representation on the IOC board (Guttmann 1984: Ch. 14). In principle, all countries were entitled to participate, to compete on an equal basis in the same arena. As the world map was covered by independent nation-states, so were the Olympic playing fields. However, the Games hardly reflected a world in which everyone agreed on the greater common good. The Soviet Union challenged IOC precedent by appointing its own representatives; African governments challenged both South African and Rhodesian participation; Indonesia threatened to organize alternative games; Israel's participation came under fire from Islamic countries. Real-world fissures greatly disturbed the Elysian visions of Lausanne. Nor were participants die-hard believers in Coubertin's internationalist vision. As the games globalized, the desire of countries to demonstrate national greatness increased as well. Medal counts counted. Otherwise modestly endowed countries like East Germany and Cuba made it a point to shine at the Games. While in its rules and ritual the Olympics enshrined the formal equality of nations, they thus also provided a forum for ideological contest and national self-elevation.

The most dramatic transformation of the Olympics occurred in the 1960s when the Games became a television event, a mass spectacle for a growing global audience. From flickering images for a primarily Western public, they grew to become a slickly produced package broadcast around the world. Only a few events, such as the World Cup football finals, could match the simultaneous, shared interest in the same event by billions of people that marked the Olympics as a global festival (Tomlinson 1996). In this regard, the Olympics uniquely demonstrated the kind of integration made possible by new advances in communication and transportation. For a few weeks every four years, the Summer Games produced an undeniable common global awareness. This increased interest was the honey that attracted the corporate bears. Abetted by the IOC, corporations sought to exploit commercial opportunities by serving as sponsors. American commercial television became the prime source of funding. The Games turned into a billboard, one giant kaleidoscope of advertisements. While the Games at least tried to keep their distance from politics, about capitalism they were never neutral.

However, their message is not only commercial. With the advent of television, organizing countries also gained a stage on which they could display themselves. The opening ceremonies, in particular, gradually turned into densely symbolic performances. From the "Spielbergian spell" cast by the Hollywood version of American history in Los Angeles in 1984, to the uplifting narrative of national revival, reconciliation, and global unity in Seoul in 1988, to the linking of Catalan and Spanish themes to a novel interpretation of Greek history in Barcelona in 1992, to the projection of the "New South" in Atlanta in 1996, to the multicultural recognition of aboriginal identity in Sydney in 2000, and the Athens 2004 emphasis on the Greek origins of the Games – these ceremonies each "arrogated" universal Olympic ideals in the context of particular histories and cultures, simultaneously celebrating the local and the global (Tomlinson 1996: 590ff.; the official Athens theme was "Celebrating Humanity"). As ritual, they both express and contain the tensions inherent in the Games themselves, tensions that are also intrinsic features of contemporary world culture.

In this way, the Olympics begin to tell our story of world culture – the culture of world society, comprising norms and knowledge shared across state boundaries, rooted in nineteenth-century Western culture but since globalized, promoted by nongovernmental organizations as well as for-profit corporations, intimately tied to the rationalization of institutions, enacted on particular occasions that generate global awareness, carried by the infrastructure of world society, spurred by market forces, riven by tension and contradiction, and expressed in the multiple ways particular groups relate to universal ideals.

To complement the example of the Olympics this chapter first describes other ways in which world culture is embedded in numerous organizations and activities, including many that are not ostensibly global in scope. We then explain how we think about culture generally and how we distinguish "world" culture from other kinds. Previewing an important theme in this book, we stress that many elements of world culture are contested. We conclude with a summary of the case we want to make and an outline of the chapters to come.

Culture in World Society

Even if the Olympics are a richly symbolic event, one could argue that they are exceptional rather than representative. A now biennial television event comprising a few weeks of entertaining competition hardly concerns most people most of the time. Does this mean that the world culture it expresses is some rarefied sphere floating above the "real world"? We argue that it is not. Many ordinary activities and institutions are saturated with it. In fact, all the things that make the world one – its infrastructure, economy, state system, law, and global problems – are deeply "cultural."

Infrastructure

For the experienced traveler, flying across oceans has become a mundane routine. That very routine represents a form of common knowledge among the wealthier classes of the world. They know all too well how to order a ticket, stand in line, find their way around airports, and go through customs. They know how to squeeze their bodies into seats and stay put for hours. As international travelers, they share a slice of world culture, a set of shared assumptions and expectations. Mistaking the reality of air transportation for a species of cosmopolitanism, they might even perceive themselves as a cultural vanguard. In the air, the American tourist, Japanese executive, and African official have more in common with each other than with their countrymen. Their cultural experience is not limited to the motions of traveling itself (cf. Tomlinson 1999: 4ff.; Iyer 2000). Crossing borders, they encounter far-flung cultures. As people move, cultures mix. At least for a privileged elite, the culture of the neighborhood may lose its appeal by comparison with the pleasures of other places. Air travel thus intensifies the "deterritorialization" many have ascribed to social life in the era of globalization (Scholte 2000). Floating routinely at 30,000 feet produces a distinct view of the world.

We would not want to deny the cultural effects of air travel or deflate its cosmopolitan potential, but our own take on it is slightly different. The very fabric of the civil aviation system is part of world culture. In less than a century, scientists and engineers have figured out how to build durable long-distance airplanes, how to operate them safely and enable them to communicate. Executives have found ways to run airlines and set schedules more or less reliably. Public officials have devised ways of monitoring safety and controlling traffic. While a portion of the airline industry serves only a domestic market, especially in the United States, much of it concentrates on international travel. The system that makes even domestic travel possible depends on close coordination of policies and procedures across national boundaries. The relevant standards, some set by governmental but many by private-sector groups, apply universally. A country or airline wishing to become part of the system is required to abide by strict norms. This is not to suggest that aviation is a cozy business: competition is stiff, and many countries deviate from the norm. However, this system does embody a conception of the world as a single place, a conception shared by engineers, pilots, officials, and executives. It is based on a vast foundation of universal, technical knowledge, authoritatively produced by experts. It functions thanks to commonly accepted norms, developed by experts and enforced by state and other authorities. Among the public at large, it commands enormous trust in the rational enterprise of moving millions of people across thousands of miles. With only slight exaggeration, we can therefore say that the infrastructure of civil aviation is an intricate world-cultural system, a highly systematized world-view given material form in a specialized, rule-bound global institution.

Economy

At the end of the twentieth century, the world economy seemed to reach a new level of integration. More than a trillion dollars' worth of currency changed hands in foreign exchange markets every day; stock markets attracted capital from around the globe; commodities were produced in ever-widening networks; newly industrializing countries sought their fortunes in international trade. Workers, companies, and countries became exposed to new competition. Affluent consumers became accustomed to a steady supply of cheap goods from foreign sources. As the web of integration tightened, the liabilities of interdependence increased as well: Western banks absorbed losses from loans to emerging markets; poor people in debtor countries particularly felt the sting of market discipline. After the end of the Cold War, the business of the world was business. Globalization, in the new conventional wisdom, meant making the world safe for capitalist free markets. As observers on the left and the right agreed, capitalism had taken over. The driving force in this system was the relentless pursuit of profit in the market. As the unintended consequence of millions of self-interested decisions by market players, the world was becoming a single economic system.

Yet this economic integration, real enough in its consequences, hardly was an eruption of blind forces. For many years, some academics and politicians in Britain and the USA had argued for the opening up of markets and a reduction in government's role – in other words, for global liberalization

(Yergin and Stanislaw 1998). As the role of international organizations like the IMF (International Monetary Fund) and the World Bank expanded to promote free markets and countries' stable growth, they operated under what came to be called the "Washington Consensus" about what constituted sensible goals and policies. However, this consensus only expressed in the form of explicit policy an increasingly shared commitment to markets as vehicles of progress, to economic competition as essential to realizing individual freedom, to GDP (gross domestic product) growth as a marker of collective value. Complementing such ideological scaffolding of capitalism, labeled "neoliberalism" by skeptical observers (see Chapter 7), was the expansion of the knowledge and categories that make a global economy run. Internationally active enterprises were to be organized in corporate form; their success had to judged by rational accounting methods; transactions depended on common understanding of contractual obligations; for the purpose of rational enterprise, labor had to be treated as a factor of production.

As in the case of global infrastructure, then, the very fabric of the global economy is part and parcel of world culture. Economic integration is more than a material juggernaut. It is, at least in part, the realization of ideas. Free markets themselves, after all, are a set of ideas, as Karl Polanyi showed in discussing an earlier period of globalizing fervor (Polanyi 1985). To seek material advancement through economic activity freed from social constraint, to encourage endless technical progress for the sake of competitive advantage, to pit workers and countries against each other in ceaseless battle, all that is part of a distinctive world-view. By the end of the twentieth century, that view had become second nature to many people around the globe. To many business people, public officials, and academics, the world-view also had become socially real: it governed a single system operating under a single set of rules. What made the system work was the very fact that, at least in their international dealings, the main players could rely on common knowledge about what constituted rational economic activity. The Washington Consensus that shaped the actions of international organizations was only one version of this larger consensus (Stiglitz 2002: 16, 53). The world economy, too, had become a world-cultural system.

Governance

By the end of the twentieth century, the United Nations (UN) had close to two hundred members. Although control over some territories was still in dispute, with the end of colonialism virtually all the world was fully governed by independent nation-states. According to some optimists, economic integration would now tie states together more intimately. They would have to pursue their interests in peaceful ways: "no two countries with a McDonald's desired to go to war with each other," as one popular version of this argument had it (Friedman 1999: Ch. 12). Others argued that new forms of governance, for example through the UN itself, would bind states together as part of a larger whole. In 1990, Iraq confounded those expectations by invading Kuwait, claiming it as its rightful possession. Concerned about Iraq's control of oil supplies and the power imbalance in the region, an international coalition beat back Saddam Hussein's forces, thus vindicating Kuwait's integrity as a state. Though the coalition acted under UN authority, the Gulf War was an exercise in hard-headed realism on all sides. It showed that states were still the prime repositories of force in the world. According to the most common form of realism, still conventional wisdom among statesmen and most academics, states are rational actors pursuing their security and power interests to the best of their ability in a world without shared norms or central authority (Waltz 1979). Order comes about through coalitions and self-help, through successful deterrence or victory in war. But in world politics nothing is really secure: underneath a veneer of civilized agreement, the war of all against all continues. What matters in that war, hot or cold, is the command of people, tanks, and missiles, as the Gulf War seemed to confirm. The world of the 1990s had yet to shed the legacy of 1648, when the Treaty of Westphalia affirmed the principle of state sovereignty among self-interested war-making states.

Once again, we accept the notion that states have interests, pursue power, and collide on occasion. But what does it mean to say that Kuwait, Namibia, and China are all "states"? Where do their interests come from, and what entitles them to pursue power as they see fit? Why should the world be anarchic in the first place? For all the hardware they have at their command, for all the devastation they can cause, states are the institutional form of an idea, namely that each part of the earth should be ruled exclusively by a single government that acts on behalf of "its" people in exercising sovereignty. However impregnable a state may seem, it exists by the grace of mutual recognition, its authority conferred by the system in which it operates. Like capitalism, enmity and political interdependence are cultural forms (Wendt 1999: 136). What states want is not something they can make up by themselves; rather, what they want depends on the range of interests their shared knowledge defines as appropriate and worth pursu-

ing (ibid.: 372). The state system, therefore, embodies a common understanding across states that they do indeed constitute a single system. Its
apparent anarchy reflects underlying common knowledge of what it takes
to be a state. This anarchy is not a condition in which "anything goes";
instead, state behavior is constrained by many shared norms, though of
course some of these have been observed very imperfectly by the likes of
Saddam Hussein, the former dictator of Iraq. As we will show in a later
chapter, global governance is by no means limited to the actions of states.
Here we only illustrate the point that the legacy of 1648 is also a cultural
one, since this dimension of world politics constitutes a world-cultural
system in its own right.

Law

In the spring of 2001, a Belgian court convicted four Rwandans, two nuns
among them, for their role in the genocide against the Tutsis. UN war crimes
tribunals for the former Yugoslavia and Rwanda had already sentenced
many others. People guilty of genocide or crimes against humanity, it
seemed, were now being held accountable under international law. Heart-
ening as those convictions might appear, the law obviously reached only a
few instances of egregious cruelty. No similar acts in Chechnya, Liberia, or
Afghanistan had yet been punished. The enforcement of international law
was still a matter of political convenience. If major powers supported legal
action, it would happen; if not, international law remained toothless doctrine. Thus realism was vindicated after all.

Or was it? The war crimes prosecutions, however selective, are only the
tip of a moving iceberg. International law already encompasses much more
than the most dramatic violations of the Yugoslav and Rwandan cases.
Business transactions are governed by rules – pertaining to contracts, insurance, and the like – that are understood across the globe. The dealings of
states are often based on treaties and conventions that have binding force.
Numerous tribunals are engaged in settling disputes. The International
Criminal Court, discussed in Chapter 10, is designed to be a permanent
body charged with pursuing crimes against humanity, war crimes, and genocide. Without claiming that international law functions as coherently and
effectively as established municipal systems, it is fair to say that at the
beginning of the twenty-first century, a new kind of "world law" is growing
(Berman 1995). This world law is rooted in the realization of relevant
judges, lawyers, and officials that there is one world, the problems of which

require the impartial application of one set of rules. It comprises expanding doctrines of contract, state responsibility, and human rights. It applies to many actors besides states as parties to be held accountable. As a systematic body of rules and principles, implemented by an ever-expanding set of institutions, world law is growing into a single tradition enveloping the globe – a part of world culture.

Global problems

In 2001, the world observed the twentieth anniversary of the discovery of HIV/AIDS as a new disease. Experts described the course of the disease in detail, scientists reviewed progress in research, reporters conveyed the hardships experienced across Africa, and activists advocated new policies on drug pricing and distribution. The UN Secretary-General called for a multi-billion-dollar global effort to combat the disease. Since the early 1980s, that effort had already greatly intensified. The expanded scope of HIV/AIDS research and drug production, combined with the political attention and organizational resources it had attracted, made the disease the object of a global campaign. Obviously, much was at stake in that campaign: without a sustained effort, many Third World countries risked losing a substantial portion of their younger generations.

The campaign paralleled similar efforts to deal with other global problems by transnational means. It was remarkable in many ways. In less than 20 years, consensus emerged among experts, officials, and indeed a large part of the public that HIV/AIDS constituted a "pandemic," a plague that involved the whole world and affected the whole world. Both in basic research and in public health studies, experts compiled a substantial body of common knowledge about origins, transmission, and possible treatments. Around HIV/AIDS grew a community of patients and advocates turning the disease into an object of global moral concern. They appealed to the human rights of patients as individual persons entitled to the caring concern of the world community. They defined the obligations of states and companies to people and principles that transcended their own interests. Once it was defined as an object of global concern, HIV/AIDS triggered substantial efforts by all kinds of international organizations, from UNAIDS (the Joint United Nations Programme on HIV/AIDS) and the World Health Organization to Doctors Without Borders and the International HIV/AIDS Alliance. In the way it dramatizes the oneness of the world, draws on authoritative science, and expands the scope of common moral concern, the global HIV/AIDS campaign is thus also a world-cultural project.

Enacting World Culture

World culture is embodied in extraordinary events like the Olympic Games and it is at work in travel, commerce, conflict, and research. However, its influence goes deeper than these examples convey. World culture also shapes all kinds of ordinary activities that do not have any ostensible global focus. Analyzing one such activity in some detail further helps to clarify what we mean by world culture.

Consider a local chess club in a small town, anywhere in the world. The players abide by global rules governing the play of the game. These rules are formally overseen by the World Chess Federation (WCF), the authoritative chess body at the global level. The chess enthusiasts study the play of international grand masters who have achieved global recognition through major tournaments and high placement in the world chess rankings, which are generated by the WCF. For the most part, local players are only "enactors" of world (chess) culture: they conform to rules coming from the global arena, they learn from external sources which master players (past and present) are to be admired and which masterful books on strategy and tactics are to be purchased, they follow tournaments in distant places they have never seen, and they read newspaper chess columns by world-famous players whose hands they will never shake. Few and far between are the local players of unusual ability and feel for the game who make even a single contribution to the core of what might be called the world chess subculture – the game as such – but some do, by making brilliant plays and winning striking victories that boost them above the local and national levels into the rarified atmosphere of world chess.

However, the game of chess as such is not the sum total of the subculture of world chess. The subculture also includes principles, norms, and models, often informal, about such matters as how to run a chess club, how to communicate about chess, proper and improper ways to approach master players, and so on. For example, the global model of a chess club points organizers to setting up a voluntary, nonexclusive, democratic organization. Anyone can be a member, all members are expected to help with the club's activities, officers (if any) are chosen by one-member, one-vote elections, and club finances and decision making are open matters. Information is to be freely shared, events are to be announced well in advance and made known to all of the members, and so on. Thus, the organizational model enacted by chess clubs tends to be fairly standardized globally; a chess player from one locale is likely to find many similarities between his club and others he might visit on, say, a world chess tour. Notable variations may occur; for example, some clubs may exclude women or particular ethnic groups. The standardized model is not wholly determinative in this respect.

Obviously, the non-chess dimensions of the culture defining and shaping chess clubs around the world are not peculiar to chess. World culture supplies formal and informal rules about such dimensions for a plethora of global subcultures, most of them overseen by one – or, in some cases, two or several – peak global organizations, usually international nongovernmental organizations (INGOs). Members of the subculture comply with the rules, for the most part willingly, because they accord with deeper principles of world culture that make these rules appear fair, reasonable, sensible, even natural. That a chess club should be nonexclusive accords with the principle of equal treatment of all, that is, nondiscrimination – and what could be more sensible and fair than that anyone who is interested in chess should be welcome to play? That a bunch of eager amateurs should not swarm about a grand master demanding autographs and advice while he is in the midst of a championship match accords not only with a basic principle of chess – a calm, quiet atmosphere is crucial for the concentrated thought required to make good moves – but also with the principle of respect for the integrity and dignity of the individual, indeed, all individuals. Thus, a complex set of elements of world culture, some of great generality that apply to many social arenas, others that apply to a number of chess-like activities, and still others that are specific to chess as such, constitute the global chess subculture. Many are implicit, understood, or taken for granted, while others are explicitly expressed in the formal rules of the game, in the constitution of the World Chess Federation, in the bylaws of the local chess club, and so on.

The example thus far illustrates the constitutive and directive capacity of world (chess) (sub-)culture. Also important is world culture's generative power, for it helps account for the dynamic aspects of global development. Because the global model of the "chess club" is widely known, it is easy for chess enthusiasts to start a club and begin organizing competitions. In this way, the world chess subculture fosters new organizations tied into global structures. Because the World Chess Federation maintains systematic rankings of world-class players, with corresponding rankings by national chess organizations, strong amateurs gain motivation to improve their play and, in some cases, eventually become innovative contributors to the game. Indeed, the structure of global chess makes innovation and evolution inevitable, since it is built around competition, intensive study, and the rapid dissemination of information about new openings, surprising defense strategies, twists on classic lines of attack, and so on.

As the chess example illustrates, most world-culture doing is enactment – individuals and organizations adopt and implement the rules, norms, and principles of global chess on a largely wholesale basis. Local variations and departures from standard models occur, in response to local circumstances and conditions, but innovation is limited and often even regretted. In this respect, world culture is like culture at any other level. Culture provides the cognitive framework by which we understand the world and orient ourselves to it. It also provides a huge amount of cognitive detail that is interpreted as meaningful by those who enact it, and it is this cognitive detail that makes it possible to manage everyday reality. We inevitably take this cognitive detail for granted; it is the very definition of reality that is provided for us by culture. If we did not treat it as natural and normal, we would find ourselves at every moment crushed by the immense load of puzzlement and confusion that would confront us in the dense social milieu in which we live.

Of course, enactment is also constructive, i.e., an indicator of "agency," but only in the limited sense that it tautologically reproduces the culture being enacted. It makes sense to reserve the notion of cultural construction for the development or propagation of cultural innovation (or cultural revival, which is rather common), that is, for departures from institutionalized rules, models, and principles. However, this form of construction or agency can occur only when actors are firmly anchored in the solid bedrock of cultural enactment. The full implications of this central feature of culture for the actors who enact, reproduce, and occasionally construct world culture will emerge in later chapters.

Thinking about Culture

In analyzing world culture, we apply a particular way of thinking about culture more generally. Since our main purpose is to show the strength of this way of thinking by example, we refrain from extended conceptual discussion. For the sake of clarity, though without attempting an overly restrictive formal definition, we briefly want to explicate the way we use the concept of "culture." Building on several sociological traditions that were famously brought together in the social-constructionist analysis of Berger and Luckmann (1966), we think of culture as socially shared symbolic and meaning systems that become embedded in objects, organizations, and people yet also exceed what particular individuals can grasp and accumulate in an increasingly systematic fashion.

Culture is often discussed as if it were essentially a complex set of abstractions. It refers to conceptions of the nature of things, principles of social organization, norms regarding proper behavior, patterned "habits" or "folkways," and similar ideas. All of these are noticeably abstract and general. Culture is thus treated like a kind of disembodied symbolism or world-view that floats freely above the mundane details of everyday life. This tendency to speak of culture as free-floating is especially pronounced when world culture is at issue, not least because the "globality" of world culture is itself considered a high-order abstraction.

A dual misunderstanding is at work here. On the one hand, regardless of the level of reality under discussion, be it "local," "national," or global, culture is always and inevitably abstract. Culture operates in and through language, whether it is guiding interaction in routine, face-to-face encounters (e.g., friends sharing coffee and gossiping about indiscretions by their co-workers) or setting the framework for the grandest global phenomena (e.g., capitalist forces impelling the IMF to impose draconian structural adjustment programs on debt-ridden states). But language is inherently abstract. For example, "friend" is a highly general category of broad applicability that can refer to innumerable past or potential instances, and any moderately competent user of a language can correctly apply this abstract category to concrete instances without having to think about it. "Gossip" is a similarly general category applicable to innumerable instances, as are "international organization" and "transnational social movement" and "global network." These latter instances, in fact, are perhaps less abstract than "friend" or "gossip" because they refer to fewer possible instances and could even be reduced to actual lists.

In this light, world culture is not more abstract than any other level of culture, and its elements may be less abstract than many elements of culture at smaller scales or more immediate settings. However, this conclusion is also misleading to the extent that it still seems to represent culture as free-floating, detached, or at some remove from everyday reality. Culture has the strikingly tautological habit of becoming incorporated into the very "stuff" that it defines, into the things that owe their existence and meaning to the cultural complex that constitutes them. Reversing the common observation that individuals, groups, and organizations are "embedded" in their surrounding cultural environments, we should also think of culture as embedded in the objects, actors, scenes, and structures whose nature and operations are culturally organized. It is embedded in purposive organizations, technical structures, formalized rules, and constitutional documents. Even the propensities, capacities, and potential pathologies of individuals are embodiments of culture. People growing up in a given cultural complex cannot turn out "any old way"; the enveloping culture sharply restricts the possibilities.

Another less noticed aspect of the "culture work" that builds culture into people, organizations, rules, and documents is the longevity of cultural construction processes, increasingly explicit and deliberate, that lead to the formalized embedding of culture in structure. For example, a set of massive, multifaceted, long-term cultural processes eventually produced (and are therefore embedded in) the limited liability corporation, an artificial entity having both legal "personality" and a range of rights and obligations that are entirely taken for granted – so much so that corporations can now be easily and cheaply created out of thin air in huge numbers by quite ordinary individuals. To understand the culture embedded in the corporation, one needs to understand the cultural processes that produced it and the subsequent processes that have changed its meaning and purpose over several centuries.

This discussion gives the lie to a third misunderstanding about culture – that it is primarily to be found "in people's heads." Socialization, acculturation, learning, and similar theories implicitly make this assumption, and we would hardly dispute the conventional understanding that cultural creation takes place above all in the head. We nonetheless insist on the cultural poverty of people's heads. As containers of culture, they are not especially helpful, in two senses. The first is trivial but still worth emphasizing: any given head is cognizant of a negligible portion of the culture in which it is embedded (i.e., the cultural complex that directly orders the daily life, meaning system, functionality, and life chances of the individual attached to the head). More significant is the extension of this triviality: no matter how many heads we put together, their collective contents will still constitute only a small, and usually negligible, proportion of all of the enveloping culture.

How is it possible that all the culture in all the heads of all the world does not approach the sum of all culture that embeds, shapes, guides, informs, and ultimately constitutes the being and meaning of all those individuals-attached-to-heads? We can leave aside history for the moment – the long legacy and vast accumulated residue of past cultures which have shaped contemporary cultures in innumerable ways. Even currently active, identifiable culture is far more than the sum of all the contents of all the world's heads. How can this be?

Four factors, at least, are important in accounting for this unlikely situation. First, as far as heads go, cultural redundancy is epidemic: most of the cultural cognizance of any particular head overlaps with that of many other heads. (The French sociologist Emile Durkheim labeled such cognitive and normative redundancy the *"conscience collective,"* which means both collective consciousness [awareness] and collective conscience.) For example, most heads have active vocabularies of only 5,000 to 10,000 of the tens or hundreds of thousands of words available in their languages, and most heads share largely the same active vocabulary – so most words are unknown to most heads, and many words are known to very few heads. Some words, in fact, may be known to no heads at all, in any active sense. The same logic applies to virtually all cultural domains: that which is culturally available is largely unknown to almost everyone.

Second, for at least the past several centuries, and for much longer in some arenas like institutional religion, ever more expansive cultural creation has been the order of the day. More people have had more time to produce more kinds of cultural elements, and they are increasingly likely to do so self-consciously, elaborately, and thoroughly. Innumerable occupations and entire industries have emerged that do nothing but churn out new or reworked culture, ranging from the obvious "culture industries" (in the narrow usage of the term) like art, literature, performance, film, and television, to the natural and social sciences, engineering, medicine, design, advertising, administration, accounting, etc. These sectors produce knowledge, information, propaganda, mathematical equations, techniques, diagrams, organizational charts, auditing systems, and on and on, all in such abundance that it has become commonplace to worry about "information overload." As a corollary, we have an expanding range of media through which to produce culture, adding to classic verbal and visual media the many new technologies that have emerged since the mid-nineteenth century.

Third, cultural accumulation is increasingly deliberate and systematized. In most social arenas, structures and organizations ensure that cultural development is recorded and preserved, accumulating on dusty shelves, in crammed filing cabinets, or in dense electronic circuitry. Not all of this stockpiled culture is constantly active, and accidental or deliberate forgetting may be common (Douglas 1986), but vast amounts of stockpiled culture are available to be activated on a need-to-know basis. The ubiquity and reliability of such stockpiling is reflected in evolving theories of the purposes of education, which has shifted from memorization and rote recitation to "learning about learning," that is, developing the ability to find information (stored culture) by familiarizing students with a (limited) range of accumulative stockpiles.

Finally, with the rise of an independent public sphere and its rapid differentiation, culture creators are increasingly likely to offer their creations to the world through commercial, professional, or informal means. Publication, in the general sense, is epidemic. Because a higher sense of reality and value is attributed to culture that appears in the public realm, and because this "value-added" impact of the public realm is generally on the rise, the urge to go public is continually intensifying. This trend produces forms of self-revelation (on radio and television talk shows especially) that in earlier times would have been considered shamefully exhibitionist but have now become humdrum entertainment in many parts of the world.

What these four factors mean, taken together, is that cultural creation occurs at an ever accelerating pace and is ever more faithfully accumulated. Who has not heard the decades-old truism that half of all science (or literature, or images, or inventions . . .) has appeared in the past two or three decades? For many newer forms of cultural production, such as computer programming, management consulting, self-improvement psychologies, how-to manuals, and so on, even three decades is much too long a span in this regard. The German sociologist Georg Simmel's observation that "objective" culture far outstrips individual "subjective" culture (Simmel 1971), already overwhelmingly the case in his day, is even more apt now: objective culture overwhelmingly outstrips all subjective cultures (the culture in people's heads) put together. This dynamic quality of culture especially pertains to modern world culture, which always and everywhere exceeds what particular individuals make of it.

Distinguishing World Culture

If not only the grand spectacle of the Olympics and such obviously global activities as managing the international aviation system but also the seemingly small-scale and interpersonally immediate activities of the members of a chess club are instances of world-cultural enactment, one might be tempted to believe that virtually all social activity has world-cultural character. After all, building contractors are enacting world culture when they pour concrete that is designed to meet the standards for compressive strength and tensile splitting strength established by ISO (the International Organization for Standardization). So too are hospital nurses who inject patients with synthetic narcotic painkillers produced by global pharmaceutical companies like Pfizer and Glaxo Smith Kline, and psychologists who turn to the globally dominant DSM IV manual to refresh their memories about the clinical symptoms of mental disorders. Each of these examples reveals a distinct aspect of social life that involves world culture, and an astonishing number of everyday activities similarly involve world culture to some degree. What remains unclear is the nature of this world-cultural involvement: how can we distinguish aspects of routine activity that reflect or engage world culture from those that do not? In other words, how do we recognize *world* culture when we see it?

To formulate a provisional answer to this question and illustrate ideas we will apply in later chapters, we use two concepts of central importance in studying contemporary world culture: the world polity (Boli and Thomas 1999) and cultural universalism (Robertson 1992). When anyone invokes the entire globe as a frame of reference, refers to global corporations or global governance IGOs (intergovernmental organizations), or explains some aspect of globalization, the social unit that is brought into play is what we call the world polity. The world polity is the conceptual vision of the world as a single social system, an encompassing "society" involving all of "humanity" in extensive webs of interaction and flows of goods, ideas, money, values, and so on, among other social units (individuals, associations, companies, ethnic groups, states, nations, INGOs, etc.). This global social system is a polity because it is integrated by and operates through a complex set of multilayered authority structures (Boli and Thomas 1997). Some of these authority structures are well-integrated and cohesive, such as international banking and financial systems, global sports federations, and world-spanning transportation and communication systems. (Like most arenas in which a definitive world champion or world ranking can be identified, the global chess arena is fairly well integrated and cohesive.) Most of the authority structures are rather disorderly and loosely interconnected, such as the international human rights regime, "global pop" culture (Taylor 1997), and international labor organizations. Whether strongly or weakly integrated, when any of these structures becomes relevant to a social situation – be it with regard to technical properties of concrete, marketing efforts of global pharmaceutical companies, or using DSM IV to make sense of a puzzling set of symptoms – the world polity is activated. That is to say, one of the levels of social reality that provides meaning, guides to action, and a sense of purpose to the actors involved is the global level and the cultural framework that is associated with the global level of reality. This occurs explicitly in the Olympics but also more implicitly in a great many other areas.

Any given social situation typically involves numerous different levels of social reality simultaneously; the global may be only one of many levels of reality, and multiple polities, more or less formally structured, may be relevant at one and the same time. For a building contractor, for example, small-scale levels of reality that are constantly at work include personal relationships with supervisors and laborers (individual-level reality), the local or regional labor market, and city and county governments (which make building codes, rules for sewer lines and power hook-ups, and the like). Provincial (state) and national levels of social reality – polities of a more familiar sort – come into play via regulations regarding employer obligations to employees, tax and pension systems, and so on. An exhaustive analysis would reveal many more levels of social reality and associated polities that are relevant to the contractor's work, and only one of these is the global level, or the world polity, and the many relevant cultural constructs that operate at the global level. However, an exhaustive analysis would also uncover many more ways in which the contractor's work situation relies on, activates, is informed by, or enacts the global level of reality (that is, world-polity governance structures and world-cultural elements) – many more if the project involved, say, a great new opera house for a national capital city than if it involved a garage that is being converted to a bedroom.

Implicit in the idea of the world polity is the correlative concept of cultural universalism. To say that a cultural element is universalistic is not to say that it is truly universal, that is, found in all cultures (the anthropological usage, now somewhat outmoded) or found "everywhere" (an exceedingly slippery concept to which we return below). Rather, it is to say that the element is presented to the world "as if" it were universally meaningful, applicable, useful, or proper. The element is presumed to have universal (worldwide) scope; it is presumed to be interpretable in a largely uniform way and to make sense both cognitively and, often, normatively, in any particular local culture or social framework. For example, the means of testing the technical properties of concrete (one of the key concerns of ISO's standards regarding concrete) are presumed to work no matter where they are used. The properties required of concrete to support a given type of building using a given construction method are presumed to be the same no matter where the building is located. The proper dosage of a painkiller is presumed to be the same (allowing for variability in age, weight, and sex) for any person in any locale; so too are the probabilities of various side effects of the drug. More controversially, but no less definitively for those who accept its authoritativeness, the DSM IV classification of mental disorders is presumed to apply to any troubled patient, regardless of cultural, ethnic, religious, or national background.

In the strongest form, universalistic elements are presumed to have literally universal (cosmic) scope. Many of the natural sciences have precisely this character: the working assumption for chemists, physicists, planetologists, and the like is that the physical laws they study are literally applicable everywhere in our universe, and even, in the spectacularly wild-eyed theories of astrophysicists and cosmologists, to universes beyond ours.

These examples, cognitive and "factual" in nature, may seem obvious, even natural (which observation in itself reveals the penetrative nature of universalistic world culture). As we move to more purely normative universalisms, such as the doctrines of human rights, conceptions of corruption, or Coubertin's vision of brotherhood, uneasiness is likely and the sense of naturalness disappears. Definitions can be at stake: one person's corruption is another person's dutiful effort to meet obligations to village, clan, or region. Tensions emerge: in the Olympics, nationalist fervor competes with transnational ideals. Similarly, implications can be troubling. The principle that all people are to be accorded the same rights and protections across all cultures and societies implies, for example, that women should have full equality with men in marriage. "Not so fast!" scream men, and clerics, and judges in many societies and cultures; women are to be subordinate to men, at least in certain aspects of the marriage relationship. Do these objections mean that women's equality in marriage is not, after all, a universal principle, and therefore not a part of world culture? No. The principle is still conceived, by both its supporters and its critics, as inherently universalistic in itself (it speaks, notably, of "all people") and as a would-be universal in its applicability. It is therefore world-cultural; but so too is the counterposed principle that, with respect to some issues and arenas, women should not be fully equal to men. World culture incorporates many controversies and contradictory claims of this sort. Like all levels of culture, it is the locus of much contention and struggle, the more so as world society becomes ever more inclusive and penetrative such that ever more diverse societies and groups become direct participants in world-cultural enactment and construction.

Contested Culture

As the disputes surrounding women's rights show, the global scope of world-cultural principles does not imply consensus. World culture is not a seamless canopy hovering over us or a cultural Gaia that warmly envelops us. Global consciousness can take different forms and global sharing is often a prelude to argument. World culture encompasses as well the competing ways in which people construct images of the world they want to live in, alternative views of global futures. In many contexts, the meaning and purpose of world order are at stake. Many conflicts in the world today are also cultural contests.

Culture is, in fact, a hot global topic. Consider a full-page advertisement that appeared in American newspapers not long ago, under the ominous heading "Global Monoculture." A series of photographs challenged readers to name the place they depicted. One showed long lines of cars on a multi-lane highway, and asked: Frankfurt or Chicago? The accompanying text spelled out the message. "[W]ith economic globalization, diversity is fast disappearing," it said. "The goal of the global economy is that all countries should be homogenized." If "any place is becoming like any place else," then "[w]hat's the point of leaving home?" The ad argued that this stifling monoculture was the nefarious work of corporations concerned only about their profits, people and nature be damned. Though bad in itself, monoculture therefore also reflected the gross power imbalance that threatened the globe. Implicitly, the ad was an effort to rally progressive forces behind another, more egalitarian and multicultural vision. In fact, it was part of a series of advertisements, all of which offered a leftist perspective on issues such as genetic engineering and economic globalization. The advertisements were published by the Turning Point Project, a broad coalition of activist organizations that had banded together for this purpose.

As arguments, these texts may leave a bit to be desired. For example, it is not clear that multinational business can thrive only on homogeneity, as Coca-Cola's grammatically challenged "Think local, act local" corporate strategy suggests. However, as exhortation they follow an increasingly familiar pattern. They contribute to a backlash against neoliberal globalization, articulated in a globally diffused critical discourse. To call the rise of this discourse a turning point in quite the sense the Turning Point Project intended may be premature. But what has changed in recent years is that globalization has turned from mantra to threat. No longer a merely descriptive term, it has become an object of ideological debate. For many groups around the world, taking a stance toward globalization has become a primary way to express their own visions of world order. The contested nature and direction of globalization show some of the fissures in world culture.

The expanding global backlash (Broad 2002) unites around certain common themes, such as those expressed in the Turning Point ads: Globalization is the process, dominated by greedy corporations, of imposing a rapacious economic system bound to produce social inequality, cultural blight, and environmental devastation. Neoliberal globalization is exploitative and therefore unjust. It serves the interests of global elites, not those of the poor. It turns democratic nation-states into empty shells. As it obliterates cultures, it denies people the very essence of freedom. The destructive power of the monoculture calls for the reassertion of diversity. Such themes find expression in movements protesting against the IMF, the World Bank, the WTO (World Trade Organization), and particular multinational corporations. Among critical academics, they have led to descriptions of globalization as "predatory" (Falk 1999), a "syndrome" (Mittelman 2000), and a "false dawn" (Gray 1998). By 2001, they had gathered sufficient support to constitute a platform for the World Social Forum at Porto Alegre in Brazil, which we discuss in Chapter 7. In a short period, backlash discourse had greatly intensified in movements, at meetings, and among academics.

However, apart from the core consensus on the discontents of globalization, the discourse takes different forms. Diagnoses of globalization express alternative world-views. For example, the critique of globalizing monoculture can take the form of a fundamentalist defense of a sacred tradition against the forces of "McWorld" (Barber 1995), a revival of national identity, or protection of the rights of "indigenous" cultures. Motives for opposing neoliberalism range from Catholic rejection of heartless materialism to neosocialist dismay at rising inequality to environmentalist concern about uncontrolled growth. Similarly, proposals to fix what now ails a globalizing world also vary greatly, some envisioning communities or states as bulwarks against global assaults, others calling for one-world solutions relying on global ethics or global governance. The very richness of global debate should alleviate fears about the advent of monoculture.

Such backlash discourse, which we examine further in a later chapter, is becoming an integral part of world culture. It is one prominent example of global debates joined by participants from many continents, focused on common problems, articulated through a shared rhetoric, and played out as a confrontation of competing world cultures. Of course, not all parties are equal; not all contributions are consequential. But what is at stake in these debates is how the world should be constituted as a single society, what counts as valid knowledge, and what principles should prevail in transnational affairs. To some extent, many such issues are up for grabs. Articulating and debating them means contributing to world culture.

The Case for World Culture

This book proposes a view of world culture as a global, distinct, complex, and dynamic phenomenon and supports this view by analyzing its different dimensions with concrete examples. As prelude to our substantive chapters, we now summarize our perspective on world culture.

World culture as global

In speaking of "world" culture, we have in effect treated it as global, as the globe-spanning culture of actual world society. Though the distinction between "world" phenomena, as properties of large geographical areas, and "global" ones, of true planetary scope, once may have mattered, world and global in these senses have practically converged. As we explained earlier, what matters for our purposes is that certain ideas and principles are presented as globally relevant and valid, and are seen as such by those who absorb them. At any rate, the claim does not have to be wholly correct as an empirical matter (for example, not all parts of the globe need to be equally enamored of chess or well-represented in the backlash discourse we have just described) to be useful as a working hypothesis (for example, because the chess subculture works on common assumptions or the backlash discourse is universally relevant).

World culture as distinct

Arguing that the world has a culture might seem to slight the diversity that still prevails today. However, our point is not that world culture obliterates all others, supersedes the local, or makes the world one in the sense of being utterly similar. To be sure, from our analytical point of view, it does have a coherence and content of its own, but this does not imply empirically that the world is on a long slide toward Turning Point's monoculture. Nor does it rule out the possibility of a "clash of civilizations" (Huntington 1997), which we discuss in a later chapter. We suggest that world culture grows alongside of, and in complex interaction with, the more particularistic cultures of the world. In relating to world culture the more particularistic ones also change. For example, as we discuss in Chapter 9, the civilizations central to Huntington's argument are always already embedded in an encompassing global civilization, which to some extent constrains their interactions and bridges their differences. Within world culture, civilizations cannot be self-centered, taken-for-granted practices, if they ever were. Actual cultural practices in particular places, as well as the thinking of particular individuals, are likely to exhibit mixtures of "world" and more local symbolism. In treating world culture as distinct, we do not claim to capture the full range of those practices. As our argument about how to distinguish world culture implies, world culture is not the sum of all things cultural.

World culture as complex

From another angle, our analysis of world culture might seem too complex, too focused on teasing out tension and difference. The monocultural scenario, after all, has numerous supporters. According to the popular "McDonaldization" argument (Ritzer 1993), for instance, institutional forces pressing for efficiency and control threaten to impose one way of life everywhere. We think the direction sketched by this argument is partly correct: rationalization is powerful, and in fact a certain kind of rationality has become an influential cultural model. But even on the culinary scene, rationalization is not a cul-de-sac. The fast-food experience takes many forms, single models of food production come in multiple versions, foods and tastes mix around the world. From our perspective, the McDonaldization thesis is not so much wrong as one-sided. World culture encompasses different domains and contains tensions among its different components. Global consciousness does not come in one styrofoam package.

World culture as an entity

We have already ascribed several characteristic to world culture. Whenever we say that world culture "does" x, the specter of reification lurks. In some instances, of course, talking of world culture as an active whole is a matter of convenience, sparing us the need to unpack it into components or into the actions of people using the symbolic resources at their disposal. Treating it in this way does not entail seeing it divorced from other realms of human activity. As we have already hinted in our discussion of "real world" institutions, we think the analytical move to distinguish the cultural from, say, the political and economic, should actually enable us to see how those aspects of human activity are mutually constitutive. However, we do not want to grant critics of reification too much. In the final analysis, we do claim that a distinct and recognizable world culture is crystallizing as a phenomenon with its own content and structure. At the same time, we do not draw tight boundaries. In exploring what issues reasonably fit under the heading of world culture, we err on the side of inclusion.

World culture as culture

As we explained, we hold a particular view of culture. We regard it as socially constructed and socially shared symbolism. Our position is "holistic" and "constructionist." This rules out subjective or purely textual views of culture – it is neither (just) in people's heads nor (just) in esoteric documents. It also leaves aside popular grab-bag notions of culture as a way of life. However, it incorporates many other perspectives, from which we borrow liberally. Our holistic constructionism directs attention to the way in which culture is created and consciousness is formed. It suggests that, once created, cultural forms do have a dynamic of their own. It requires analysis of how cultural elements come to be shared, notably through the work of institutions that carry abstract ideas into practice. It points to the fault lines and tectonic stresses that may become sources of change. We argue in the next chapter that this perspective builds on and complements much previous work on world culture. We apply this perspective heuristically. Our purpose in this book is to marshal available resources to illuminate our problems, not to engage in scholarly polemics by advocating one theory to the exclusion of others. We hope that our view of culture is sufficiently ecumenical to be useful to a wide range of readers.

World culture as dynamic

Our opening example of global sports showed how rules, ideas, and symbolism surrounding this transnational practice have grown over the years. The world culture of sports is always being constructed and reconstructed. The point applies more generally. World culture is not simply a finished structure, a done deal. Certainly, some world-cultural patterns display continuity over many decades, as the global commitment to the nation-state form illustrates. But world culture is open to new ideas, vulnerable to new conflicts, and subject to continual reinterpretation. Even the apparent convergence of people and countries from many regions on the merits of liberal democracy as a model for organizing societies hardly counts as the "end of history" (Fukuyama 1992). Much as we appreciate the value of the model itself, we lack the Hegelian confidence to think of contemporary world culture as the fully formed end point of humanity's ideological evolution, or as the irreversible progress of reason that has achieved a system immune to future contradictions.

World culture as significant

Needless to say, we think world culture is significant in many ways. We argue against the view that it is a veneer, a set of fairly abstract notions only variably relevant in real people's lives. Examples such as the globalization backlash, one could argue, still refer to the concerns of a relatively small elite. Models such as neoliberalism or even the nation-state would seem irrelevant in West African states on the verge of collapse. We agree that the relevance of world culture can vary in this way, but this does not diminish its significance as a feature of world society. Without grasping world culture we could not understand the direction of world affairs, as we have already suggested. However, it is also vastly more pervasive in particular places than ever before. Anti-globalization discourse affects African dealings with international organizations, neoliberalism shapes development strategies even of countries with few resources, and the nation-state has become the operative model for groups not naturally hospitable to living within one political system. Even more concretely, as our earlier examples show, many regular activities now embody world culture in some way. World culture matters for the world as a whole and for the world in all its varied parts. That is what this book seeks to show.

Structure of the Book

In the next chapter we review relevant literature on cultural globalization and world culture and describe several partially complementary perspectives that will guide our analysis. Chapter 3 selectively recounts the recent history of world culture, tracing some of its important contemporary features back to the nineteenth century. Chapter 4 jumps forward to the contemporary era to examine how elements of world culture are constructed, specifically through the global ritual of major international meetings. Distinguishing between the "hardware" and "software" of world culture, Chapter 5 shows how world culture is carried by both a technical and an organizational infrastructure. Focusing on the issue of national identity, Chapter 6 argues that world culture fosters difference. Chapter 7 expands upon the "global backlash" referred to above to demonstrate how certain kinds of cultural critiques are part and parcel of world culture. In Chapter 8 we use the case of global Pentecostalism to illustrate how particular groups creatively expand world culture. Disputing the "clash of civilizations" argument, Chapter 9 analyzes militant Islamism as a form of opposition to world culture. Chapter 10 returns to the issue of global governance by studying how the International Criminal Court institutionalizes world culture. Finally, in the Epilogue we offer some general reflections on world culture that tie together central themes of the book.

Chapter 2

Analyzing World Culture: Alternative Theories

After 1989, images of world culture featured prominently in public discussion of global affairs in the United States. Would moves toward a "new world order" explode in a "clash of civilizations"? Would the triumph of liberal democracy inoculate the world against ideological conflict, leading to the "end of history"? Would the forces of Hollywood-inspired Coca-Colanization produce a "McWorld," against which tradition-bound adherents of "Jihad" would continue to rail? Would global commitment to a technically proficient, freedom-loving "Lexus" culture uproot communities cherishing their distinct "Olive Tree" cultures? For a time, making provocative claims about the state of world culture seemed a sure way to write a nonfiction bestseller. Successful books on world-cultural themes, such as those by Barber (1995), Friedman (1999), Fukuyama (1992), and Huntington (1997) tapped into a widespread sense that culture mattered. They affirmed and shaped a growing consciousness of the way the world was drawing together, or might implode, culturally. Their common message was unmistakable: one could no longer understand world society without understanding world culture.

Looking beyond American bestsellers, we find parallel trends in more conventionally academic work. While many students of global affairs continue to focus on economics and inequality, state policy and military conflict, and other ostensibly more serious problems, the study of culture as a global phenomenon has become increasingly popular. A scholarly discourse on world culture is emerging. In this chapter, we describe this trend with four goals in mind. First, we see the work of scholars as part of the culture they try to grasp: as they make sense of world culture, they also advance a new kind of global awareness. Intense reflection on the direction of cultural change is a feature of world culture itself. Second, rather than accentuate the differences among scholars, we stress that there is a common thrust in the empirical and theoretical work on world culture. We think of the work we review here as the beginning of a promising tradition, perhaps a paradigm in the making. Third, we locate our own contribution in this emerging tradition. A brief analysis of prominent studies of world culture conveys how we extend current work. A more detailed look at four theoretical accounts of world culture shows how we build on their combined insights. Finally, by juxtaposing and synthesizing different lines of inquiry into world culture, we devise a framework to guide our own study of world culture in subsequent chapters. This analytical chapter thus serves to relate scholarly trends to world culture, review relevant literature, locate our study within it, and prepare for the substantive work that lies ahead.

Studying World Culture

How should we understand world culture? Innovative scholars investigating the subject do not yet have a ready-made answer. To call their collective efforts a paradigm for studying world culture might attribute too much consensus to a burgeoning field. Yet in the way they go about answering the question, scholars have much in common. For example, they typically assume that the rise of world culture is an outcome of globalization: as the world becomes more intimately connected in complex ways, growing links are given meaningful form. They agree that this is largely a new phenomenon, both in scale and content: there is a culture that begins to span the actual globe, and it is no longer defined only in European terms. Scholars also display the anxiety of difference: for fear of implying that cultural globalization snuffs out diversity, they invariably stress the multiple ways in which people respond to putatively global ideas and symbols. A hallmark of the emerging research on world culture is that it advances awareness of global awareness. However, as we will illustrate, scholars differ in how emphatically they claim that world culture is now a global reality worthy of study in its own right. On the spectrum we review below, our work stands at one end.

The *Dictionary of Global Culture*, edited by Kwame Anthony Appiah and Henry Louis Gates, Jr. (1997), partly illustrates the new thinking. As the editors say in their introduction, "we all participate, albeit from different positions, in a global system of culture" (xi). That culture, they immediately add, is "increasingly less dominated by the West, less Eurocentric" (ibid.). As European dominance declines, it becomes possible to recognize its former evils more forthrightly while taking pleasure in the benefits of a culture initially created under the steam of European ideas (ibid.). The "emerging shared culture" does not consist "simply of the sum of the thousands of traditions of the local cultures of the past" (xiv). However, the *Dictionary* itself, as Appiah and Gates acknowledge, does present global culture as the sum of many contributions, from "Abakwa, Sociedad" (secret society of African extraction based in Cuba) to "zydeco" (hybrid musical style). It does little to explain what makes global culture global. Between "Hugo, Victor" and "Hurston, Zora Neale" there is no entry for "human rights"; between "McCullers, Carson Smith" and "Meiji Restoration" there is no "media" entry. Of course, the sheer juxtaposition of miscellaneous items, giving equal regard to many regions, itself makes a point about the direction of cultural change. But the editors present it as a starting point only, "for a more open and equal participation by Westerners in that emerging global civilization" (xiv). The *Dictionary* helps to lay the groundwork for understanding world culture but does not address the subject head on.

In his book *Globalization and Culture* (1999), John Tomlinson comes closer to doing so. He uses the example of supermarkets in Western cities (120ff.) to illustrate how globalization, defined as "complex connectivity," turns the world into a "single social and cultural setting" (ibid.: 10). The customers' experience becomes "deterritorialized" because they are no longer limited to local produce or a national diet. By the sheer variety they offer, supermarkets symbolize the absence of a single dominant style; world cuisine is inherently pluralistic, not homogeneous. Selecting from the wide range of options available, customers partake in a global food system; reverberating in far-flung places, their actions have consequences for what gets produced, and how, worldwide. But with the options comes the problem of forming a new diet, defining a new culinary identity. In principle, at least, even mundane shopping can turn customers into cosmopolitans, people who are able to "live in both the global and the local at the same time" and recognize both that "there are no others" and that the world consists of "many cultural others" (194–5). The spread of food items and their reassembly into new dietary styles thus shows one way that culture globalizes. In the food scene, we can observe world culture as the "context of integration" of cultural practices and experiences across the world (71).

However, can world culture be more than common context in this sense? Tomlinson is skeptical. In a strong sense, global culture means "the emergence of one single culture embracing everyone on earth and replacing the diversity of cultural systems that have flourished up to now" (71). "Well, pretty obviously," he adds, "such a culture has not yet arrived." A "single, unified" global culture is not about to emerge (105). Most attempts to delineate it enter into merely speculative discourse (72). Somewhat paradoxically, then, Tomlinson suggests that culture can globalize without producing a global culture. But his skepticism depends on the idea that the only way to represent world culture is as a "single, unified" monolith replacing all that came before. Not only does that assumption create the paradox, it prevents Tomlinson from fully addressing world culture as such.

World culture is explicitly on the agenda of the international team of scholars that wrote *Many Globalizations: Cultural Diversity in the Contemporary World* (Berger and Huntington 2002). More emphatically than Tomlinson, the project assumes that "[t]here is indeed an emerging global culture" (Berger 2002: 2). We can see it emerging, according to one contribution to the book, in the work of globe-trotting Americans who consult for multinationals, monitor foreign elections, build a music television network, or spread the Gospel (Hunter and Yates 2002). Whether they work for the firm Porter Novelli or for the Carter Center, for MTV or Campus Crusade for Christ, these leaders share a vocabulary and worldview. They envision a shrinking world bound to make progress through market competition and respect for diversity and human rights. Of course, Americans are not the only globalizers, but they do have disproportionate influence: world culture is "heavily American both in origin and content" (Berger 2002: 2). But it is not a single thing. As the varied work of globally active Americans illustrates, world culture has four "faces": the "Davos" culture of free-market business and political elites, the "faculty club" culture of progressive nongovernmental organizations, the popular culture of entertainment and consumption, and the new transnational movement culture produced above all by Pentecostalism.

This model of world culture, proposed by Peter Berger, frames the studies in the book. These studies assume the existence of certain subcultures of world culture and ask how these play out in different countries. The book reviews many "localizations": how China incorporates the Davos business culture, how nongovernmental civil society takes a particular form in Turkey, how Hungary responds to Western pop culture, how Chile has welcomed evangelicals, and so on. The findings also complicate the four-faces model. World culture is not just American, as "emissions" like religious movements originating in India show (Berger 2002: 12–13). To some extent, the faces are a mask, hiding a "wild substructure" of behavior that does not fit official global models, as in the case of South Africa. Global models are not universally accepted, and in fact provoke criticism and resistance. The argument, as the title indicates, is that there is no one pattern of cultural globalization, that cultural diversity reigns even in the global age. Only briefly does Berger reflect on common traits in the four faces, such as an increasing global interest in enhancing "the independence of the individual over against tradition and collectivity" (ibid.: 9). The organizing device of the book, namely to study national variations in cultural globalization, reflects another common trait, namely the universal right of nation-states to define their own particular identities, but the book does not examine it. It addresses not what makes global culture global, but rather the local multiplicity of global cultures.

In his book *La Mondialisation Culturelle: Les Civilisations à l'Épreuve* [Cultural Globalization: The Challenge to Civilizations] (2000), the French scholar Gérard Leclerc takes a further step in analyzing world culture as such. In an elaborate history of ideas, Leclerc shows how European intellectuals discovered and defined "the world" through their encounters with Asian civilizations. Whether these were treated as alien others, as early stages of human evolution, or as colonial subjects, Europe was always on top; world culture, naturally, was European culture. Only in the twentieth century, as decolonization proceeded, did Europe's natural assumption of superiority dissipate, and with it the European version of world culture. Given that irreversible demise, recreating some version of the old world is not an option. Today, there are no new civilizations to discover, no new territories to incorporate, and, as a result, there is only one humanity on a single planet. How, in this finite world without a center (ibid.: 7–9), will the many cultures form a single whole? How will some unity in plurality become possible?

To this problem of globality (8) Leclerc offers no easy solutions. Yet, he implies that Europe's loss may be the world's gain, for some universal values first associated with Europe may flourish more easily as their association with European control diminishes (286). For example, secularism and tolerance (474) may be more effective components of world culture, facilitating essential unity-in-difference, precisely because they are no longer tainted by Europeans acting in total disregard of what they preach. Europe's loss also has another implication for thinking about world culture. Leclerc reminds us that the very experience of losing their central position led some Western intellectuals to think more creatively about the new world situation. Once, intellectuals thought of world culture in terms of exchanges among civilizations, but increasingly they had to see these as embedded in a larger whole. In the 1950s, the German philosopher Karl Jaspers was already arguing that civilizations could not simply proceed along separate cultural tracks; all were now part of a movement toward unification, a single universal history (316–17); in the 1960s, his colleague Kostas Axelos called for a new kind of planetary thinking, effectively unifying all previous traditions (467–8). From an aesthetic standpoint, the French author André Malraux grasped the new global condition with his idea of the "imaginary museum," suggesting that the modern era draws all art out of its communal or religious context and brings it together, as products of human creativity, in a single imaginary space (300–3). These highbrow speculations on what a world culture might consist of are harbingers of a broader shift among sophisticated intellectuals. Constructing some simple, static picture of "the other" is now frowned upon; seeing all "others" as fellow contributors to a shared cultural project fits the demands of the age. Though he has doubts about the role of Muslims in this process, Leclerc optimistically envisions a new International of intellectuals who join in the work of creating a common culture (478). However, now that the intellectual scaffolding for "planetary thinking" about culture exists, what can we actually see from that vantage point? To use Leclerc's terms, how do universal ideas crystallize into an actual "global civilization," and how does such a civilization work? An empirical sociology of world culture would have to assume that it grows not just in the fertile minds of philosophers.

The German scholars Joana Breidenbach and Ina Zukrigl chart this growth by example in their book *Tanz der Kulturen: Kulturelle Identität in einer globalisierten Welt* [Dance of Cultures: Cultural Identity in a Globalized World] (2000). From its roots in Western Europe, Christmas has become a global holiday, but Germans might be surprised by the way it is celebrated in Trinidad (ibid.: 194–5). Feminism may have started in the West, but it, too, has gone global, adapted by groups in the South to advocate a form of emancipation distinct from that of Western liberals (217–21). As English became the global lingua franca, other languages died, yet there is also a global movement afoot to preserve and support the indigenous languages of small groups (227–32). Such examples illustrate that cultural globalization is a double process. On the one hand, it differentiates (35). It offers new options, new goods, ideas, and lifestyles, new ways to mix the new and the old. People interpret globally circulating symbols very differently according to their own needs and customs. On the other hand, differences now play out within a common framework. The metaphor in the title makes a point: the world now has a common set of standards and concepts, a symbolic "reference system" (206), which enables more and more people to participate in a joint "dance." Guided by global ideas and norms, people become more similar in the way they identify themselves as different. Global culture helps them both to bridge and to articulate differences.

Much of Breidenbach and Zukrigl's book is devoted to clearing away misconceptions about this global culture. Global culture is not all-encompassing, since many ideas and lifestyles are disconnected, many differences not bridged (213). For example, celebrating Christmas need not prevent anyone from celebrating a local holiday. World culture is not created by stirring old ideas into a melting pot: it represents something new over and above previously existing cultures (36). World culture is no mosaic, since that metaphor conveys a picture of neatly juxtaposed and unchanging cultures; the whole point of their book is to show that differences are fluid and relative when they are caught up in an ever-shifting global dance. World culture is not an alien force suppressing difference; as long as global symbols are freely appropriated, they can be anyone's authentic culture (37). World culture is not the opposite of diversity; rather, it organizes diversity (89). Certainly, some things do get lost, as the language example suggests, but, on balance, world culture stimulates difference. Christmas in Trinidad, feminisms in Africa, and the revival of the Maori language in New Zealand are cases in point. Far from hovering abstractly above the planet, world culture provides ideas and symbols, concepts and models that seep into daily life and thereby add a layer to people's experience.

Scholars thus picture world culture in different ways: as the sum of cultural contributions, as globalized identity, as a composite of forms of globalization, as global civilization, and as a shared reference system. We do not want to overstate their differences for, as we pointed out, these studies have much in common. On the basis of shared assumptions, they all aim at greater understanding of how the one-ness of the world now takes symbolic shape, a deepened consciousness of global consciousness. In this way, scholarly analysis also serves as an indicator of the ongoing growth of world culture.

This book is part of the global discussion of world culture and therefore, in some small way, part of its subject as well. It extends the ongoing work by picking up where Breidenbach and Zukrigl leave off. We share the assumptions of many of our colleagues and will draw on some of their terms and ideas. However, as we indicated in the first chapter, we do push in a different direction. More than our colleagues, we present world culture as a coherent domain worthy of study in its own right. More emphatically than others, we aim to convey the content and structure of world culture as such. We show by example how it can be studied empirically and systematically. To organize our work, we draw throughout this book on four influential accounts of world culture, to which we next turn.

According to one influential view of world culture, it constitutes the ideology of the capitalist world-system. It is a culture shaped by Western interests, a form of hegemony that sustains an unequal system. This account does allow for difference: political divisions in a competitive system require cultural distinctions among states, and the system's very presuppositions inevitably provoke resistance. A second theory treats world culture as the rules of world society, a set of models that constitute the legitimate global actors and provide scripts for them to follow. This culture has its origin in Western thought, but it now has a truly global character. While this account recognizes sources of difference, such as local constraints on implementation of global models for state action, its main thrust is to argue for the surprising similarity in the lives of individuals, states, and international organizations. The third perspective we discuss mainly approaches world culture as the domain in which various groups come to terms with the way in which a process of globalization reshapes the world as a single place and redefines their positions within it. While world culture has a minimal common core, for example in the form of some universal standards, the thrust of this account is to argue that world culture does not crystallize as a single set of values or ideas, since its hallmarks are contention among opposing conceptions of world order and highly variable involvement in globalization by particular cultures. Finally, we turn to an anthropological account of world culture, according to which the various flows of cultural material intersect in multiple ways in the lives of particular collectivities that creatively mix indigenous and exogenous elements to form new identities. Though this account recognizes the common building blocks groups have to work with and the centripetal pull of a cultural apparatus, it stresses that world culture is not a thing produced by world society but rather the set of processes by which diversity is organized globally.

Table 2.1 (p. 56) summarizes the main points of each of these accounts, which we will now describe in greater detail. While we will draw on all four perspectives, the ideas of John Meyer and Roland Robertson will be especially important in framing our own approach to world culture.

World Culture as Ideology of Capitalism

When Immanuel Wallerstein tried to explain the difficulties encountered by newly independent African states in achieving economic development and national integration, he concluded that they were not simply recapitulating the experience of European states (Wallerstein 1974: 4–7). Understanding the record of both African and European states, he found, required seeing them as part of something larger: a capitalist world-system. The relative power of European states derived from their leading role in the rise of that system; the difficulties of African states stemmed from the way they had been forcibly incorporated into that system. But how did the system itself work? What was its history? From the late 1960s, studying the history of capitalism as a world-system became Wallerstein's primary task.

Since the "long" sixteenth century, Wallerstein argued in his subsequent work, capitalism had expanded as a world-system. When European powers began to conquer or trade with other parts of the globe, they built a new economy based on private ownership of the means of production, geared toward capital accumulation by operating for profit in world markets. This modern form of capitalism was a world-system because it contained a single division of labor that transcended distinct political units. The division of labor took geographic form: various parts of the globe contributed differ-ent resources or performed different kinds of work. European "core" coun-tries became centers of accumulation. Their superior position initially depended on small advantages in technology and location. Over time, cap-italists required the support of strong states to consolidate these advantages. Such states helped to account for the system's success: while underwriting the success of various groups of capitalists, no single state could dominate the system as a whole, and the resulting competition made the system ever more expansive.

Did the system have a culture? The world-systemic picture of capitalism suggested several reasons for a negative answer. To start with, Wallerstein argued that Europe's early success had little to do with cultural distinc-tiveness. For example, any difference in values between China and Europe, exaggerated in any case, had not prevented the former from exceeding the latter's accomplishments for centuries; no Western "ideology of individual-ism" could account for Europe's unexpected advance (1974: 62). Similarly, Protestant values had little influence: while they might have helped to over-come some obstacles to innovation, such values were essentially mani-pulated by powerful groups to suit their interests. Any link between Protestantism and capitalist development was therefore largely accidental (ibid.: 151ff.). Culture did matter in one respect, namely as a unifying force in emerging states. The main case in point was the revolt of the Nether-lands against Spain, for here religion served to bring together a previously divided population in a struggle that set the stage for a period of Dutch economic hegemony (ibid.: 204–5). But the Dutch example also indicates another reason that the system lacked a culture of its own: its dynamism derived initially from the competitive pursuit of economic advantage by states that, as part of this competition, used cultural means to create differences by setting boundaries. Henceforth, strong states would try to create national cultures in the interest of ruling groups; as a result, homogeneity within nation-states would go hand in hand with the creation of cultural difference across the globe (ibid.: 349).

Insofar as the early world-system had a "geoculture," it was a remnant of the feudal age, a hierarchical ideology of ascribed privilege. Even by the eighteenth century, there was not yet a world culture of the system's ruling bourgeois class (Wallerstein 1980: 289). The development of a true world culture, a culture of the system as a whole, had to await the French Revolution (Wallerstein 1995: 147). That revolution minimally legitimated social change and popular sovereignty. It articulated principles in a universalistic fashion. It enshrined liberty, equality, and fraternity as core elements of a new, liberal world-view, one that was to become dominant by the mid-nineteenth century. Allied to the view that progress could best be obtained by marshaling state power, "centrist liberalism" eventually became a global ideology, defeating its prominent challengers, conservatism and radical socialism. This geoculture embodied the universalism of revolutionary dreams, but, according to Wallerstein, it was a false universalism. Its tenets were formulated by and for an elite minority within the world-system (1998a: 24); it was the faith of the cadres serving the interests of the powerful (1998b: 80). Liberal universalism was also false because it was particularist in its application: liberal tenets applied to some nations and races more than others, partly as a way to pacify the demands of white male workers in core countries (1998a: 20ff.). Because this universalist geoculture could only be sustained by a racist and sexist system, it was inherently contradictory.

In the twentieth century, the old geoculture's false pretensions increasingly were exposed, as subordinate groups turned the tables on the core by shaping their particularisms into tools of confrontation (Wallerstein 2000). While oppositional movements like socialism were still beholden to universalism, the "revolution" of 1968 dethroned liberalism and discredited the old challengers (1998a: 29). By contrast, new antisystemic movements, such as the "Khomeini option" of religious fundamentalism, are often profoundly illiberal in the way they reject the premises of capitalist civilization (1998a: 58; 1998b: 92). Since the world-system is becoming more and more polarized, according to Wallerstein, cultural differences are bound to intensify as well, fueling new kinds of identity politics as the main form of antisystemic activity (1998b: 159). Even though, in Wallerstein's judgment, such oppositional movements do not pose a "fundamental ideological challenge" to capitalist geoculture (1995: 245), he does expect the increased resistance to lead to transformation. Wallerstein applauds the demolition job performed by antisystemic movements, looks forward to the demise of capitalist culture, and holds out hope for a more equal world society, but he has tempered his residual revolutionary fervor by stressing that the outcome of capitalism's crisis is highly uncertain.

Thus (world) culture has once again become a key "battleground." This is nothing new, Wallerstein has pointed out, because "cultures are... arenas where resistance to hegemony occurs" (1980: 65). This resistance takes the form of "appeals... to the historical values of established 'civilizations' against the temporary superiorities of the market" (ibid.). Airs of superiority always take cultural form, for cultures are "the ways in which people clothe their politico-economic interests and drives in order to express them, hide them, extend them in space and time, and preserve their memory" (ibid.). Culture, then, is both weapon of the powerful and tool of resistance of the weak (Wallerstein 1991a: 99).

With his analysis of geocultures, the contradictions of capitalist civilization, and culture as battleground, Wallerstein has produced an increasingly elaborate picture of world culture. Yet the thrust of his argument has remained consistent: Culture matters insofar as it is part of the reproduction of a system. Cultures reflect the interests of groups. The culture of a system is the ideology of its dominant constituents. In the culture-as-battleground imagery, the battle reflects the contradictory economic and political interests of contending parties. While Wallerstein has called for the conceptual dissolution of economic, political, and economic "spheres" as misleading artifacts of capitalist culture (2000), his own analysis thus inherits the constraints of historical materialism. In that tradition, culture is ideology, serves interests, legitimates a system, and reflects underlying conflicts. In short, culture has an instrumental quality, and its dynamism derives from "deeper" forces. Reasoning within that tradition, world culture *must* be the culture of capitalism.

If we interpret Wallerstein's stance with the tools of his framework, we can see world-system analysis as the reflection of a particular kind of struggle within and about world culture, rooted in nineteenth-century conflicts. The key to that tradition was exposing bourgeois culture as an instrument of capitalist oppression. As a vantage point, this tradition is important, but for an adequate understanding of world culture it is too confining. We agree with the common criticisms of materialist treatments of culture – that they are crudely functionalist in assuming that culture's primary role lies in maintaining a system, that they miss dimensions of culture not reducible to struggles over material interests, that they reduce the process of culture construction to a feature of hegemonic control, and so on. We therefore depart from the instrumental view of culture as ideology. As our next sections make clear, there are other, more encompassing views of culture. These entail a more inclusive picture of world culture, not limited to features directly related to the reproduction of or the fight over global capitalism. This means that we also differ in our judgment of various historical episodes.

At the same time, we do not want to overstate our differences with Wallerstein's line of thought. Rather than engage in polemics, we aim to incorporate several of his substantive insights. In a general sense, we agree that world culture is one dimension of an expanding global system – "carried" by a growing global infrastructure and "pushed" by groups that have a stake in its success. Like Wallerstein, we think world culture contains homogenizing tendencies, for example in the spread of institutional forms like the state, as well as differentiating ones, such as the pressure toward distinct definitions of national identities. We therefore also see a tension in world culture between universalizing principles and particularizing counterthrusts. As a result, we agree that culture can become a prime battleground, though major battles are not necessarily driven by well-defined material interests.

Wallerstein's version of the materialist story is only one of many. It shares a resemblance with others that portray world culture as ideology sustaining a system, as a symbolic reflection of hegemony. For instance, Peter Taylor agrees with much of Wallerstein's analysis of the world-system and presents its culture as a form of hegemony. However, his picture contains subtle differences (Taylor 1996, 1999). His main claim is that the world-system has always had a form of cultural hegemony, beginning with the Dutch version of the seventeenth century. When Dutch power declined, the British took over, to be succeeded in the twentieth century by the United States. In different historical periods, therefore, world culture consisted of different kinds of hegemony. In each case, the vision of a core state became a feature of the system as a whole. In other words, the most powerful states have exercised " 'moral and intellectual leadership' within the inter-state system which has had a fundamental impact on the socio-cultural nature of the modern world-system" (1999: 31). The three versions of world culture, Taylor has also argued, were similar in essential ways. Of course, they all depended on the notion that what is good for the hegemon is good for the world (1996: Ch. 3). Internationally, they all promoted an ideology of economic freedom. Within particular nation-states, they valued the inclusion of different groups as citizens in a state with limited powers. Therefore, hegemons "have been the modern world's liberal champions both economically and politically" (1996: 35) since well before the nineteenth century. Dutch, British, and American hegemony constitute versions of one tradition, distinguished chiefly by the specific economic activity they gave priority – commerce, production, and consumption, respectively. To probe this liberal thrust further, Taylor examines actual cultural products in some detail, interpreting Dutch paintings, English novels, and Hollywood movies. In these most characteristic cultural forms, he shows, the hegemons celebrated the lives of individuals, the comforts of material satisfaction, the very ordinariness of existence. In their aesthetically seductive ways, hegemonic cultures represented the cutting edge of global change, defining what it meant to be "modern" in each era. Of course, Taylor points out, hegemonies provoke reaction, notably from rival particularisms (1996: 34), such as Germany's protectionist response to English laissez-faire. Such reactions fuel conflict that contributes to hegemonic succession. Partly due to such conflict, Taylor anticipates the end of the American-dominated liberal era and the rise of a very different kind of world culture.

Like Taylor, Leslie Sklair regards consumerism as the "culture-ideology" of the global capitalist system. He describes a world in which transnational corporations "produce commodities and the services necessary to manufacture and sell them" and an increasingly united transnational capitalist class "produces a political environment within which the products of one country can be successfully marketed in another" (Sklair 1995: 60). This now fully global system needs eager consumers: the culture-ideology of consumerism "produces the values and attitudes that create and sustain the need for products" (ibid.). It binds these consumers to the system, for "[w]hen we experience the need for a global product we are engaged in a typical cultural-ideological transnational practice" (ibid.: 7). With the active support of transnational corporations the culture-ideology penetrates even societies where actual consumption cannot satisfy externally created desires (ibid.: Ch. 5). While the grossly asymmetrical system might seem to produce the material conditions for socialism, it also "closes down the political and cultural-ideological space for it" (28). However, like Taylor and Wallerstein, Sklair believes the current global system is unsustainable and therefore holds out hope for a "democratic feminist socialism" as a potential "Third Way" (269).

Having sketched materialist views of world culture in some detail, we now turn to the first of three perspectives that provide counterpoints and together shape our own approach.

World Culture as Ontology of World Society

In the 1970s, John Meyer and his colleagues faced a puzzle about the spread of formal education around the globe. Why, they wondered, did states with very different needs and resources adopt very similar educational institutions and methods, even when these did not obviously suit their particular situations? Meyer's previous work on educational organizations suggested a way to address the issue. He had argued that in modern societies organizations are not so much tools deliberately designed to solve problems as institutions driven by outside pressure to implement practices defined as "rational" (Meyer and Rowan 1991 [1977]: 41). Organizations are "dramatic enactments" (ibid.: 47) of rules that pervade a particular sector of society. By adopting these rules, ceremoniously as it were, by operating according to the official "myths" of rationality, organizations increase their legitimacy (41). Because all organizations in a particular field experience the same institutional pressure, they are likely to become more similar over time.

The insight Meyer and his colleagues brought to bear first on education, and ultimately on world culture as a whole, is that this "institutionalist" account also works at the global level. What, then, are the rules and assumptions built into the globalization of formal education? First of all, education has become the obligatory work of states. States themselves are constrained by global rules to act in rational fashion for the sake of progress: according to prevalent global models, states have ultimate authority in many areas of life, and they must exercise that authority by building "rational" institutions that promote "growth" (Meyer 1980). Formal public education is one such institution. Any modern state must have it, even if, as in the case of Malawi (Fuller 1991) and similar countries, the country has few resources to sustain it and its people have basic needs not served by this foreign import. Second, education seems so compelling in part because it is inextricably linked to great collective goals. According to the global script, learning increases human capital, educational investment raises growth, the spread of knowledge is the road to progress. Third, education has to take a certain form. A "rational" system is not one specifically designed to produce growth and literate citizens in a way that suits a particular country, but rather one that implements certain kinds of procedures and curricula, certain styles of teaching and studying. Thus, Malawi strives to implement a modern curriculum with professional teachers who exercise authority in their classroom, however difficult this may be when books and pencils are lacking (Fuller 1991). In globalizing education, form trumps function. Fourth, education reflects particular ideas about the people involved in it, especially the students. They are to be treated as individuals capable of learning, entitled to opportunity, eager to expand their horizons. Education must foster individual growth, but it must also connect students to their country: both implicitly and explicitly, it is always a kind of citizenship training. Around the world, formal education is one large civics lesson. Here again, Malawi is a case in point, even if individuality is unlikely to be fostered through mass teaching in drafty classrooms (ibid.).

The example shows several characteristics of world culture as institutionalists view it. It is the culture of a decentralized "world polity," in which many states are legitimate players but none controls the rules of the game (this account is therefore often called "world polity theory"). It contains rules and assumptions, often unstated and taken for granted, that are built into global institutions and practices. When we illustrated in the first chapter how many features of world society are "deeply cultural," for instance in the case of world chess, we already were applying an institutionalist insight. Moreover, no single person, organization, or state chooses the rules it follows; these are, to a large extent, exogenous – features of the world polity as a whole. In part for this reason, institutionalists sometimes describe world culture as composed of "scripts." Of course, a script does not simply create itself. It is the joint product of teachers and administrators, ministry officials and consultants, UNESCO representatives and NGO advocates. Like many aspects of world culture, it is the focus of much specialized professional activity, notably in international organizations. Finally, world culture is universalistic: the same assumptions, the same models are relevant, indeed valid, across the globe. To return to our example, this is not to say that actual educational practice exactly lives up to a single global model, but, institutionalists claim, the power of world culture is evident in the extent to which local practice depends on global norms.

Because these scholars view world culture as a deep structure underlying global practices, they have described it as a kind of "ontology." In using this term, they do not imply that global actors routinely speculate philosophically about the nature of being, but they do think there are now powerful, globally shared ideas about what is "real" in world society. Ontology, in their sense, comprises a set of rules and principles that define, among other things, the very actors that can legitimately participate in world affairs. "Culture has both an ontological aspect, assigning reality to actors and action, to means and ends; and it has a significatory aspect, endowing actor and action, means and ends, with meaning and legitimacy" (Meyer et al. 1987: 21). It "includes the institutional models of society itself" (ibid.). It specifies what the constituent parts of world society are and what kinds of things are to be considered valuable in the first place. This culture constitutes the array of authoritative organizations carrying out its mandates (Boli and Thomas 1999: 14). Because the world cultural order shapes not only the nation-state system but also other organizations and even human identities, Meyer and his colleagues ultimately present the world as the enactment of culture (Meyer et al. 1997: 151). Of course, this implies that world culture is not simply made by actors, the product of contending groups in a given system; it does not necessarily sustain a particular type of political economy or justify the position of actors within it, as the materialist account would have it. World culture cuts deeper.

What is the content of this ontology? As the education example shows, one prime tenet of world culture is that the world consists of states – corporate actors in control of territory and population, endowed with sovereignty, charged with numerous tasks, and expected to operate rationally in pursuit of globally defined progress (Meyer 1980). Though states encounter many difficulties, the idea has a powerful grip on global practice. But states are not the only actors, for the second main tenet of world culture, again evident in the education example, is that the world also consists of individuals – human actors endowed with rights and needs, possessing a distinct subjective consciousness, moving through a common life course, and acting as choosers and decision makers (Frank and Meyer 2002). Of course, Meyer does not mean that world culture somehow creates flesh-and-blood persons. However, how we understand and express ourselves as persons, the way we assert our rights and needs, does depend on globally relevant ideas. States and individuals are inextricably linked through a third tenet, the global principle of citizenship, which requires the cultivation of individual capacities as a basis for societal growth, respect for the equal rights and status of all members of society, and the creation of commonality among individuals as a way to integrate society. In short, the way we belong to a society is not simply an accident of birth or a result of personal choice; to some extent, belonging fits a global mold. Yet individuals are not merely citizens of states: since in principle all have the same rights and duties, may pursue their own interests freely, and can contribute to solving collective problems, they are construed as citizens of the world polity as a whole (Boli and Thomas 1997: 182).

The origins of this world culture clearly lie in the core Western cultural account, itself derived from medieval Christendom (Meyer et al. 1987: 27–8). Notions of individual value and autonomy, the importance of rationality in the pursuit of secular progress, and the status of states as sovereign actors, have deep roots in European history. Even in the nineteenth century, such basic ideas were still applied first and foremost by and for Westerners. However, this culture is now effectively global, both because its main structural elements are similar across the globe and because they are deemed to be universally applicable (Boli and Thomas 1997: 173). It has become global due to a decades-long process of institutionalization. Intergovernmental organizations enshrined many of the tenets we have described, for example in international conventions and declarations (some of which we will discuss in Chapter 4). After the Second World War, state building proceeded largely according to global scripts, resulting in a world of sovereign, rational, nominally equal states. Institutions focused on cultivating individuals have expanded rapidly. These include, of course, the educational institutions we have referred to in this chapter, but many others as well, such as the sports organizations we mentioned in the first chapter. International nongovernmental organizations – voluntary associations of interested individuals – have assumed increased influence in articulating global principles. Many people, groups, and institutions, in short, have done the work of world culture. A key consequence of that work is global isomorphism, the increasing institutional similarity of differently situated societies. Where materialist accounts of the capitalist world-system would expect variation by economic status and historical trajectory, institutionalists find homogeneity, for example, in the way organized science spreads to all corners of the globe (Drori et al. 2003) or in the way women's rights gain recognition within many states (Berkovitch 1999a).

Since institutionalists treat world culture as constitutive of reality, as a symbolic structure that shapes the ways people act and feel, they do not need to assume any widespread, explicit agreement on the fundamentals of world culture. They would suggest that even ostensible critics of existing world culture, such as environmentalists or feminists, ultimately conform to important tenets. However, this is not to say that world culture is a seamless web. For one thing, institutionalization is always incomplete, due to numerous local constraints, as we already noted in the case of formal education in Malawi, which resembles the supposed global script in only some respects. World culture also provokes genuine conflict. Thus, the assertion of equal rights for women has been challenged by Islamic groups as incompatible with their tradition (Berkovitch 1999a). The notion that world culture is now global, universally shared and applicable, is itself subject to challenge in practice, insofar as it is disproportionately the product of powerful states. A case in point is the expansion of education, at least in part a consequence of America's exercise of hegemony (Meyer 1986: 215). World culture could not be seamless in any case, since many of its principles are contradictory, as is evident in the well-known tensions between equality and liberty, efficiency and individuality, and expectations for states to "be themselves" and "act alike" (Meyer et al. 1997: 172). World culture thus creates a culturally dynamic world: "Ironically, world-cultural structuration produces more mobilization and competition among the various types of similarly constructed actors than would occur in a genuinely segmental world. Increasing consensus on the meaning and value of individuals, organizations, and nation-states yields more numerous and intense struggles to achieve independence, autonomy, progress, justice, and equality" (ibid.: 172–3).

The institutionalists agree with the Wallersteinians on several empirical features of the modern world-system, but they account for the origins and reproduction of that system in different ways. As our brief summary has shown, the institutionalists give culture much greater weight. It becomes, so to speak, base rather than superstructure. As an analytical standpoint, this carries its own risks. For example, it is tempting to find evidence of deep culture at work in the activities of various institutions and then use the understanding of culture thus acquired to explain the evidence that served to generate the independent cultural variable in the first place. While avoiding such circular reasoning, we will partly rely on the institutionalist argument for guidance.

World Culture as Definition of the Global Condition

In the late 1970s and early 1980s, fundamentalism was much in the news. The Islamic revolution in Iran had overthrown the Shah and established the Islamic Republic. In the United States, the so-called New Christian Right exerted unexpected influence in politics. Conventional wisdom held that in both cases discontented groups, previously excluded from full participation, reasserted themselves by trying to turn back the clock in public life and impose a particular religious truth on their society. Surveying the ways in which people brought religion to bear on society at large, Roland Robertson questioned that interpretation of fundamentalism as backward and out of step with the times. Without endorsing the substance of their ideas, he proposed that fundamentalists were grappling with important global dilemmas and advancing distinct views of world society. In their own way, they were creative global actors. Robertson's interpretation illustrates key features of what he came to call globalization theory, a theory in which world culture figures centrally.

Robertson noted, first of all, that the "search for fundamentals" (1992: Ch. 11) was by no means limited to hard-line Islamists; rather, it was a universal phenomenon, expressed in many kinds of church–state tensions across the globe. The search was universal because it reflected a global predicament. The very frequency of such searches, he thought, contained a message: fundamentalisms were one way for particular societies to deal with dilemmas they encountered in the process of globalization (Robertson and Chirico 1985). As the world became compressed into a "single place," each society and tradition had to redefine its place within it. Fundamentalists confronted in more dramatic fashion a problem many others grappled with as well. In a threatening world, they claimed to define a society's "own" identity by relying on its "own" tradition, and to put forth alternative views of world society itself (ibid.). On the surface, it seemed that fundamentalists were trying to withdraw from the wider world, but in fact they were joining a global discussion or "discourse" about how to construct a new kind of world order (Robertson 1992: 113). Of course, fundamentalists often presented themselves in an oppositional mode, as storm troopers against a world culture they regarded as the product of the evil West (an issue to which we will return in Chapter 9). Yet even this was somewhat misleading, for Robertson argued that fundamentalist movements often invoked globally diffused ideas (ibid.: 166–7). One basic argument of many fundamentalists, namely the right to preserve the integrity of their own tradition, itself drew on a global idea – that peoples and societies are entitled to their particular identities, and indeed are expected to develop some form of cultural distinctiveness. Particularism had been universalized (102). In Robertson's reading, fundamentalism was thus a globally diffused means of responding to problems inherent in globalization, producing images of world order while invoking existing global principles.

As this view of fundamentalism illustrates, Robertson was among the first scholars of his generation to advocate systematic analysis of the world considered as a meaningful whole. Understanding the worldwide religious resurgence evident in fundamentalism, in particular, required "a definitely global focus, a focus on the world as a whole" (1992: 2). To understand the "world as a whole" in turn required that we see it as the result of a long process of globalization. That term refers to "the compression of the world and the intensification of consciousness of the world as a whole . . . the increasing acceleration in both concrete interdependence and consciousness of the global whole in the twentieth century" (ibid.: 8). As this definition suggests, culture does not somehow exist apart from globalization; it is not a dependent variable, subject to the play of independent forces. Instead, Robertson thinks of culture as integral to the very process itself. Globalization partly consists of the extension of global consciousness (1998: 218). It is not simply an objective process of integration, a way of connecting people and places. Essential to the process is the very way people make sense of it. And they must make sense of it, as Leclerc also stresses, for globalization poses a problem, namely of "the form in terms of which the world becomes 'united'" (Robertson 1992: 51). At a fundamental level, everyone "knows" that the world is one; but what holds it together is a question. For Robertson, world culture consists first and foremost of answers to that question.

Unity is a problem because all the "players" on the world scene have found themselves undergoing what Robertson has called "relativization" (1992: 27). These players or core units of global analysis include national societies, individual selves, the world-system of societies and humankind. In the modern era, individuals fit into nation-states as citizens; but this relationship becomes relativized, in Robertson's sense, when citizenship becomes subject to general norms derived from human rights standards pertaining to humankind as a whole. In the case of the United States, for example, its treatment of citizens in criminal cases, especially when the death penalty is a possible outcome, now receives critical scrutiny from outsiders. Similarly, as they become economically and technologically more integrated into a larger system, particular societies must define their places in the larger world-system. A case in point is the experience of the People's Republic of China in recent decades: no longer the self-centered Middle Kingdom or isolated keeper of the Marxist faith, it redefines itself ambiguously as an aspiring superpower that observes common economic rules while challenging the applicability of human rights standards in Asia.

Naturally, as Robertson's interpretation of fundamentalism already suggested, different groups will respond to these predicaments in different ways. They share a common global condition, and they all face the "problem of globality," but they construct different images of the world they live in and of the order they envision. Not only does globalization bring different forms of life in ever-closer conjunction with each other (1992: 27), but out of this conjunction emerge different visions of how to build global order, different "explicitly *globe-oriented* ideologies" (ibid.: 78–9; emphasis in original). Islamic fundamentalists, for example, typically view the desirable world society as a collection of closed communities, in which the realm of Islam is marked off clearly from that of the infidels; in a way, the clash-of-civilizations model fits their vision, as we will elaborate in Chapter 9. Others, by contrast, envision a more organized world community, in which, for example, nation-states would be held accountable in terms of common rules; the International Criminal Court, which we analyze in Chapter 10, would be a step in the right direction from this perspective. Because none of these visions yet prevails, globalization has been, and is bound to remain, a contentious process. What matters for Robertson is not the resolution of the problem – for him world culture is the domain in which this contention plays out.

In proposing this analysis of globalization, Robertson drew on ideas he first developed in a critique of studies of "modernization" in the late 1960s. He and his colleague J. P. Nettl were dissatisfied with then-current accounts of social change that predicted convergence over time due to inexorable pressures on societies to "modernize" (Nettl and Robertson 1968). Modernization did not have to happen, they suggested. It did not need to follow a single path or lead to a common goal. Instead, they argued, societies find themselves in a global field of other societies that provide a kind of reference group. Each society pursues its own path by selectively incorporating examples or standards set by others. In global competition for status, societies engage in continuous comparison. Peter the Great's Russia and Meiji Japan are early instances of extensive borrowing in jockeying for global position, but their experience became universal. From this critique of modernization theory Robertson drew lessons that shaped his thinking about globalization and world culture. Rather than a natural, domestic, evolutionary process, modernization turned out to be inherently "relative," because societies develop only in relation to an international system of societies, notably by deliberate comparison and emulation. The process is also "reflexive," because elites necessarily reflect on how to position their nation-state in world society, to varying degrees picking and choosing from options presented to them. It is "constructive" because pursuing modernization is a kind of reality construction. And it is global, because it is embedded in what Robertson later called a "global culture of modernization" (Robertson 1991: 211; cf. 1992: 91ff.). Each of these features carried over to Robertson's thinking about the formation of world culture.

As we have seen, for Robertson world culture is not something set apart from "real" globalization but rather a critical dimension of the process itself, because globalization partly consists of the way in which people collectively reflect on it. World culture is the domain in which the world gets constructed, at least symbolically. That construction does not follow a single design; rather, the many would-be architects are always at odds. To be sure, they share a common project, since they all must come to terms with the question of how to live together in a single place. They share a minimal common culture, for example insofar as they all must articulate what they take to be the interests of humanity as a shared reference point. But this commonality is limited, for even universal standards, such as those pertaining to modern state building, are necessarily subject to local interpretation. Hence, the content of world culture in practice always takes "glocalized" form (Robertson 1995). World culture is, so to speak, a mold rather than a model: it contains the various ways in which individuals and collectivities relate to the world as a whole. This relationship gets expressed in many different ways, ranging from very abstract "world images" to concrete forms of "glocalization" (ibid.). World culture is therefore the sum total of ways to define the global situation, the ways in which people around the world express their global consciousness.

Since Robertson's analysis of globalization is "cultural" through and through, it is not surprising that he has occasionally criticized the Wallersteinians for being too materialist. He has pointed out, for example, that the political-economic expansion of the world-system has itself been subject to competing definitions of the situation, that it has been a culturally contentious process (1992: 69ff.); but he has also noted a kind of thematic convergence with their work, for example when it comes to "antisystemic" movements, even if the analytical lens through which they look at these themes still produces some distortion. Though Robertson agrees with the institutionalists on the constitutive role of culture, he nevertheless differs in his assessment of that role. To him, culture is not so settled, not a collection of ready-made scripts. He regards world culture as more inherently contentious and globalization as more open-ended.

In our own analysis, Robertson's work serves as a guide along with that of the world polity theorists. We will elaborate the constructive, contentious, and reflexive features of world culture he has emphasized. To the empirical examples and historical references that support his analysis of globalization we will add more detailed study of empirical cases. We now turn to a fourth type of account, one that closely fits with Robertson's and exemplifies efforts to analyze world culture in a more fine-grained manner.

World Culture as the Organization of Diversity

In his study of McDonald's in Hong Kong, James Watson (1997) demonstrated that its customers across the globe do not consume fast food in the same way. Some features of McDonald's "system," such as the taste of the hamburgers and the division of labor devised to produce them, do seem to be universal. However, when Hong Kong consumers enter a McDonald's restaurant, differences from American practices quickly appear. Instead of displaying congeniality, workers project unflappable competence; while expecting fast service, consumers are likely to hover or linger; young people occupy the place as a kind of youth center. To succeed in particular markets such as Hong Kong, McDonald's itself has adopted a "multilocal" strategy, varying its menu and management style as needed. Partly as a result of this strategy, its restaurants no longer appear to be exotic in Asian cities; rather, they become one element in a diverse culinary scene. That scene is changing in any case, for example due to new tastes and technologies prevalent among younger generations. Since the "local culture" is itself complex and fluid, the impact of McDonald's is actually difficult to gauge. In terms similar to Robertson's, Watson describes that impact as a form of "localization" and argues that this is a two-way street, implying changes in both local culture and the company's operating procedures (ibid.: 37). Reflecting on his observations, Watson notes that "the ordinary people of Hong Kong have most assuredly *not* been stripped of their cultural heritage, nor have they become the uncomprehending dupes of transnational corporations" (107–8). Instead of passively receiving a prefabricated transnational culture, he concludes, the people of Hong Kong are themselves producing it.

Watson's argument is open to objections. For example, Hong Kong has long been an unusually cosmopolitan place, so the selection of this case already favors the point he wants to make. Small changes in consumer behavior need not undermine the McDonaldization scenario, and Watson may well underestimate the extent to which customers across the globe do adopt a fast-food mentality toward meals. Rather than pursue such objections to his case study, we focus here on the type of analysis Watson offers. That analysis reflects an important thrust in anthropological thinking about world culture. In seeing local cultures as changing and open to the outside world, treating ordinary people as active participants, analyzing the transnational as something that is produced in particular locales, and describing global standards as subject to multiple interpretations, Watson conveys a macroanthropological model of world culture. We caught a glimpse of it in our discussion of Breidenbach and Zukrigl's *Dance of Cultures*. While not all anthropologists working on these issues accept that model, it has become increasingly influential.

One reason for the model's rising appeal is that anthropologists have found that in some respects Hong Kong is not unique. When Ulf Hannerz examined life in Kafanchan, a town in central Nigeria, his observations did not fit traditional notions about culture. Anthropologists customarily envisioned the world as a mosaic, each small place having its own culture (Hannerz 1996: 4–5). Culture itself they treated as the fixed property of particular groups, a distinctive symbolic repertoire that is learned across generations and coherent within any one place (ibid.: 8). However, Kafanchan was rather more complex. Located at the intersection of rail lines, it had grown along with modern infrastructure and was connected to world markets. Its population consisted of different ethnic groups. The Nigerian state made its presence felt through several institutions, notably the schools and the army. Most books available in Kafanchan are in English; several bookshops were started by Protestant missions. Even before the advent of electricity, Lagos newspapers had linked a Kafanchan audience to the nation's center; with electricity came modern mass media, transmitting both Western and Nigerian entertainment products as part of a vibrant popular culture. It was implausible, Hannerz thought, to ascribe a single culture to Kafanchan, a particular "package" characteristic of this particular place. Rather than seeing culture as necessarily coherent and distinctive, Hannerz proposed to view it as the "organization of diversity" (1992: 13). In the Kafanchan case, this meant tracing the variable impact of state and market on more-or-less settled "forms of life" there. If Kafanchan had a culture, it consisted of the ongoing, creative interplay of indigenous and imported elements (1996: 4), of a "moving interconnectedness" (1992: 167).

Through the movement of people and the flow of media images, through the institutions of state and market, Kafanchan had developed numerous "transnational connections," as the title of one of Hannerz's books indicated. It had become embedded in a "global ecumene" (1992: Ch. 7). The culture of that ecumene is the global organization of diversity. But what does this culture consist of? Drawing on his Kafanchan experience, Hannerz argued that there is no single set of ideas that prevails everywhere. Rather, world culture is a culture of creolized cultures, in which diverse, initially alien outside influences are absorbed by various collectivities relying on internally diverse frameworks (1992: 261–2). The various streams of culture are thereby refracted differently depending on what frameworks operate most strongly in any one context, leading to both the absorption of universal ideas ("saturation") and distinct mixtures of the indigenous and the imported ("maturation"). One restraint on the free play of creativity suggested by the creolization metaphor is that among the operative frameworks are institutions that are part of the "cultural apparatus" of the state, including formal education, and these usually channel ideas in a very asymmetrical way, e.g., from elite policy maker to rural student (cf. 1992: 83). In the ecumene as a whole, culture also flows through an asymmetrical center–periphery structure, and this means that there is bound to be great variation in how collectivities are exposed to "alien" content and in the resources they have to process the influx (ibid.: 261–2). But the "center," though still able to set some cultural standards, is not what it is often presumed to be: all cultures are creolized to some degree, and the periphery, as in Kafanchan, definitely talks back. Rather than a rigid center–periphery structure, world culture displays a "creole continuum" (67).

Like Hannerz, Arjun Appadurai sees a world of greatly intensified cultural flows that impinge on different groups in different ways. The combined effects of global media and international migration have produced a kind of cultural rupture – more and more groups now must confront the question of how to cope with the onslaught of exogenous cultural pressure. In this situation, the work of the imagination becomes "a space of contestation in which individuals and groups seek to annex the global into their own practices" (Appadurai 1996: 4). But "annexing" the global is always an active, creative process; for example, even the consumption of mass media products throughout the world "often provokes resistance, irony, selectivity, and, in general, *agency*" (ibid.: 7; emphasis in original). To describe the process as local cultures contending with global forces is actually somewhat misleading. For one thing, culture is never a given, never fixed for all time. Appadurai challenges the idea that culture is a substance, the possession of a localized group (ibid.: 12–13). He proposes to focus on culture as adjective, as a dimension of all group practices that show how a group is distinctive and expresses its collective identity. Difference-making and identity-expression are always ongoing, so it makes sense to see culture as inherently dynamic. The "local" aspect of culture is similarly problematic, since what a place means, how a group occupies it, and whether place even matters to its identity, are all subject to cultural definition. Locality itself is always "produced" (ibid.: Ch. 9). Under global conditions, therefore, culture shifts to being "a rather more volatile form of difference" (ibid.: 60).

In arguing for the volatility of difference, Appadurai does not mean to imply that cultures are now at the mercy of global models. To be sure, there are homogenizing trends, but in the end these are outweighed by an opposing thrust toward greater heterogeneity. Older bulwarks of commonality are in decline – the USA is no longer a cultural puppeteer (1996: 31) and nation-states are under siege (ibid.: 40). Commoditization also has its limits, for "at least as rapidly as forces from various metropolises are brought into new societies they tend to become indigenized in one or another way" (ibid.: 32). In fact, the new global cultural economy "has to be seen as a complex, overlapping, disjunctive order that cannot any longer be understood in terms of existing center–periphery models" (ibid.). The main source of variety in world culture is the disjuncture among different cultural flows or "scapes." Ideas, people, capital, media content, and machines all move quite independently and get distributed differently across the globe: they follow "nonisomorphic paths" (1996: 37). They also constitute building blocks, to be assembled in multiple new imagined worlds by differently situated groups (ibid.: 33). Particular "scapes" may also diversify internally; for example, the so-called "ideoscape" once provided a coherent Euro-American master narrative to shape political action, but this tale has lost its internal coherence (36). There is no single pattern to the flows, for their relationships "as they constellate into particular events and social forms will be radically context-dependent" (47). In the macroanthropological model represented by Hannerz and Appadurai, then, world culture does not appear as a single substance produced by world society; rather, it is the set of processes by which diversity gets organized globally.

As our brief summary has shown, macroanthropology differs from world-systemic views of culture in its critique of center–periphery models and its emphasis on the production of difference. Against the world polity perspective, it would urge greater attention to the deep sources of heterogeneity and the concrete processes of local adaptation. It does have an affinity with Robertsonian globalization theory, in effect treating "glocalization" as a hallmark of all world-cultural processes. Though we will not pursue the ethnographic research strategy of most anthropologists in this book, several of their themes guide our work: specifically, the tension between homogenizing and differentiating forces, the dissolution of centers and peripheries, and the reproduction of difference as a global process in its own right. By comparison with Hannerz and Appadurai, we will put more stress on the "organization" in the "organization of diversity"; where they see mainly creolization, disjuncture, and flow, we note more constraint, pattern, and structure.

To consolidate this review of influential accounts of world culture, we summarize them in Table 2.1.

Table 2.1: *Summary of theoretical accounts*

Account	World system theory	World polity theory	Globalization theory	Macroanthropological theory
Key figures	Wallerstein	Meyer	Robertson	Hannerz/Appadurai
Concept of culture	Ideology	Ontology	Reflexive interpretation	Symbolic organization
Approach	Materialist: world culture is instrument of legitimation or arena of struggle	Institutionalist: world culture constitutes actors, purposes	Pragmatic: world culture comprises definitions of situation, common reference points	Interpretive: world culture is made up of reconfigured cultures, niches in global scapes
World-view	Culture embedded in hierarchical system	Culture integral to universal polity	Culture in reflexive relation to ongoing globalization	Culture at intersection of multiple flows
Content	Liberalism/universalism, Racism/sexism, nationalism	Models of states, individuals, formal organizations as actors	Contending views of world order; common conception of humanity	Multiple forms of linking local–global practices
Key processes	Hegemonic imposition, resistance	Isomorphic institutionalization	Relativization, selective emulation, glocalization	Creolization, glocalization
Illustrative instances	Antisystemic movements	Educational expansion	Fundamentalisms	Urban cultures

Toward a Synthesis

In view of the differences among the various accounts, a reader might now question our assumption that students of world culture are in fact talking about the same thing. Can Wallerstein's hegemony be squared with Hannerz's creolization? Does Robertsonian contention fit with Meyer's iso-morphism? Clearly, the four accounts derive from distinctive intellectual traditions. Wallerstein's Marxist, materialist lineage favors treatment of culture as ideology, Robertson and Meyer draw on Max Weber and Emile Durkheim in stressing the centrality of culture, and the anthropologists relate critically to their discipline's tradition of seeing culture as the sym-bolic way of marking group distinctions. These authors therefore also make contrasting claims about processes central to world culture, ranging from Wallerstein's dialectic of dominance and resistance, to Meyer's institution-alization of models, to Robertson's forms of relativization, and Appadurai's intersecting flows. Their interpretations of concrete events are bound to vary as well. For example, the rise of fundamentalist movements matters to Wallerstein as an instance of antisystemic activity, while Meyer might treat them as unwitting carriers of common global assumptions, Robertson stresses their active role in global discourse about the desirable world order, and the anthropologists would point to their irretrievably hybrid nature. These scholarly differences are real. They are also valuable insofar as they prevent premature consensus and stimulate creative explorations. We there-fore do not want to argue that these accounts fully converge on a common perspective or a single paradigm, or that there already is a grand synthesis under the surface only waiting to be revealed. What we do claim is that, in some respects at least, these accounts overlap and that their family resem-blances can point the way to a more coherent perspective on world culture.

Viewed as producers of cultural products, these observers of world culture have much in common. With one exception, they are white males of Euro-American background. Their vantage point is the Western academy. While this certainly restricts their range of vision in some ways, it would be misleading to pigeonhole them on the basis of a crude sociology of knowledge. Their work carries the imprint of Western intellectual tradi-tions, but it is driven in the first instance by empirical questions, by an inter-est in the world as it is. For most, these questions stem from critical reflection on the actual process of "modernization," especially as it has affected non-Western countries. As a result of their engagement with these questions, they all have questioned the relationship of center or core to periphery. Like many of their colleagues, they have become intensely reflexive about the once-standard enlightened Western narrative account; for them, no "end of history" is in sight. For all of them, the fact that messy history continues only increases the importance of culture in the process of globalization, for it is there that competing views of the world and its history are hashed out. At the same time, they have not made a postmodern turn insofar as they continue to search for structure and pattern. They also have not "gone native"; they have avoided romanticizing the "other," if only by questioning the very meaning of native or local culture in the wider world setting. It is not unreasonable, then, to view their accounts as branches of a single, critically self-reflexive tradition of social science scholarship. Our work continues in this tradition.

Do these accounts share anything in the way they analyze culture? In this regard, the family they represent may be too extended to show much resemblance, but we would suggest three analytical features that tie them together, even if the precise meaning of the dimensions differs from case to case. First, these accounts are constructionist, in the sense that they incorporate the kind of process famously described by Peter Berger and Thomas Luckmann in *The Social Construction of Reality* (1966). Culture is reality as socially constructed, the product of a collective process of defining a common situation. The constructive part of the process is apparent, for example, in Wallerstein's view of the way core classes created centrist liberalism as dominant ideology, in institutionalist studies of the role of international organizations in formulating global principles, in Robertsonian analyses of movements creating world images, and in Hannerz's creole cultures' creative use of multiple building blocks. Second, from the Berger/Luckmann model follows a dialectical view of culture: the very form of culture construction contains seeds of its antithesis or fosters opposing tendencies that challenge any cultural template. Thus, liberalism requires racism and calls forth particularist resistance, global models pit state against individual and liberty against equality, relativization leads to glocalization rather than the dominance of any one world image, and continuing global flows undermine any settled local culture. As these examples of "dialectic" already indicate, these accounts share with the Berger/Luckmann model a processual approach to culture. While it can have a structure of its own and acquire a certain autonomy from the vagaries of social conflict, it is never fully congealed but always subject to reinterpretation; construction invites reconstruction.

Beyond such highly abstract convergence, we find more specific agreement on the what, when, and how of world culture. For example, with respect to the content of world culture all accounts recognize the individual and state as globally legitimate, culturally constituted units. Similarly, with the partial exception of the institutionalists, they find difference proliferating within the geoculture. With regard to history, the sociological accounts identify the late nineteenth century as a critical period in world culture development, the "take-off" period, as Robertson has called it, in which Wallersteinian liberalism achieved dominance and the institutionalists' rational models first crystallized, as we will explain in the next chapter. After the Second World War, all agree, world culture became fully globalized. Of course, the various interpretations have their own ways of explaining the dynamics of culture, but they depict similar methods by which world culture spreads. For example, Taylor's "rival particularisms" have an affinity with Meyer's competitive rationalization (1983: 271), Robertson's selective emulation, and the deliberate difference-making anthropologists attribute to creole cultures. Such historical and empirical points inform several of our chapters.

What these accounts share above all is the idea that world culture is inherently contentious – a "battleground" of sorts. To be sure, they differ on what battles they find most important, but they agree that world culture is shot through with conflicts. Particularists oppose universalists, defenders of individual rights take on state interests, nations hold out against global pressures, defenders of the indigenous challenge would-be imperialists, advocates of justice challenge the claims of liberty. These conflicts take specific forms: they are about certain issues, involve particular actors, employ an evolving global rhetoric, and lead to collective mobilization. Forces seemingly at loggerheads are also often deeply entwined with what they ostensibly oppose. In describing culture as battlefield, then, these accounts do not describe a world torn apart, for the very form of conflict helps to bind groups around the globe into a common life.

We describe these overlaps and resemblances to suggest that through different lenses different observers nevertheless show common features of a common object. These we propose to study more systematically. Yet, as we have shown, the accounts we build on do not fully agree. Since we have been involved in work related to two of these, we are not impartial. While we aim to analyze world culture in a way that does justice to the concerns of a broad range of scholars, we do take sides. When the chips are down, we favor playing the institutionalist and Robertsonian cards. However, our strategy in the following chapters is to draw liberally, yet critically, on all the main ideas we have reviewed in this chapter. Having laid out our analytical tools, we now turn to more substantive investigation of world culture, beginning with a closer look at the recent history of world culture.

Chapter 3

Tracing World Culture: A Brief History

On September 14, 1793, Lord Macartney, the English diplomat leading an embassy to China, was finally received by the aging emperor Ch'ien-Lung in his magnificent tent at Jehol. As the emperor was carried inside, Macartney noted in his journal, "all the Chinese made their usual prostrations," while the British "paid him our compliments by kneeling on one knee" (Cranmer-Byng 1962: 122). After giving the emperor a large gold box with a letter of congratulations from King George III, Macartney exchanged presents with him. The visitors were then treated to a sumptuous banquet, a five-hour ceremony that seemed to "resemble the celebration of a religious mystery" and displayed "the sober pomp of Asiatic greatness, which European refinements have not yet attained" (ibid.: 123–4). In the following days, Macartney was allowed to enter one of Ch'ien-Lung's elaborate parks and attend his birthday celebrations. The emperor also granted the ambassador another audience at one of his palaces. Yet, in spite of the apparently gracious reception, Macartney soon began to feel that his discussions with Chinese officials were leading nowhere. An imperial edict dismissing the embassy confirmed his fears. Realizing his mission had failed, Macartney left Peking on October 7, traveling down the Grand Canal to the south before setting sail for England.

Macartney had left England the previous year with two ships and an entourage of 95, charged by the British government to seek diplomatic relations with the Chinese empire, negotiate a treaty of friendship and commerce, establish a permanent presence in the Chinese capital, and open new ports to trade (ibid.: 3, 30). By engaging China in diplomatic relations, England had hoped to draw it into its sphere of influence. By expanding trade opportunities, England had hoped to make more money in a potentially enormous market. Unstated in the formal charge to the ambassador was a key factor behind his mission: tea. Since the seventeenth century, the

English had become addicted to it, and China had become their key sup-plier. Yet, China needed little that Britain had to offer. It also consciously sought to keep foreign goods out by charging high fees and tariffs. Since the Chinese demanded payment in precious metals, the China trade had become a huge drain, the "tomb of European silver" (Sahlins 2000: 425). The embassy's goal was to improve the balance of trade and create a more equal relationship.

This was no easy task. Though Macartney had studied most available sources on China, he knew how incomplete they were. None of his party spoke Chinese, making them dependent on the translation services of a Chinese priest, recruited from a college in Naples, who understood Latin and Italian but not English. Reflecting on his experience, Macartney com-plained about the "difficulty of obtaining correct information." However, lack of knowledge was only one obstacle. The embassy's behavior was another. Ignoring precedent, Macartney bypassed Canton and went ashore closer to the capital in northern China instead. Claiming to represent an independent sovereign, Macartney insisted to Chinese officials that he would not kowtow to the emperor. Eventually, he was allowed to kneel as he would for his own king, but, as Chinese court documents put it at the time, this "unwarranted haughtiness" marked the visitors as "ignorant barbarians" who did not deserve Chinese generosity (Cranmer-Byng 1962: 33). By their own behavior, the barbarians complicated their mission.

Yet it never really had a chance. Even before Macartney stepped ashore, Chinese officials had drafted an edict ordering his dismissal (Cranmer-Byng 1962: 337). Delivered to the ambassador on October 3, the exquisitely con-descending edict expresses a world-view Macartney barely fathomed. "We, by the Grace of Heaven, Emperor, instruct the King of England to take note of our charge," it begins (ibid.: 337ff.). Though complimenting the king for the "humility and obedience" in his message and for the "sincerity" shown by the congratulations and "local products" conveyed by the ambassador, the edict resolutely refuses the English requests. Having an English subject reside in China's capital "does not conform to the Celestial Empire's cere-monial system, and definitely cannot be done." He could not be allowed to go in and out, he would not be understood, "we have nowhere to house him," and soon other "Western Ocean countries" would make similar demands. "How can we go as far as to change the regulations of the Celes-tial Empire, which are over a hundred years old, because of the request of one man – of you, O King?" Such a change is not necessary to conduct trade, the edict states, and trade itself is unimportant: "The Celestial Empire . . . simply concentrates on carrying out the affairs of government properly, and does not value rare and precious things." Of course, other kingdoms have offered precious things in tribute, but "we have never valued ingenious articles, nor do we have the slightest need of your country's manufactures." Dismissing the embassy and its requests, the emperor then commands the king to "act in conformity with our wishes by strengthening your loyalty and swearing perpetual obedience" and to "reverently receive" the special gifts bestowed upon the envoys.

Ch'ien-Lung's edict constitutes a classic statement of the Chinese view of world order. In this view, China was the center of the world, the "prototype of civilization" (Cranmer-Byng 1962: 341), confident in its accomplishments and superior in virtue. At the apex of its hierarchical social order stood the Son of Heaven as the supreme symbol of unity and harmony, whose authority was sustained by the proper ceremonial forms, to be observed by both the Chinese elite and by other rulers (Fairbank 1968: 6–8). From the emperor radiated a mystical influence that transformed others with the blessings of Chinese civilization and brought order and peace to humanity (ibid.: 8–9). By promulgating a new calendar, weights and measures, and a musical scale, the recipient of a new Mandate of Heaven could even institute "human time and space, economy and harmony – all as the extension of the imperial person" (Sahlins 2000: 426). An old Chinese image presents this view of world order as a series of concentric rectangles, with the royal domains at the center and a zone of cultureless savagery at the periphery (Sahlins 2000: 437, citing Needham). The whole world, in short, formed a hierarchy. In this world, the center always held. "Rare and precious things" only mattered as confirmation of the emperor's power and virtue, as tribute to the goodness of the order over which he presided.

Macartney thus confronted a wholly different civilization with its own distinctive conception of world order. When he refused to kowtow, he at least realized that he risked giving offense by violating sacred ritual rules. In other ways, he was clueless. Wanting to get down to the business of negotiating after attending numerous ceremonies, he did not realize that, from the Chinese perspective, the essential work was done, since the ceremonies were the business (Sahlins 2000: 428). Far from impressing the Chinese with English "pre-eminence" (Cranmer-Byng 1962: 191), Macartney's presents were received as tribute to be added to the already rich displays in palaces and parks of products from around the world. Those displays, which he was not allowed to see, did not celebrate foreign science and ingenuity but rather, by their sheer inclusiveness, demonstrated that "the whole world was the work of the emperor and within his power" (Sahlins 2000: 432). "[I]f ever anyone carried coals to Newcastle," the anthropologist

Marshall Sahlins concludes, "it was British people carrying signs of civilization to the Chinese" (ibid.: 430). To them, dismissing Macartney was simply the civilized thing to do.

Yet, just as Macartney misunderstood the Chinese, they, in holding fast to their own conception of world order, also underestimated him. Macartney was in effect the carrier of an ambitious civilization with an expansive view of its potential role in the world. His thinking reflected assumptions about politics and economics, about history and progress, about power and values that would increasingly mold world culture. As a diplomat seeking to establish relations with China, he assumed that the world consisted of equal, sovereign states capable of concluding mutually beneficial agreements. In this order, neither kowtow nor tribute had a place. Promoting trade seemed an utterly natural goal – not merely a concession by a benevolent ruler but an intrinsically valuable advance in the material well-being of different peoples. If England could be the first to establish a permanent presence in China, it would gain a great advantage in the global competition among great powers that increasingly shaped world affairs. The embassy's carefully chosen presents, such as clocks and globes, and the scientists brought along to impress the Chinese with contraptions like balloons and submarines, symbolized creativity and enlightenment. In this way, the mission demonstrated that "it was in vain attempting the progress of human knowledge" (Cranmer-Byng 1962: 191). The advancement of knowledge was tied to power: if China were to "interdict us their commerce . . . we have the means easy enough of revenging ourselves, for a few frigates could in a few weeks destroy all their coast navigation" (ibid.: 210–11). From the "progressive" British point of view, China in fact appeared like an "old, crazy, First rate man-of-war [sic], which a fortunate succession of able and vigilant officers has contrived to keep afloat . . . and to overawe their neighbours merely by her bulk and appearance, but whenever an insufficient man happens to have the command upon deck, adieu to the discipline and safety of the ship" (212–13). If it were to fall apart, Britain could still gain, for as Britain "from the weight of her riches and the genius and spirit of her people, is become the first political, marine and commercial power on the globe, it is reasonable to think that she would prove the greatest gainer by such a revolution as I have alluded to, and rise superior over every competitor" (213). Though he was disappointed about the failure of his mission, as the representative of a rising power Macartney was confident in his judgment that the Chinese dismissed him at their peril. In the world-cultural tidal wave to come, the old man-of-war could not hope to stay afloat.

That tidal wave did not simply begin in 1793. The cultural baggage Macartney brought along, literally and figuratively, had a history. When he took pride in completing European knowledge of the northern Chinese coastline, he placed himself in a long Western tradition of explorers and mapmakers. His confidence in the progress of human knowledge reflected views that had become increasingly common during the European Enlightenment. The embassy's scholars and artifacts demonstrated British scientific and engineering prowess, rooted in what is now called the Scientific Revolution (Goodman and Russell 1991). British faith in trade, long a driving force behind the expansion of the world market in which China already had a "notable place" (Adshead 2000: 234), had been bolstered by eighteenth-century thinking about political economy, which had produced a doctrine of free trade that would gain influence in the century to come. Macartney's diplomatic world-view had even deeper roots in the culture of European states, shaped above all by the Treaty of Westphalia of 1648 that had settled the Thirty Years War by recognizing the equal sovereignty of states – a "watershed" in European thinking about the responsibilities of states both within their territories and toward each other (Hall 1996: 52–3). The embassy thus represented a number of important cultural currents. Only in the decades after its return to England did these already strong currents, pushed along by the kinds of economic and political considerations that were Macartney's own chief motives, combine into a single world culture.

The very mission to China undertaken by Macartney was not unprecedented either. In fact, he benefited from earlier missions to China by having a Chinese Catholic priest, Jacobus Li, serve as his interpreter. These earlier missions by Western "religious internationals," first the Jesuits, then the Dominicans, had expanded European knowledge of China and exposed the Chinese elite to the culture of the lands far to the west (Adshead 2000: 234). Generations of Catholic missionaries had to engage in delicate negotiations similar to those Macartney faced (Wills 2001: Ch. 11). Precisely because Macartney was well aware of the religious impulses behind earlier Western forays into China, and the tensions these produced, he assured his Chinese hosts that he had no ulterior religious motives. After all, the embassy had not brought along any clergymen. Lacking the "zeal for making proselytes" of the Portuguese, he said, the English "never attempted to dispute or disturb the worship of tenets of others, being persuaded that the Supreme Governor of the Universe was equally pleased with the homage of all His creatures when proceeding from sincere devotion, whether according to one mode or another of the various religions which He permitted to be published" (Cranmer-Byng 1962: 167). Submitting their documents to missionaries for translation, and receiving answers via Jacobus Li, Chinese officials were not persuaded. Subsequent efforts by Protestant missionaries, more zealous than Macartney, to save Chinese souls, fed Chinese official skepticism by giving the West's world-cultural thrust a distinctly religious cast.

As the residues of missionary activity at the time of the embassy showed, throughout the era of "first globalization" (Gunn 2003) China and the West had already been drawn into sustained contact. Yet the impact of the missionaries' message had remained "limited and local" (Wills 2001: 139). Contrasting trends in Europe and China over the century and a half preceding the embassy, exemplified by a "breakthrough" in British science versus a "breakdown" in Chinese science, had deepened the cultural gulf (Adshead 2000: 251ff.). In 1793, there certainly was no single world culture. China and Britain in effect inhabited different worlds, understood in different terms. In the following century, the assumptions that informed the embassy grew in influence. The world became more unified, and this unity took symbolic form. By the time the Chinese empire collapsed and made way for a republic in 1911, after a century of turmoil in which the world-view of educated Chinese had changed dramatically (Fitzgerald 1964: 38), a single, dominant world culture had coalesced. China and Britain had come to inhabit the same world, understood in similar terms. Though modified and elaborated in ways we will describe in later chapters, the world culture of the nineteenth century is still with us. It has provided a template for contemporary world culture. Drawing on the theoretical perspectives we discussed in Chapter 2, this chapter shows by example in the following sections how the template formed. Awareness of the world as a "single place," a hallmark of world culture according to Robertson, grew in this period. Global "scripts," essential to institutionalist views of world culture, were written in many spheres. As different regions participated in the emerging world culture, they exhibited the varying versions anthropologists have stressed. Yet, for all its global reach and inherent diversity, this was largely a world culture made in and by Europe, for reasons emphasized by world-system theorists.

One World

Among the presents carried by Macartney's embassy were beautifully crafted globes that reflected the recent discoveries of Captain James Cook in the South Seas. The globe still had many blank spots. The polar regions had not been explored. Europeans knew little about central Africa, Asia, or South America. Lewis and Clark had yet to survey the western part of North America. Macartney himself counted greater knowledge of the Yellow Sea as one of his accomplishments. As late as 1848, large areas were "marked in white on even the best European maps," showing that "there was not, even in terms of geographical knowledge, *one* world" (Hobsbawm 1975: 49; emphasis in original). In the decades to come, the blank spots were rapidly filled in, though explorers only reached the poles in the early twentieth century. However, what Cook's travels conveyed to the British public – a sense that the world was now known as a whole – became an increasingly common insight throughout the nineteenth century. Geography came into its own as a discipline (Livingstone 1993: Ch. 6), building on the work of generations of explorers to complete its description of the earth. Overcoming the crude efforts of amateurs and replacing culturally biased pictures that were typical everywhere in earlier times, geography produced a scientific, rationalized image of the world, hallmark of a new kind of global consciousness. By the beginning of the twentieth century, humanity occupied a single space and had mastered it intellectually.

The practical mastery of space also advanced. Macartney left England in September, 1792; after stops in Brazil and Java, he arrived 10 months later in East Asia. By the middle of the next century, he still would have needed some 11 months to circumnavigate the globe (Hobsbawm 1975: 53). However, as steamships overtook sailing ships and the railway network expanded, travel became far easier. In 1889–90, the American journalist Nelly Bly traveled around the world in 72 days, beating the 80-day mark set by Jules Verne's legendary hero Phileas Fogg (Kern 1983: 212–13). Her feat proved that distance was not what it used to be. Of course, one no longer had to travel to the ends of the earth to prove that point. The spread of the telegraph since the 1830s allowed information to travel faster than people and goods. Coordinating activities across space became easier; awareness of distant events intensified. In journalism, the "middle ages ended in the 1860s when international news could be cabled freely from a sufficiently large number of places on the globe to reach the next morning's breakfast table" (Hobsbawm 1975: 60). Whereas it took Macartney months to convey the emperor's edict back to England, by 1872 messages from Tokyo could reach London via telegraph nearly instantaneously (ibid.: 59). Soon after, commentators noted that simple villagers had "a wider geographical horizon than the prime minister of a century ago" (Kern 1983: 70). Horizons broadened into an awareness of living in a single world.

This intellectual unification also created a new world time. Macartney wanted to show the Chinese that Britain had found a rational way to keep time. He was proud of the clocks he brought along: a watch was one of the first presents he gave the emperor, and he included a watchmaker in his party. However, the measurement of time varied from place to place. As long as people at a distance operated in different worlds, this was not a problem, but as the world became connected in many practical ways, the temporal disjunctions became an obstacle. The telegraph made people simultaneously aware of events at a distance and thereby demonstrated that events took place at different times as measured locally. Railroads struggled to operate efficiently and on schedule as long as localities along a route kept different times. To overcome the chaos of diverse times, engineers began to press for uniform time, which American railroads adopted in the USA in 1883. The following year, representatives of 25 countries gathered in Washington for the Prime Meridian Conference, which "proposed to establish Greenwich as the zero meridian, determined the exact length of the day, divided the earth into twenty-four time zones one hour apart, and fixed the precise beginning of the universal day" (Kern 1983: 12). Over the following decades, much of the world gradually adopted standard time. By sending signals that enabled localities to adapt to the uniform standard, the telegraph once again proved crucial. In 1913, "the Eiffel tower sent the first time signal transmitted around the world" (ibid.: 14). The globe's single space now also had a single time.

Macartney sought the right of Europeans to settle in China and to trade on equitable terms, pursuing a treaty with the empire as an equal partner. His mission, as we have seen, faltered in the mismatch of distinct civilizational standards. But as Europeans like Macartney increasingly entered non-Western regions, and as major Western powers extended their influence across the globe, the standards of global interaction had to be clarified, at least in the view of Western elites. Over time, a single standard of civilization crystallized in a body of international law that grew out of the culture of European states and their diplomatic interactions. The standard defined the world as a community of civilized states. Civilized were those states that guaranteed certain basic rights to their citizens, operated as competent bureaucracies, adhered to the precepts of international law, fulfilled their international obligations, and accepted "civilized" norms (Gong 1984: 14–15). European and American liberals promoted this project. While advocating liberty in all spheres, they also strove to centralize society by means of an efficient state apparatus capable of molding individuals into citizens. In international relations, they saw trade and diplomacy among formally equal sovereign actors as the rational path to peace and progress. As responsible actors guided by reason, both individuals and states had to abide by universal norms essential to the exercise of liberty. Embedded in international law, the "liberal revolution" (Stone 1984: 15ff.) helped to change the cognitive map of the globe by symbolically constructing new actors and assigning special value to them. It also expressed a moral aspiration, a scale by which individual states and indeed world society as a whole could be measured (Gong 1984: Ch. 3). The Western-derived standard of civilization purported to be universal, both in the sense of describing the actually evolving community of qualified states and in the sense of claiming superiority over existing civilizations. The concentric rectangles of the Middle Kingdom's image of the world thus had to make way for a new image of multiple actors rationally pursuing their goals governed by universal norms (cf. Gong 1984: Ch. 4). As Macartney had already intimated, "barbarous" China (Gong 1984: 57) did not measure up to the new standards.

It was not only China that failed to measure up. Even domestically, the self-styled "civilized" nations rarely practiced what they preached since they protected only some liberties of some favored groups. In international relations, many deviated from civilized norms in pursuing imperial ambitions and engaging in brutal conflict. Purporting to establish a universal civilization, while ignoring existing civilizational differences, was not itself very civilized (Gong 1984: 22–3). At least some of the failures, more apparent in retrospect but already challenged at the time, became cause for global concern. The liberal revolution spawned a kind of reformist internationalism. The international anti-slavery movement defined slavery as beyond the pale of civilized norms; the suffrage movement claimed equal political rights for women; the Red Cross sought impartial, humane treatment for injured combatants and protection for civilians in time of war (Lyons 1963: Ch. 4). In the process, such movements changed what it meant to be "civilized" by arguing for the common humanity of blacks and whites, men and women, citizens and noncitizens. Non-Europeans similarly expanded the meaning of presumed universal standards. For them, the standard of civilization became a critical lever in demanding equal treatment, national independence, and full recognition – a basis for inclusion in world society (Gong 1984: 8). The emerging world culture thus created critical tensions as individuals, movements, and even whole countries measured messy reality against global standards. By its contradictions and incompleteness, which resulted in global redefinitions of global terms, the world culture of

Robertson's "take-off" period in the late nineteenth century further intensified the spreading consciousness of the world as a single place.

Actors on the World Stage

The intellectual mastery of world space was in part a deliberate project. By funding journeys such as those of Cook and Macartney, some great powers fostered exploration that provided a basis for knowledge of the planet. Domestically, civilized states seeking to gain control over their own territories instituted surveys, following the example of the first complete British Ordnance Survey begun in the early 1790s. States also promoted geographical knowledge, for example via atlases used in their growing public education systems. Expanding such knowledge became the work of professionals such as surveyors and geographers. Their expertise became codified, their fields turned into full-fledged disciplines. Though amateurs such as the polar explorers could still contribute, specialists claimed the authority to define global space. Such specialists cooperated across national boundaries in new international organizations. For example, in the 1860s the International Geodesic Association undertook the measurement of the earth as a whole; in 1909, the International Committee for the Map of the World proposed to compile a map on the scale of 1:1 million or sixteen miles to the inch (Lyons 1963: 229, 234). State policy and professional initiative, often coalescing in international congresses and organizations, thus combined to raise global spatial consciousness. A similar story applies to world time, though in that case, as we have seen, private railroad companies provided a major impetus. In establishing global communication across larger distances, state officials proved more important; a case in point is the international organization of postal services, symbolized by the founding of the Universal Postal Union in 1874 as a model of cooperation among states (Codding 1964).

Elaborating a global standard of civilization was an equally deliberate venture. In a number of influential texts, Western scholars proposed the standard as a bedrock of international law, in the sense that specific norms were taken to derive from a single universal principle and only those who qualified as civilized were properly subjects of international law (Gong 1984: Ch. 2). With their treatises and journals, experts raised the status of international law as an academic field (Lyons 1963: 217). To codify principles of international law in a "scientific" manner, prominent figures joined forces in the Institute of International Law, founded in 1873, whose wide-ranging work was rewarded with a Nobel Peace Prize in 1904 (ibid.: 219–20). A partner organization, the International Law Association, also founded in 1873, focused on influencing public opinion and reforming private international law (ibid.: 221). States supported such efforts by applying principles of international law in their diplomacy. To advance the peaceful settlement of disputes as part of civilized international behavior, they also gathered at major congresses, such as the Hague Peace Conferences in 1899 and 1907. Private groups, notably the growing peace movement (ibid.: Ch. 5), exerted pressure by advocating new norms for international behavior. In these ways, more and more actors were involved in determining who belonged to the community of nations and how it should be organized. Just as importantly, in this and other areas a number of "actors" – states, science, international organizations – were constituted as legitimate elements of world culture in their own right. The writers of the global "scripts," emphasized by world polity theorists as key elements of world culture, became major players in making those scripts authoritative throughout the world.

The work of world culture, such as implementing surveys and time zones, was partly carried out within states. They proved themselves worthy of acting on the global stage by demonstrating their capability as organized actors. Out of heterogeneous groups they constructed cohesive "imagined communities," inculcating a common identity through formal education and print media (Anderson 1991). They constituted themselves politically by adopting constitutions, expanding state bureaucracies, and instituting parliamentary assemblies. They pursued progress by promoting industry and trade, developing professional expertise, and expanding education. All sectors of society were rationalized in the states' organizational revolution. In short, independent countries turned into instances of "civilization" – coherent, rational, secular, progressive nation-states, in principle committed to, and capable of, abiding by universal norms and competing with rivals within a peaceful world community. While states often strayed from such scripts, they thus bootstrapped themselves into becoming the key actors on the global stage, the chief elements of a new world polity.

In many fields, as we have noted, experts began to play a leading role. While science had long been a highly legitimate international enterprise supported by major states and organized in special societies (McClellan 1985; Wuthnow 1987: Ch. 8), in the nineteenth century its status and influence increased enormously. To some extent, this followed from developments within scientific fields as new discoveries demonstrated the cognitive power of science. Though science only indirectly contributed to the early industrial revolution, it promised great material advances, partly realized in the chemical industry at the end of the nineteenth century. In the organizational revolution across several sectors, ranging from law and business to education and communication, scientific knowledge could be used to rationalize reform. Competition among civilized states put a premium on the advancement of science, which received increasing resources. Scientists themselves furthered their cause by organizing in professional associations that defined the identity and marked the boundaries of disciplines. Even as science became more nationalized, it also "expanded into the international arena as never before"; with more than 30 international associations in basic science alone, "internationalism became common stock for scientists" by the late nineteenth century (Crawford et al. 1993: 13). In the liberal transformation of Western societies, science and scientific expertise also commanded ideological support. They embodied the most systematic use of secular reason and reinforced the conception of individuals and states as rational actors (Drori et al. 2003: Ch. 1). By the end of the nineteenth century, science's procedures had been further systematized, its practitioners organized, its applications made more useful, its international scope expanded. As a result, its cultural authority became deeply institutionalized as a major feature of the global cultural frame (ibid.: 10, 42).

By acquiring this authority, contested though it was throughout the nineteenth century, modern science left its imprint on the global understanding of the world itself. It represented the world as a natural order, a system of cause and effect amenable to theoretical understanding based on observation and experiment. The Christian belief in a single, rational Creator had been important for the discovery of physical laws – historically a limitation of otherwise advanced Chinese science – but it produced knowledge of a cosmos operating impersonally, without design or intent (Goodman 1991: 421–2). Though "for the great majority of European scientists God remained important" (ibid.: 423), assumptions about the Creator ceased to be crucial to charting the planets or examining electricity or explaining evolution. Whereas Catholic missionaries in China had used science in part to convey knowledge of God's creation as a path to faith, in keeping with long-standing European tradition, Macartney, like many of his generation, made a clear distinction between scientific knowledge and religious faith. As he assured his hosts, there were many ways to worship the Supreme Governor of the universe. Differences in religion need not prevent a common appreciation of the hard knowledge the embassy's experts possessed. Religion, his position implied, concerned a separate, compartmentalized realm of the spirit. Science offered knowledge of the real world. Macartney favored science's godless cosmology. In this regard, too, his position would become characteristic of world culture, though as we will see in a later chapter this left ample room for distinct religious contributions to world culture.

Scientists were not the only ones to get organized internationally. The reform movements we mentioned above had their own organizations, such as the International Women's Suffrage Alliance (1904) or the International Committee of the Red Cross (1864). Workers banded together in Workers' Internationals (first in 1864) and the International Co-Operative Alliance (1895). The peace movement had its International Arbitration League. Protestant groups formed the World Evangelical Alliance (1846) and the World's Student Christian Federation (1895). Some companies joined cartels, such as the International Rail Makers Association (1904); in 1907, Royal Dutch Shell became one of the first true multinational corporations. States also addressed their common problems in new organizations, such as the International Telegraphic Union (1865). Thus, an intricate network of international organizations was in place (Murphy 1994: 47–8), culminating in the founding of the Union of International Associations in 1910 (Lyons 1963: 205). They did some of their most dramatic work at innumerable conferences and congresses, from the International Anti-Slavery Conference in 1840 to the peace conferences of 1899 and 1907; less dramatic but equally important were many conferences on issues of trade and infrastructure (Murphy 1994: 57–9). These highlighted new issues, declared principles, agreed on conventions, or resolved disputes. They were the workshops of world culture, precursors to the kinds of meetings we discuss in the next chapter.

The explosion of such gatherings shows that by the end of the nineteenth century, world culture work had become regular and routine. Civilized nation-states elaborated the rules of the emerging world polity and were themselves increasingly bound by such rules. Science interpreted the world authoritatively while promoting and operating according to internationally accepted procedures. Intergovernmental organizations and nongovernmental groups pushed issues onto a global agenda and mobilized across national boundaries, following increasingly standardized organizational rules. For China, this world-cultural work had fateful consequences. By the standards of international law, it lacked the capacities of a proper civilized state, which to Europeans justified the imposition of unequal treaties at the time of the Opium Wars (Gong 1984: Ch. 5). Although China once had a distinguished scientific tradition (Needham 1954), the indifferent response to the scientific curios brought by Macartney signaled that China would long remain outside the new global cultural frame. Though China stayed nominally independent, it hardly played a part in the organizations and meetings that became staples of international life, only joining the Universal Postal Union in 1914 after the demise of the empire (Codding 1964: 239). The world of 1914 would have been utterly alien to Ch'ien-Lung.

A World of Difference

While China was unable to fend off Western intrusions in the decades following the Macartney embassy, Japan still adhered to its long-standing policy of closure. However, when in 1859 Commodore Perry appeared in Tokyo Bay with his infamous black ships, demanding the right for foreigners to trade in Japan, the Tokugawa Shogunate had to concede access. This forced intrusion reverberated deeply throughout Japanese society. The military superiority of the foreigners marked Japan as inferior. Unequal treaties, like the ones imposed on China, deprived Japan of jurisdiction over Westerners on its territory. As long as Japan continued its feudal ways, would-be modernizers recognized, it could not hope to count as a civilized society. Such problems motivated a group of reformers to overthrow the Shogunate and usher in the Meiji Restoration in 1868 (Westney 1987: 18–19). Assuming direct control over the whole country in 1871, the new government began an ambitious program of borrowing from the West by sending delegations to major countries to seek out the best modern practices (ibid.: 3, 13). After wearing traditional dress at an awkward meeting with the American president, an early delegation decided to wear Western clothes only – a small decision that symbolized Japan's willingness to jettison traditions in order to be taken seriously. From Britain, Japan adopted the postal system; the Paris police became a model for Tokyo; the new primary school system followed American precedent. The military mixed features of several European models. The new Japanese press was even more innovative, publishing newspapers that barely resembled their Western models (ibid.: Ch. 4). While Japan hardly underwent a liberal transformation, it did institute some liberal institutions, such as a parliament. Proudly reviewing the remarkable progress Japan had made in the 50 years after Commodore Perry's arrival, a distinguished group of Japanese experts described how across a range of institutions they had adopted Western models, as new "buds" on a home-grown tree, but also felt an ever-stronger need to adapt them to "our nationality and our customs" (Okuma 1909: 204, 280). Japan thus engaged in selective emulation. Its distinct blend of institutions and practices was composed of variations on several themes. Japan took its place under the canopy of world culture via glocalization, in the manner anthropological accounts have stressed.

The very fact that the government's delegations could pick and choose from numerous examples already suggested that world culture did not contain simple, clear-cut recipes. In many domains, it came in particular, mainly national, versions. For example, states did not converge on a single model for their internal organization, as illustrated by the difference between decentralized policing and education in the USA and the centralized approach in France. The versions of global models were themselves evolving. Germany was becoming a full-fledged nation-state at the same time as Japan. European newspapers were becoming a mass medium while Japanese publishers were experimenting with the new mediascape as well. This evolution took place through active comparison, each state and organization checking its own status against the advances made by others. Japan, of course, did this most deliberately and most dramatically, but so did many other countries, from Latin America to Russia. World culture grew through comparative glocalization.

In Europe the fact of national difference had turned into a principle – that it was right and proper for civilized states to manage their own affairs, to cultivate their own traditions, and to defend their own sense of nationhood. In the age of nationalism, each state had to "become national" (Eley and Suny 1996), displaying its own "soul," a unique combination of "a rich legacy of memories" and "present-day consent" (Renan 1996 [1882]). In claiming recognition as a civilized nation, Japan also claimed the right to be different. It could bolster this claim because its organizational revolution paid off. In 1895, the country defeated its old enemy China; in 1905, it shocked the world by humiliating Russia. Of course, the victories strengthened Japan's geopolitical position and increased its regional influence, but its success also had cultural consequences. Its institutional reforms and military prowess enabled Japan to claim to be a member of the community of civilized nations. Appearing to satisfy all the criteria of the conventional standard and acting competently as a nation-state in the international arena, its claim could not be denied. By staking this claim, Japan's glocalization also helped to universalize the standard of civilization. This package of world-cultural rules had been devised by white Europeans and Americans who extended a European tradition into the international arena; their aspirations for a peaceful world reflected a kind of Christian ardor in secular form. As an Asian, and non-Christian, yet civilized actor, Japan demonstrated that the standard could indeed be universal: Asians could be global actors in just the same way as Westerners. To be civilized no longer meant having to be white and Christian. The right-to-be-different, while also being the same, was not a European privilege but a universally valid principle.

Japan's early impact on world culture contrasts with China's experience. Macartney's dismissive attitude toward the backward and exotic "other," bound to be overtaken and transformed by the progressive West, fore-shadowed how China would fare in the "clash of civilizations" his embassy helped to unleash. Yet, however hesitantly, China, too, sought to resist undue Western influence, reform its institutions, and adapt to world-cultural principles. In spite of its military weakness, it maintained its formal independence. In the latter days of the old regime, Chinese intellectuals such as Sun Yat-Sen charted a path to a republican nation-state. China's experience reinforces what the Japanese case shows most clearly: namely, that the world culture Macartney represented did not spread as a tidal wave washing over what he considered "crazy" old men-of-war. It did not calmly diffuse from an enlightened center to a benighted periphery. Though many of its elements did originate in the West, its shape and meaning evolved in tense encounters with "others," who emulated, changed, or resisted the symbolic presents Macartney's successors had to offer. Japan may have been unique in modernizing independently, but in this respect its experience represents the rule rather than the exception in the history of world culture: far from being passive, the Rest talked back to the West. In this way, as anthropologists have stressed, world culture became an organized yet diverse culture of cultures (Sahlins 2000). Anthropology itself, a discipline that came to the fore in the "take-off phase" of world culture, embodied the globalizing awareness of this organized diversity.

Imposing World Culture

In June 1897, Queen Victoria celebrated her Diamond Jubilee with a week of elaborate festivities (Briggs and Snowman 1996: 164–6). A Chinese diplomat attending the occasion might well have marveled at how Western pomp had come to match Asiatic refinements. He would have recognized the expressions of loyalty the Empress received from her far-flung subjects. He would have been impressed with the splendor of imperial troops in national dress, symbolizing her government's unprecedented control over a quarter of the earth. The monarch, dressed in black with only a simple bonnet on her head, might have appeared to embody virtue in a manner reminiscent of her Chinese counterpart. In the 60 years of her reign, Britain had fashioned itself into a new kind of Middle Kingdom, spreading its values while enhancing its power. The very maps its explorers had helped to complete, with borders drawn by imperial edict and imperial domains marked in red for the edification of schoolchildren, showed how even global space was now organized by a new center. Britain had greatly extended its political and cultural reach, exceeding the boldest dreams officials like Macartney might have had a century before.

From the middle of the nineteenth century, Britain had advocated free trade as a norm for global economic activity and seeded new markets with its investments. Politically, it strove to achieve a balance of power among sovereign states while claiming to take on the civilizing mission of preparing others, such as India, for full participation. Its bureaucrats brought clean, rationalized administration to foreign lands. Its missionaries exported the blessings of a faith that promised individual salvation. Its merchants set up new enterprises around the globe. Its leading intellectuals extolled the virtues of liberty. Beginning with the pioneering international exhibition at the Crystal Palace in 1851, promoted by Victoria's husband, Albert, Britain vaunted its accomplishments in applied science. Appealing to universal humanitarian standards, it had employed its navy to shut down the slave trade. Increasingly, English became the lingua franca of international discourse. To be sure, many other parties helped to craft world culture. Latin American countries pioneered the new form of the nation-state. Many liberalizing ideas came from America and France. Japan, as we have seen, left its own imprint on world culture. Yet in many spheres, the empire celebrated in 1897 had been the primary, though by no means the only, vehicle for the spread of the new world culture (cf. Ferguson 2003: xxvi–xxviii).

Based on his own nation's experience, the Chinese diplomat might also have regarded the Jubilee with some skepticism. Britain had cunningly used the standard of "civilization" on which it prided itself to justify the forceful submission of China. While claiming to pursue transcendent goals, it intruded into the country and imposed unequal treaties for profit and power – the actual goals of British *realpolitik* about which Macartney had been so forthright. In China, Britain tried to spread a taste for opium, not freedom. Its liberal ideology of formally equal states and morally responsible individuals did not extend to China, let alone to its imperial domains.

Instead, Britain used seemingly egalitarian principles to establish a global hierarchy that diminished the status of non-Christian non-whites. Civilization had become a racial prerogative (Ferguson 2003: 264) and, in Kipling's famous exhortation to America, the "white man's burden." The task was made less burdensome by the comforts of empire, whose bourgeois officials enjoyed the ministrations of their darker-skinned servants. As Winston Churchill, defender of the empire until the very end, acknowledged not long after the Jubilee, the "beautiful ideal" of the civilizing empire was everywhere soiled by the "sordid appetites of the conquerors" (Ferguson 2003: xxviii). As world-system theorists would put it less charitably, the spread of world culture was a self-contradictory imperial project that served the material interests of core powers.

Like Macartney in China, an observer of the Jubilee might have detected signs of weakness in Britain, foreshadowing the eventual decline of the empire. Around 1900, Britain already faced numerous external challenges. By most measures, the United States had become the greatest economic power; Germany vied ever more assertively for political superiority; in the East, the rise of Japan signaled fresh competition. Even at the height of its power, Britain could not dictate the terms of world culture to such rivals. Thus, Britain's right to rule, and the particular values it sought to diffuse, were not universally acknowledged truths. Nearly as fateful were the challenges from within. For example, soon after the Jubilee, the Boer Wars, in which Britain tried to annex Afrikaner republics in South Africa, tarnished the imperial project, as anti-war activists like Emily Hobhouse denounced the British use of concentration camps and Liberal politicians like David Lloyd George abhorred the savagery of extermination tactics (Ferguson 2003: 278–80). The British-trained lawyer M. K. Gandhi, a stretcher-bearer in the Boer Wars who was gaining fame as an opponent of discrimination against Indians in South Africa, would soon return to India to lead a movement against British rule. Speaking for the native Africans, a group of black intellectuals (including the American W. E. B. DuBois) who gathered for the first Pan-African Congress in London in 1900, claimed for blacks the principles Britain had preached, demanding equality for Africans as citizens of independent states. Around the world, the elite who graduated from British schools used institutions planted by the British to undermine the empire itself, whose inconsistently applied liberal principles made it a "self-liquidating" enterprise (Ferguson 2003: xxv).

Outside the empire proper, anti-imperialist forces were slowly gathering as well. Around the Islamic world, al-Afghani denounced the culture of the

West and called for Muslim unity in opposition to Western imperialism (Keddie 1968), in a manner that later inspired other Islamist critics of world culture, such as those we discuss in Chapter 9. In China, Mao Zedong would soon write his first analysis of Chinese politics as the empire expired, adapting the revolutionary principles developed by Marx in London to a movement that would establish China as a communist power in opposition to the capitalist world economy built by Britain and her fellow core states. Just as Macartney mocked China as a crazy old man-of-war, a later Chinese colleague might have compared the British empire around 1900 to a magnificent Indian palace, splendid on the outside while "downstairs the servants were busy turning the floorboards into firewood" (Ferguson 2003: 218).

As the British empire tottered, world culture became an arena of struggle, as world-system theorists have stressed. Rival core states sought to put their stamp on that culture, however much they already shared. The liberal content of world culture, so at odds with cruel reality, provided fuel for critique and resistance (Schama 2002). The exploited were bound to rise up in protest, exposing the hypocrisy of world culture in its imperial phase. The struggle would change but not erase the mark Britain left on world culture.

Conclusions

Our brief history of world culture shows that the Olympic Games, the example we started with in Chapter 1, fit a pattern. Coubertin followed in the footsteps of other reformers dreaming of human brotherhood in a more unified world community. The organization he devised drew on a repertoire for international action that had become familiar to his elite supporters. The uneven representation of countries was only one small example of the greatly variable participation of different regions in new global fields. Emanating from the core of the world-system, the Olympics also self-consciously universalized a Western tradition. Without the prior nineteenth-century growth of world culture, the Games could not have succeeded.

This chapter has also illustrated the historical assumptions that underlie the influential perspectives on world culture we discussed in Chapter 2. We have seen how in the nineteenth century more and more people became conscious of living in a single, "compressed" world and that this consciousness intensified through invention and discovery, confirming part of the historical scenario sketched by Robertson. We also described how parts of world culture solidified through deliberate organization, for example by numerous intergovernmental and nongovernmental bodies, that also constituted the actors stressed in Meyer's institutionalist interpretation of world culture – issues we will elaborate in Chapter 5. Echoing themes from anthropological accounts, we showed how from the outset world culture came to be adopted, modified, and glocalized through tense interaction and selective emulation. Finally, we partly affirmed a world-system theory argument by illustrating how the self-serving imposition of world culture by great powers shaped its initial contours. Combining such accounts leads to an ecumenical picture of the origins of world culture: creativity and cooperation, copying and coercion all played a part.

Our selective history sets the stage for the rest of this book. It suggests that the form and content of contemporary world culture derive from nineteenth-century precedent. The way we now imagine world time and space is not new. Individuals and states, along with business organizations, remain key actors on the global stage. In economics and politics, the effects of the liberal revolution are still with us. Many organizational forms, both national and transnational, follow earlier models. The dynamics of world culture, from comparative glocalization to critical struggle, also show continuity. Specific chapters will convey such continuity. For example, the UN summits we treat as instances of culture creation in Chapter 4 partly hark back to international meetings of over a century ago. When we discuss differences and the problem of national identity within world culture in Chapter 6, we again revisit nineteenth-century themes. The antiglobalization movement we analyze as a contemporary form of immanent critique in Chapter 7 embodies ideas familiar to earlier generations of world culture critics. World culture, as sociologists say, is path dependent. Of course, we do not argue that there is nothing new under the sun. In fact, our agenda for the rest of this book is precisely to show the ways in which world culture has grown and changed since the Second World War.

The First World War marked the end of the early formation of world culture this chapter has summarized. At the time, optimistic liberals envisioned a future liberated from the "great illusion" that military conquest could advance the interests of civilized states (Angell 1913). Participants in the wave of self-conscious European internationalism we illustrated above, Coubertin among them, believed all humanity could finally be at peace. Many on the left thought workers had no country, but only universal, globally shared interests that would make any conventional war impossible. The Great War proved them wrong. That very conflagration shows that the growth of world culture did not spell harmony. Global consciousness did not entail consensus. The actors that became legitimate players on the global scene often were opponents; the differences inscribed into world culture carried explosive risks. Civilizing empires also pursued their interests through violence. A "world unified" was not a world without conflict. That sobering lesson puts the dualistic impact of cultural frameworks in perspective. It is a lesson that applies all too well to the even more intricately unified world of the twenty-first century.

Chapter 4

Constructing World Culture: UN Meetings as Global Ritual

The Earth Summit

Hopes were high when representatives of 172 countries gathered for the United Nations Conference on Environment and Development (UNCED) in June 1992. In an unprecedented show of collective concern, more than a hundred heads of state had promised to come to Rio de Janeiro. Lengthy negotiations prior to the meeting had produced several agreements that seemed ready for signing. Maurice Strong, the Canadian chair of a ground-breaking conference on the environment in Stockholm 20 years earlier, would be at the helm again, prodding delegations to meet their shared responsibilities. Expecting major action on environmental problems, thousands of journalists would cover the event. Parallel to the official proceedings, hundreds of nongovernmental organizations would stage a large meeting, aiming to raise global consciousness and pressure states into action. In the end, some 30,000 people converged on Rio for the largest international meeting to date (Grubb et al. 1993: 13). As a global event of historic proportions, devoted to the future of the planet itself, it certainly earned its nickname, the "Earth Summit."

Could the conference meet the high expectations? The first signs were not promising, as developed and developing countries resumed long-standing disputes (Grubb et al. 1993: 26ff.; Panjabi 1997: 129–31, 176–7). While delegates from the North called for protection of forests, many from the South stressed their sovereign right to use resources such as timber for urgent development needs. When the North argued for strong environmental protection, the South demurred or asked for financial support. These large groups of countries were also internally divided. The USA, for example, differed from its European allies in its reluctance to acknowledge a right to development or assume new environmental obligations (Panjabi

1997: 14, 171ff., 238ff.). As a result of such tensions, the meeting did not reach agreement on a forest convention and its final Declaration and Agenda for future action represented a compromise. Many states registered reservations even about the compromises. Financial commitments from the wealthy countries hardly met the needs identified at the conference. From the point of view of one high UN official, these problems did not outweigh such accomplishments as the "action programmes, the political commitment, the open and transparent process [of cooperation], and the [increased] public awareness" (Grubb et al. 1993: 49). Even some environmentalists were pleasantly surprised by such gains and judged UNCED a success (Von Weizsäcker 1994: 169). But for many others, it is fair to say, the conference did not yield the inspirational consensus they had hoped for.

Yet, neither UN self-congratulation nor environmentalist disappointment convey the whole story of the Earth Summit. Legal or political scorecards also cannot do justice to the meeting's legacy. Its chief impact is cultural. Officially "non-binding," the Rio Declaration on Environment and Development expresses a distinct view of environmental problems. Recognizing the "integral and interdependent nature" of the earth, "our home," it proclaims that "human beings" are central to concerns about "sustainable development" and entitled to a life in harmony with nature. States, it continues, have both the "sovereign right" to their resources and a responsibility to prevent environmental harm. It calls for the "right to development" to be fulfilled in an equitable manner. To make development sustainable, "environmental protection" must become integral to development policies. Not only is environment critical in development, it is indivisibly linked to peace as well. In all areas, women and "indigenous people" have a crucial role to play. Further, states must cooperate in a "global partnership" to protect the "integrity" of the globe's ecosystem. States should also discourage unsustainable consumption patterns. And so the Declaration continues, for 27 more-or-less-ringing principles.

Agenda 21, the other main conference document, complements the Declaration. Its many hundreds of pages address socioeconomic dimensions of environmental problems, suitable management of resources, roles to be played by various groups, and means of implementation. It expresses the hope that a "global partnership for sustainable development" will not only protect ecosystems but also lead to fulfilling "basic needs." It applauds the role of trade in improving the environment but calls for "new and additional" money to go to developing countries. It perceives both population growth and wasteful consumption as threats to the environment. It describes specific ways to protect specific parts of the global ecosystem. And it proposes a new UN Commission on Sustainable Development to monitor implementation of the Agenda. As a comprehensive analysis of environmental issues, the Agenda reflects decades of growing environmental analysis and awareness around the world.

Measured against the hopes of idealistic environmentalists, these texts still leave much to be desired. They abound in vague rhetoric. Stressing the rights and roles of states rather than the needs of the planet, they formulate aspirations more than obligations, raising doubts about the pace of government action (Conca 1996: 103). Reflecting the need for compromise typical of "package deals" in a UN forum, they balance different views without radically altering the world's environmental perspective (McCormick 1995: 257; Imber 1996: 142–3). They show how nationalism foiled a noble exercise in idealism (Panjabi 1997: Ch. 1). Skewed toward economic interests, the texts do not easily translate into deeds (Finger 1994: 209). At the same time, as several observers have noted, they have great symbolic significance. They contain "an important early expression of the emerging changes in collective self-understanding" associated with a new wave of ecological thought (Alker and Haas 1993: 164). They mark the rise of a new "dominant global discourse," centered on the notion of sustainable development (Dryzek 1997: 123). They draw "lines in the sand" regarding the principles that guide governments in environmental management (McCormick 1995: 257). This "near-global agreement" on basic principles is bound to have broad repercussions (Grubb et al. 1993: vii). Rio may not have healed the global environment, but it did much for world culture.

UNCED's cultural role goes beyond the substance of its texts. Rio was a catalyst in many ways. Planning UNCED spurred the UN apparatus into action. To prepare for the conference, governments had to scrutinize their environmental records. Ongoing intergovernmental deliberations and negotiations intensified considerably in anticipation of the key meeting. Ideas and phrases expressing global concern took more definite shape as all parties focused on laying the groundwork for a successful meeting. The scale and scope of the meeting attracted heavy media interest; having a global audience in turn raised the stakes at the conference. Invited into the planning process, NGOs found new avenues for influence; Rio became their stage as well.

By mobilizing interested parties worldwide in a collective effort to address a global problem, by symbolizing global concern through the drama of its actions, and by articulating global self-understanding through the substance of its texts, the Earth Summit crystallized significant elements of global culture. The record of Rio shows that UN meetings of this kind are more than just another opportunity for the pursuit of state self-interest, more than just another round of bargaining (cf. Young 1994: Ch. 4). They are also instances of what the Irish diplomat Conor Cruise O'Brien called, with a certain rhetorical flourish, the UN's "sacred drama" – the way in which it attempts to make "an impression on the imagination of mankind through a spectacle presented in an auditorium with confrontations of opposing personages [and in which] the personages, individually or collectively, symbolize mighty forces, [and in which] the audience is mankind and the theme the destiny of man" (1968: 10). World meetings, in other words, are rituals, scripted performances that lend special meaning to shared symbols and create a collective sense of the sacred through direct experience of the larger social whole. Global ideas and norms can originate in many places, but constituting them *as* global, *as* deserving of universal respect, requires deliberate collective effort by participants in world society. In the nineteenth century, as we saw in the previous chapter, meetings of this sort became a common feature of international life. Since 1945, carefully staged, periodic UN meetings on symbolically charged topics by the authorized representatives of key entities within world society have been peak events in those now more globally inclusive collective efforts. They are among the chief rituals of world society. They display world culture under construction.

World Meetings and the Construction of World Culture

While we focus on UN summits as peak events that show concretely and dramatically how world culture gets constructed, there are now many meetings that explicitly constitute ideas as global, as deserving of universal respect. Many people in a wide variety of fields now make deliberate efforts to arrange global rituals that sacralize new concepts or principles. Before we return to our main empirical case, we briefly illustrate this variety.

One of the largest and most influential exhibitions of contemporary art is the *Documenta* show staged once every five years in Kassel, Germany. Since its inception in the 1950s, it has expanded enormously. It displays the work of dozens of visual artists from many countries. High-profile curators shape the show by identifying a theme at the cutting edge of current trends. The exhibit routinely draws crowds in the hundreds of thousands. Both a popular success and an aesthetic bellwether, *Documenta* has become one of the most prominent art shows in the world. Its role was solidified in 2002 when Nigerian curator Okwui Enwezor took a deliberately global approach to the event. Prior to the show in Kassel, he organized symposia or "platforms" on several continents. As the curating team put it, their purpose was to "probe the contemporary problematics and possibilities of art, politics, and society" (www.documenta.de 2002). For example, a platform in Lagos drew more than 80 international "cultural practitioners" to address the realities of African cities by formulating a "critical model that joins heterogeneous cultural and artistic circuits of present global context." The Kassel show itself had a global agenda as well. It was "insistently transnational, interdisciplinary and transgenerational in its concerns," ultimately aiming to steer "the international discourse onto new pathways." The pathway of *Documenta 11*, again in the words of the curators, was to show how the ideological hegemony of democracy was being called into question by capitalism, by the rise in nationalism and fundamentalism, by new forms of citizenship, and by old colonial legacies. In his catalog, Enwezor also wrote that "the exhibition counterpoises the supposed purity and autonomy of the art object against the rethinking of modernity based on ideas of transculturality and extraterritoriality" (Kimmelman 2002). The very inclusion of many non-Western artists helped to make his point. Enwezor, in short, wanted to "produce knowledge," of art and of the world (Shatz 2002). Though the impact of this single event has yet to be gauged, it clearly had a world-cultural ambition: to transform the world culture of art by redefining who and what counted as art, by redefining the purpose of objects and exhibits. In the language of the curator, it constituted a "public intervention" – from our standpoint, an intervention in the construction of world culture.

In 1993, more than 6,000 representatives from a variety of religious groups met in Chicago for a Parliament of the World's Religions, marking the centennial of the 1893 Parliament of Religions at the Chicago World's Fair. In the spirit of the earlier meeting, the new Parliament celebrated interfaith cooperation and the role of religion in solving the world's problems. Its main order of business was to consider and affirm a "Declaration toward a Global Ethic," prepared by the Catholic theologian Hans Küng (1998: 108ff.). The Declaration identified a consensus among the religions about "binding values, unconditional standards and personal attitudes," constituting the core of a global ethic and a foundation for a better global order. It assumed that "every human being – without distinction of sex, age, race, skin color, language, religion, political view, or national or social origin – possesses an inalienable and untouchable dignity," and therefore argued that everyone had a right to be treated humanely. Not only the "human person is infinitely precious and must be unconditionally protected," but also "the lives of animals and plants which inhabit this planet with us deserve protection, preservation and care." The Declaration further urged the use of power and resources in "the service of humanity," a life of truth-fulness and tolerance, and "a Culture of Equal Rights, and Partnership Between Men and Women." The participants had high expectations: "We are convinced that the new global order will be a better one only in a socially-beneficial and pluralist, partner-sharing and peace-fostering, nature-friendly and ecumenical globe." Five years later, a similar Parliament in Cape Town followed up on the Declaration with a "Call to Guiding Insti-tutions," containing specific injunctions for governments, media, and the like. Both meetings invoked global ideas, for example about justice, the indi-vidual, and humanity, in order to formulate a global vision. By giving form to an interreligious discourse about global order, they added elements to world culture. Of course, they were nothing if not bold in claiming that the ethic they proclaimed represented an actual consensus of all religions. Even at the meetings themselves, some participants complained that not all reli-gions were included and that a specifically religious perspective on global issues might be missing from the Call (Solheim 2000). The Parliaments hardly had sufficient authority to make the Declaration binding on all believers. Yet, as we will see, their themes resonated with several ideas that crystallized at the UN summits.

Football's World Cup produces no high-minded declarations of the kind composed by Küng. Unlike the Olympics we discussed in Chapter 1, orga-nized football does not trumpet its contributions to peace and brotherhood. Yet, even this tournament contributes significantly to world culture. The competition itself, of course, depends on universal knowledge of the rules of the game and of procedures set by FIFA, the world football association. Pitting national teams against each other, it expresses and intensifies national sentiment. At least in the minds of many fans, their country's place in the world depends in part on how well its team does in qualifying rounds and in the tournament itself. Televised to an enormous audience, the World Cup solidifies the game as an appealing commercial product in the global market. For FIFA, the event is an occasion to institute new rules to regulate the game worldwide. The competition further establishes what styles and strategies work best, new norms for what makes teams successful. As teams from different continents have become competitive, the game has lost its Western character and truly has turned into the "global game" (Giulianotti 1999). The Cup has become the key event in a globalized sports system that has rules and rhythms of its own, shaping global life by creating a four-year cycle familiar to many millions of people. Perhaps even more than the Olympics, the World Cup intensifies global consciousness as a large audience follows the same event with the same knowledge and passion.

As our brief examples show, what constitutes an art object, an ethical principle, or sound football strategy is now subject to global debate organized around global ideas held to be universally applicable. As we will see, the same goes for population control and human rights, for environmental protection and equal status for women. Beyond these domains, we could cite many more events framing particular issues in global terms, from engineers setting standards for international aviation to lawyers and diplomats devising standards for international criminal justice, to mention only some forms of world culture we described in Chapter 1. In all these spheres, an elaborate apparatus for producing global knowledge and principles has emerged. The specific meetings we treat as culture construction sites have fashioned a sturdy cultural framework.

Without arguing that everything in world culture gets invented on particular occasions, this chapter proposes that we can indeed observe world culture being made at such specific events. From our analysis of UN conferences we draw several lessons that apply to other kinds of meetings as well. We show, first, that construction is indeed ongoing. Many different kinds of players are continually involved in an extensive process of defining global problems in terms of shared global principles. Second, this process is not haphazard but has taken on definite forms. Because the world now has a kind of repertoire for addressing a wide range of problems, constructing world culture to some extent has become a deliberate exercise, though of course no single party controls the outcome. Third, out of gradually accumulating concepts, knowledge, and principles emerges a common "frame." The meetings show the growth of a world-cultural edifice as they add layer upon layer of cultural material. Fourth, that frame hangs together precariously since the construction crew is internally divided and follows no single blueprint. Summits lay bare fissures within world culture; the global consciousness they raise is by no means harmonious.

In our analysis, we are guided especially by two of the theories we described in Chapter 2. With regard to the point we just made about repertoire and frame, world polity theory calls our attention to the increasingly rationalized process by which increasingly similar models and concepts are formulated across a number of different domains, resulting in a common ontology that underlies global communication about a wide variety of specific issues. With regard to ever intensifying global cultural work and accumulating layers of global culture, Robertsonian globalization theory calls our attention to increased pressures to define issues in global terms, according to specific visions of global order, even if those visions clash in some respects. World-system theory, by contrast, accounts for culture construction not as a fairly autonomous process but as driven by the interests of the players, which also helps to explain the nature of the fissures.

World Conferences as Global Ritual

By focusing on UN summits as illustrative cases we do not mean to imply that such meetings somehow generate world culture by themselves. As we will reiterate, they are embedded in an elaborate process of preparation, implementation, and reconsideration. Regional "prepcoms," for example, often involve state and NGO representatives in rounds of negotiation. Implementation of formally adopted policies depends on state follow-up, and since this invariably leaves much to be desired, meetings have encountered understandable skepticism about their impact and cost effectiveness (Schechter 2001). As instruments of the UN apparatus, they also have little autonomy, since the UN remains beholden to the interests of its most powerful members. A case in point is the influence China exerted at the Vienna human rights conference in 1993 to limit its critical impact. During actual summits, the "action" is not only at the official meeting but is usually just as intense at the nongovernmental forum accompanying it. "Parallel summits," involving thousands of domestic and international NGOs, have themselves become routine; their most notable role is to engage in "critical dialogue" with regard to issue-framing and rule-making, and they can thus affect both the agenda and the outcomes of conferences (Pianta 2001). The Earth Summit, as we saw, attracted a vast number of NGO participants, many intimately involved in negotiating on key issues; conferences on women similarly have attracted steadily increasing numbers of activists to parallel events (Berkovitch 1999b: 122–3). We will return to the creative role of INGOs in the next chapter. Outside of the UN process, many kinds of groups hold hundreds of international gatherings in less-heralded ways. For example, while in the 1980s only one "summit" meeting addressed population control, by one count about a hundred other major international meetings dealt with the issue (Barrett and Frank 1999). To think of politically motivated delegates at world conferences as creative intellectuals might give them a little too much credit, in any case: their gatherings often rely on knowledge produced independently by experts and elaborate ideas that germinated among citizen groups. Almost none of the terms and ideas we cite below as cultural contributions of world summits wholly originated during the event. For all those reasons, then, our purpose in this chapter is not to celebrate the UN as a singularly effective force in world society but rather to aim the spotlight at one particularly revealing kind of world-cultural construction site.

What makes this site revealing? One reason is that, since its founding in 1945, the United Nations has had not just a political but also a symbolic function in world society. To be sure, it has served as a forum for diplomacy, an instrument for settling major conflicts, and a vehicle for political transformation in the Third World. However, some of the founders also intended it to contribute to a different kind of world community, one in which universal principles could diminish political discord. Though it had a whiff of compromise about it, the organization's very name expressed recognition of nation-state sovereignty together with a desire for cooperation in an international system. The adoption of the Universal Declaration of Human Rights in 1948 demonstrated the moral ambition to reshape the world by articulating what humanity had in common. From the outset, the UN agenda included issues that transcended the conflicts and crises of the day. The organization's bureaucratic apparatus could address some of these reasonably well, yet over time it became clear that ordinary negotiation might not suffice to articulate a global direction on key issues of common concern. If the UN were to play a role in setting that direction, it needed a special method for doing so. From the late 1940s, therefore, it began organizing world conferences on specific themes. After modest beginnings in expert meetings, preparing, staging, monitoring, and reviewing intergovernmental conferences became central to the UN's work. By selecting topics to be addressed, mobilizing collective attention, holding special but regular meetings in a distinctive format, developing a method for highlighting new concerns, and organizing a process of assessment, the UN has created a form of secular ritual that has served to crystallize new global understandings and invest them, at least in principle, with the authority of "humankind."

Of course, meetings of government representatives are nothing new. Even within the United Nations there are several ways for governments to do business and make their views heard. While world conferences build on experience in these settings, they typically focus on issues for which no specific diplomatic solution is at hand. Their intent is as much to articulate views or set an agenda as to solve problems. They are set apart from ordinary matters, for instance by being held in venues away from regular UN locations. They require special attention from governments and organizers alike, evident in an increasingly elaborate preparatory process. At the meetings themselves, conventional horse-trading occurs, to be sure, but in "elevated" speech and style participants often try to rise to the perceived significance of the grand problem at hand. Though results may include the signing of a treaty, the main outcome of a conference is a set of documents symbolically proclaiming principles and programmatically outlining a plan of action. Those texts, consecrated by the meeting process, represent the conferences' chief contribution to world culture.

Special and set apart though they are, world conferences also have become regular features of international life. Between 1960 and 2000, the United Nations organized 70 major meetings on themes such as trade, crime, human rights, population, children, and technology. Since the 1970s, the UN has averaged about two major meetings per year; in the 1990s, after the end of the Cold War, summits became especially prominent (Schechter 2001). The organizing process, as we noted, has become highly regular as well, involving appointment of a secretary-general, several regional "prepcom" committee meetings, the drafting of meeting documents, and so on. Though details vary by issue, the script for staging conferences is now widely known. The substance of conferences also has come to fit a definite mold. Meetings address only a specific set of generally recognized Big Issues. They address them in terms that usually draw on established UN practice, invoking principles and phrases in standardized form. Conferences, in short, have assumed all the trappings of secular ritual, as anthropologists have come to describe such gatherings (Moore and Myerhoff 1977).

Of modest scale initially, UN conferences have expanded tremendously. As many developing countries gained independence after decolonization, the number of conference participants grew. In principle, conferences allow all voices to be heard, and those voices represent, though not always democratically, larger and larger portions of the world population. By the 1970s, conferences enabled "the world" to address the most pressing issues of "the world." They thus acquired great symbolic weight. Not only do meetings now routinely attract nearly 200 government delegations and thousands of participants, they also involve thousands of issue activists and many hundreds of journalists. In recent decades, the NGO role has grown tremendously, in quality and quantity (Frank et al. 1999), though this NGO role is larger in some areas than others (Schechter 2001: 192). Ties to NGO networks, now a routine feature of meetings, produce a ripple effect throughout the world community, since meeting themes become a focus of further NGO action as well (ibid.: 221). Media coverage reinforces conference messages to a worldwide audience. The sheer scale of the meetings itself magnifies the attention they draw; coverage in turn makes their substance appear more significant.

What do these rituals affirm? The process they have established itself contains a message. Naturally, within the UN context, states are the chief participants. Their authority is paramount: only what states agree to can be adopted as principle, only what states are willing to do can become part of the "official" world agenda. Increased participation by newly independent countries helped to reinforce their status as legitimate states entitled to full recognition. Even when meetings preach unity across borders, in practice states are still sovereign. Conference actions also convey another message: underneath all the rhetoric, they say that this is how the world community must define its shared concerns, resolve its differences, and set a joint agenda. As ritual accommodating differences in power and worldview, they provide a model of pacification, a way to address common problems in a civil, reasoned way. By the very selection of issues, finally, the process identifies some problems as worthy of special concern, establishing at least a minimal common understanding. Conferences, in sum, affirm the authority of states, the importance of the meeting process itself, and the significance of shared problems.

Over the years, certain terms, ideas, and principles also have become sacralized. Among them is, of course, the notion of human rights: as individuals, human beings have many inalienable rights. They are equally entitled to have these rights protected. In recognition of their usually subordinate status, women enjoy special rights as a condition for their empowerment. Human rights have come to include the right to development, but any development countries pursue must be sustainable. To be sustainable, it must serve the basic needs of the poor while protecting the common heritage of mankind. Individual rights, equality, women's empowerment, sustainable development, and the common heritage of mankind are only some of the central themes that serve to frame conference approaches to different issues. At the same time, UN meetings also invariably venerate state authority, both by vesting special responsibility in states and by invoking sovereignty to limit the obligations imposed on governments by universal principles.

The ritual invocation of common ideas does not silence all disagreement, but disagreement itself has taken particular forms, as we will show below. Specific issues provoke specific types of debate. Certain themes recur; certain countries predictably line up on opposing sides. On women's rights, Islamic countries tend to counter Western initiatives on the grounds of respect for distinct traditions. On development, Third World countries tend to oppose "sustainable" restrictions on the grounds of sovereign state rights to exploit their resources or serve the needs of their populations. Though in some instances such ritualized disagreement has threatened the success of conferences, it has not prevented some creative elaboration of shared understanding. With respect to issues such as human rights, the environment, population, and women's rights, UN conferences have done more than sacralize old notions or entrench old differences. They have helped to formulate and legitimate new ideas as well. They have shaped a global common sense of what humanity's problems are and what must be done about them.

We now turn to a comparison of the first and more recent world conferences on four selected issues to illustrate further some important features of the construction of world culture. We summarize the highlights in the four tables in the Appendix to this chapter.

Human Rights

When the International Conference on Human Rights met in Tehran in May 1968 to "review the progress made in the twenty years since the adoption of the Universal Declaration on Human Rights and to formulate a programme for the future" (UN1995: 247), the international scene was very different than it had been in 1948. Decolonization was nearly complete. The Cold War had divided erstwhile allies. The USA was caught in a hot war in Asia, Israel had just defeated its Arab attackers, and remnants of white rule in Africa were being challenged. In spite of such world tensions, the UN had passed two major Covenants on human rights in 1966, one dealing with economic, social, and cultural rights, the other covering political and civil rights. To solidify that advance and chart a path toward implementation, UN members agreed to celebrate an International Year for Human Rights, of which the conference would be the high point.

In his opening address, UN Secretary-General Thant set the tone for the conference by focusing on the scourge of racial discrimination. Apartheid in South Africa received special condemnation at the meeting, though some Western countries resisted labeling it a "crime against humanity." Israel also came in for criticism from Arab states complaining about its treatment of people in occupied territories. Allying itself with Third World states, the Soviet Union pledged to support all resistance to imperialist aggression. The conference resolutions reflected the basic dividing lines, indicative of a world no longer dominated by Western powers. Resolution I, for example, found Israel's conduct in occupied territories to be a violation of human rights. Resolution III took aim at apartheid, and several others further challenged race discrimination. Other resolutions seemed less controversial. Resolution IX recommended measures to promote women's rights, linking improvements in their status to national development. Other resolutions called on states to meet their international obligations while recognizing their prerogatives. In one typical instance, states "were invited to comply with their United Nations Charter obligations by regarding implementation of the Charter provisions on human rights and fundamental freedoms not only as a matter of national obligation but also as a matter of international obligation" (UN 1968: 542).

The Proclamation of Tehran echoed such points by finding it "imperative that members of the international community fulfill their solemn obligations . . ." and urging that states "reaffirm their determination" to enforce human rights principles. It also expressed grave concern about the evil of apartheid and all racial discrimination. It found that armed conflict and a widening economic gap between states greatly contributes to human rights violations. However, in tone and substance, the Proclamation did something more. It stressed a "need for human solidarity" in the face of ongoing violent conflict. The Universal Declaration, it reiterated, contains a "common understanding." Recent agreements have added to it "new standards and obligations to which states should conform." They articulate rights that are "indivisible." Their aim remains "the achievement by each individual of the maximum freedom and dignity." Of course, such high-minded expressions of concord did not suppress ideological differences. Tehran produced no neat consensus, but it did solemnly restate common principles in commonly used language, providing a universalizing framework for addressing particular divisive problems. These symbolized at least one way in which the common understanding of human rights had expanded since the 1940s, namely by framing race discrimination as an especially odious type of violation. A minute of silent tribute on the first day to Martin Luther King Jr., assassinated only a month earlier, signaled this shift from the outset.

The world convening for its next conference on human rights, in Vienna in 1993, was once again very different from that of 1968. Apartheid and the Soviet Union were no more. Israel had made peace with Egypt. Formal colonialism had ended. No longer embroiled in armed conflict, the USA stood out as the lone superpower. Industrializing Asian countries and some oil-exporting countries had gained influence. The new world that gathered counted many more states, 171 of which were represented. However, state delegations were not the only actors on the scene: hundreds of NGOs attended and participated in a parallel meeting of their own (Dias 2001: 31). Since the 1950s, human rights had become the active concern of many groups rather than just the pious content of UN texts. This shared concern, combined with the disappearance of old divisions, seemed to justify expectations of greater harmony. A ringing affirmation of a core world commitment seemed a most appropriate way to mark the end of the Cold War. At this juncture, said Secretary General Boutros-Ghali in his opening address (UN 1995: 441ff.), the international community can focus on human rights as a way to discover its "innermost identity," asking "questions about humanity and about how, by protecting humanity, it protects itself." For human rights, he affirmed, are the "irreducible human element" constituting the world as a "single human community." While counseling against the "naive approach" of viewing such rights as expressions of universally shared values, he nevertheless emphasized their status as the ultimate and universal norm of politics. What the world needed, he thought, was a stronger international apparatus for guaranteeing rights in practice. That apparatus need not include a special UN high commissioner for human rights, a proposal floated by some Western groups. It also could not decree universality, he added. As for the business of the meeting, it should not be "country-specific." In all, these comments represented less than wholehearted affirmation of the agenda urged by human rights advocates.

The Secretary-General had reason to be cautious: he knew member states were divided. Some, notably China and Islamic countries, had expressed reservations about the ostensible purpose of stating human rights as universal. How human rights are interpreted, they stressed, depends on any society's own tradition. Even when development threatens to violate human rights, it often must take priority. Examination of their record, these countries made clear, would not be welcome. The supposed universality of human rights, their reservations implied, was but another expression of a biased Western world-view. From the outset, the meeting was cast as a battle between universalists and particularists.

The particularists' view found its way into parts of the conference documents. According to the Vienna Declaration (UN 1995: 448ff.), the right to self-determination means that peoples can "freely pursue their economic, social and cultural development." The right to development is itself declared a human right. Though states have a duty to promote all human rights, "the significance of national and regional particularities and various historical, cultural and religious backgrounds must be borne in mind." Standard references to conformity with the UN Charter signal state claims to sovereignty. The Declaration condemns rights violations but cites none. The UN must improve international cooperation, according to the Programme of Action, but the conference only recommends that the General Assembly begin "consideration of the question of the establishment" of a high commissioner for human rights.

However, division and compromise are not the dominant tone in the Declaration. It affirms that "the universal nature of human rights is beyond question." They are the objective and indivisible birthright of individuals, the primary responsibility of governments. Even the right to development, which ostensibly pertains to countries, has "the human person" as its "central subject." The Declaration also goes beyond reinforcing tradition. Much more firmly than in the past, and building on the record of other meetings, it specifies the rights of women and children. It extends special recognition to indigenous peoples. It views democracy as a condition for fully realizing human rights. And it commends NGOs, most of which are strongly universalist, for their contribution to the cause. The battle at Vienna took place within a shared framework that put the burden of proof on would-be particularists. Instead of deepening divisions, it allowed a resolution in terms that broadened the collective understanding of human rights, at least by comparison with 1968.

Environment

The Earth Summit was not the first major meeting devoted to the environment. The watershed event had occurred in 1972, when the UN convened its Conference on the Human Environment (UNCHE) in Stockholm. After years of consciousness-raising by groups of activists and tentative steps toward environmental protection by states, this meeting was designed to turn the environment into a truly global concern. More than a hundred states sent delegations; representatives of more than a hundred NGOs were involved in the official proceedings as well. The chief organizer, Maurice Strong, introduced the conference as the beginning of a new "liberation movement" that would help the world escape from destructive growth (UN 1972: 319). He argued for a new concept of sovereignty to achieve growth that enlarges "the opportunities of all mankind" by being "in dynamic harmony with the natural order."

In Stockholm, the movement acquired a manifesto, the Declaration on the Human Environment (UN 1972: 319ff.). It offered "a common outlook" and "common principles" to guide environmental preservation.

"Man," according to its first principle, has the "fundamental right" to an environment in which to live with dignity. Various forms of oppression, it held, infringe on that right. It proclaimed improvement of the environment to be a "major issue" affecting everyone's well-being. It pointed to growing evidence of "man-made harm" around the earth, attributing some of it to underdevelopment. People and institutions at "every level" must share in "common efforts" for environmental defense. Less adventuresome than the opening address, it recognized the sovereign right of states by saying that national institutions must be entrusted with rational resource planning. At the same time, it called for increased international cooperation to safeguard resources for future generations. An Action Plan for the Human Environment complemented the Declaration. It addressed more prudent ways to manage human settlements, natural resources, and potential pollutants. It also proposed specific measures, such as an international program for measuring environmental problems. The Action Plan intended to spur action by states but especially wished to mobilize a new UN apparatus.

While the conference did formulate a "common outlook," that commonality had clear limits. For one thing, many countries registered reservations about elements of the meeting texts (UN 1972: 321–3). The United States objected to provisions calling for financial compensation to developing countries. These objections reflected the underlying debate between developed and developing countries, with the latter insisting on their right to exploit their own resources to suit their economic priorities. China wished to blame superpower plunder for most environmental harm, one instance of geopolitical conflict coming to the fore. On the issue of requiring states to inform others of potential damage originating in their territories, the conference deferred to the General Assembly. The common outlook also did not translate into definite commitments, either to pay for UN action or to set targets for pollution reduction. A large part of the world was not represented: the Soviet bloc declined to attend due to a dispute over East Germany.

Such limits disappointed some activists, an experience they were to relive 20 years later, but as a performance for a world audience the conference was quite successful. The very fact of staging it established the environment as a common concern worthy of worldwide attention. Stockholm accelerated a shift toward new "fundamental world-level understandings about nature," centered on the idea of a life-sustaining ecosystem (Frank 1997: 421). It was Stockholm that set in motion, at the international level, a broad range of activities to deal with environmental issues. However woolly the rhetoric, the meeting articulated at least some relevant norms states are expected to follow. It accomplished, as one prominent participant put it, a "revolution in thought" (*New York Times*, June 18, 1972). As creative performance, then, this ritual proved effective. Not coincidentally, many states rapidly created agencies and specific policies for environmental protection after 1972 (Frank et al. 1999: 98).

Stockholm was a beginning; Rio dramatically added momentum, as recounted above. The Earth Summit resembled UNCHE in some of its principles and conflicts, but it was bigger in the scale of proceedings and the scope of relevant issues. This dramatized the extent to which "the environment" had become institutionalized as a global concern embedded in common norms and organizations. The rhetoric also had shifted: sexist language was excised, women's rights were explicitly incorporated into the environmental agenda. In this way, the meeting affirmed a global conception of women's rights and needs that had emerged during earlier world meetings on women, discussed below. The old North–South conflict had not disappeared, but an artful compromise, "sustainable development," had become a sacred principle. Thus, in spite of the disagreements it amply displayed, Rio also showed how much the world had come to take for granted with respect to the environment in just a few decades. Precisely because the "common outlook" had in fact evolved since 1972, Rio could fulfill a substantial part of its ambitious agenda and serve as a catalytic event.

Population

From the outset, population issues were part of the United Nations' social mission (Barrett and Frank 1999: 214). It had a division and fund devoted to them. In 1954, and again in 1964, the UN organized a world meeting of experts to lend urgency to the task of population control. The first UN world conference on population, however, took place in 1974 in Bucharest. In addition to delegates from 136 nations at the official conference, a related meeting of NGOs and independent experts attracted more than 1,200 participants. Preparations for the conference had been mostly technical, focusing on how best to check population growth around the world. The concern about population as a social problem seemed widely shared. Organizers anticipated a productive conference along the lines of the Stockholm environment meeting, leading to adoption of a previously drafted plan. Instead, the meeting became one of the most contentious gatherings in the history of the UN.

Algeria and Argentina, leaders of the so-called nonaligned nations, pro-posed early on to reframe the debate (Finkle and Crane 1975; Singh 1998: 8–9). The key world problem, they argued, is not population growth but lack of development due to inequality in wealth and power. As long as developing countries are denied economic opportunity in a system that favors the rich, they will be unable to support their populations adequately. The solution to the presumed population problem, therefore, is building a more equitable New International Economic Order. Fostering genuine development in this way will prove more effective than family planning. This line of argument, supported by communist nations that saw no need for population control, undermined the traditional UN view and challenged the interests of Western states. The resulting conflict reflected the height-ened world tensions of the early 1970s as well as the greater influence of the many new Third World countries.

Far from showing the world coming together, the conference seemed to deepen divisions. Its World Population Plan of Action showed the strain. According to one of its central provisions, population and development are interrelated. The Plan "reflects the international community's awareness of the importance of population trends for socio-economic development, and the socio-economic nature of the recommendations . . . reflects its aware-ness of the crucial role that development plays in affecting population trends" (Singh 1998: 10). The Plan contained few targets and no definite commitments. In fact, it stressed that the "implementation of population policies is the sovereign right of each nation" and that recommendations must "recognize the diversity of conditions" among countries (ibid.: 11). It only invited states to "consider adopting population policies . . . consistent with basic human rights" (ibid.). More constructively, it adopted language from the Tehran conference in saying that family decisions should be made freely by individuals and couples. This represented a meager harvest, and especially Western observers echoed the complaint of a leading newspaper that the meeting's result was "feeble." Notwithstanding its global scope, as inspiring and unifying ritual, this conference had failed.

Only ten years later, the 1984 world conference on population in Mexico City showed some bridging of the earlier divides (Demeny 1985; Jejeebhoy 1990). Nonaligned nations no longer considered development the best contraceptive. A new US administration now favored growth to solve population problems. As some geopolitical tensions dissipated, so did conference acrimony. The ongoing UN Decade for Women, meanwhile, had provided new notions of the role of women in society that could help to frame a more consensual approach to population control. While abortion became a hot-button issue, the overall meeting marked a shift in tone and substance.

This thrust continued at the 1994 International Conference on Population and Development in Cairo. Once again, abortion dominated much of the meeting and its coverage, yet the conference as a whole appeared to affirm a "new paradigm" on population (McIntosh and Finkle 1995; UN 1997: 39). Its Programme of Action explicitly relied on the "considerable consensus" that had been building since 1974. Part of this consensus derived from other meetings (UN 1997: 41): policies now had to satisfy the key norms of "sustainable development" and "gender equity." Achieving gender equity required that women be empowered through free access to reproductive health services. Their health and autonomy were central to the success of any policy. Acting on the new consensus required a "global partnership" in which all players would bear "shared but differentiated responsibilities for each other and for our planetary home." Not all of the consensus was new: "population and development" remained the mantra. The conference also reiterated some recommendations from earlier meetings, giving them greater weight as international norms. Policy implementation, of course, remained the sovereign right of states that legitimately protected their distinct cultural heritages. The reservations of Islamic countries indicated that reproductive health services, in particular, would not become easily available to all women. The Plan simply urged that governments "should" carry out its many recommendations. By comparison with 1974, however, the 1994 Plan displayed a major shift in tone and substance. More focused on individual rights and needs than on collective provision or demographic predicaments, it articulated an agenda long pursued by women's groups around the world (McIntosh and Finkle 1995: 225). The elaborate preparations of a UN apparatus eager to avoid another debacle clearly paid off. The inclusiveness of the meeting (179 states attended) and the simultaneous NGO forum (involving more than 1,500 groups) served to reinforce the message. In the way it creatively extended a tradition while affirming an emerging consensus, Cairo turned out to be a far more efficacious ritual than Bucharest had been.

Women

In all its major documents, the UN expresses a belief in the equality of men and women. The preamble to the Charter refers to their equal rights; the Universal Declaration includes provisions supporting the principle. Since

1947, a Commission on the Status of Women has also been actively promoting women's equality. In 1967, the General Assembly added to the original texts a Declaration on the Elimination of Discrimination against Women. Women's rights thus gained prominence by the late 1960s. The work of many women's groups reinforced the trend: their advocacy stimulated the UN to focus on the status of women more than it had done in the past. In discussions of human rights, population, environment, and especially development, women took center stage. To mark this trend, the General Assembly decided to make 1975 the International Women's Year, observe the first Women's Day in March of that year, and hold a conference on women in Mexico City. One hundred and thirty-three states attended the meeting, most represented by women; 6,000 NGO representatives participated in the related Tribune, seen by some as "history's largest consciousness-raising session" (UN 1996: 34). As its title implies, the Mexico Declaration on the Equality of Women and Their Contribution to Development and Peace reaffirmed the importance of full gender equality and valued women's contribution to development and peace. Obstacles to women's full integration must be removed; equal access to education and work were essential. National policies that address women's needs and a new economic order ensuring global equity must overcome the underdevelopment that harms women most. Since women also have equal responsibilities, the Declaration called on them to reject intervention in the domestic affairs of states and to promote complete disarmament. The accompanying World Plan of Action, supplemented by numerous resolutions, stated in detail what nations must do to achieve equality. It also urged more pervasive concern for women in all the activities of international organizations, and it demanded UN action to bring about a binding convention on discrimination against women. Its most concrete proposal was to declare 1975–85 the UN Decade for Women.

The triad of equality, development, and peace brought together ideas that had circulated in UN deliberations for many years. By thus framing women's problems and rights in terms of their role in the wider society, the conference symbolized a long-term shift in the nature of women's rights (Berkovitch 1999a). The triad also marked the high point of an egalitarian, progressive movement rooted in the 1960s, carried by both activist groups and Third World states, that envisioned a new world order and regarded concerted international action as the way to get there. Of course, the path was not smooth. In Mexico City, for example, women's rights, like other issues previously, were linked to a controversial condemnation of Zionism. In addition, Islamic states took exception to provisions against discrimination in the family (UN 1996: 42). However, debate on such issues did not diminish the galvanizing effect of the unprecedented event. Its effect was more than symbolic: the General Assembly declared the Decade and passed a convention, NGOs received a major stimulus, and states conformed to at least some of the norms set at the meeting (cf. Berkovitch 1999b).

The UN Decade encompassed two more meetings, at Copenhagen in 1980 and Nairobi in 1985. The Nairobi meeting culminated in an ambitious strategic plan on "Forward-Looking Strategies." When implementation of these strategies appeared to be highly uneven, the General Assembly decided to hold another conference in 1995 to review what the Decade had accomplished. The very name of the Fourth World Conference on Women in Beijing established a link with Mexico City: "Action for Equality, Development and Peace." Like its predecessors, the meeting linked women's rights to the progress of society as a whole and tied sustainable development to addressing women's needs (UN 1997: 57). Perhaps more emphatically than before, this fourth conference also affirmed in its Beijing Declaration that "women's rights are human rights." It not only opposed discrimination but also called for elimination of violence against women. While the declaration went beyond earlier statements in such areas, overall it firmly restated themes from other documents, referring explicitly to the consensus of two decades that supported its principles. The accompanying Platform for Action, though intended to improve implementation, also recapitulated older themes. Its objective was the "empowerment of women." Noting that changes since the 1970s might aid this goal, it specified many actions to be taken by states and international organizations to reach targets in areas like health and education, including gender-sensitive initiatives to deal with sexually transmitted diseases. Among the human rights of women, the Platform submitted, is the right "to have control over and decide freely and responsibly on matters related to their sexuality." The overriding message, says a UN account, was that the Platform issues are "global and universal" (UN 1997: 57).

Beijing did not resolve earlier disagreements, especially between Islamic and other states. Rights of inheritance, the role of religion, and the position of women in the family remained controversial, as a series of reservations made clear. The divisive issues were similar to those of the 1994 population conference. Not surprisingly, intense debate resulted in a Platform statement recognizing the "significance of and full respect for various religious and cultural backgrounds" in achieving equality. State sovereignty, of course, also received its due. Such limitations did not prevent Beijing from working as ritual. It represented a worldwide effort to articulate, more forcefully than before, a common understanding of women's rights and needs. The very repetition of key principles and recommendations affirmed their normative authority. The Beijing process lent significance to its outcome: its preparations had been "perhaps more participatory and inclusive than any in history" (UN 1996: 64). The sheer scale of the conference further signaled a common commitment. Delegations from 189 states attended, joined by some 5,000 representatives of 2,100 NGOs and 5,000 journalists; the parallel NGO forum attracted 30,000 people. In just a few decades, women had risen to the top of the world's agenda and women's rights had become unquestionable doctrine. Whatever their "real" effects, the women's conferences had done their sacralizing work well.

Conclusions

Somewhat defensively, a UN document asserts that the series of UN conferences is more than an "extravagant talk-fest" (UN 1999). They have had a "long-term impact," it says, in mobilizing organizations, serving as a forum, stimulating government commitments, and setting international standards. As a public relations effort, such self-congratulation may not be persuasive enough to assure the future of summits, but it contains a kernel of truth. As peak events in a broader process, world conferences have served as a kind of global ritual. Not only the women's conferences have been effective at sacralization; so have many others. In fact, by recycling themes and reaffirming principles from one meeting to the next, the meetings reinforce their collective messages. The whole of the ritual apparatus is more than the sum of conference texts. UN world conferences have functioned as secular ritual by periodically focusing world attention on selected topics through events in a particular format that lead to the affirmation and promulgation of knowledge and principles guiding global action. As part of a larger whole, they have helped to make a culture that transcends regional traditions. Enshrining certain ideas and symbols as "totems" of world society, they have contributed to defining a global reality. In these events, we thus recognize some of the power the sociologist Emile Durkheim attributed to religious ritual, namely to express and reinforce a society's sacred beliefs.

Taken together, these conferences tell us much about the construction of world culture. They show, first, how over the past half-century this construction work has become a regular feature of international life, involving thousands of organizations and tens of thousands of participants. The very coming together of so many people in the conference process is made possible by premises they share, ideas they take for granted. Second, their work has become highly structured: contributing to world culture now requires going through certain kinds of motions. Third, this work has a cumulative effect. The carry-over of themes and principles from one meeting to the next points to the elaboration of certain core elements of world culture, to which we will return in the next chapter. Fourth, world culture takes explicit form through confrontation. It encompasses contested knowledge and conflicting principles; the parties engaged in building it are themselves divided by values and interests. In the case of the conferences, we saw how certain issues provoked recurrent debate. Finally, over the last half-century a certain definition of the global situation has emerged, one we will examine further in the next chapter. Through the UN meetings, along with many other fora, knowledge of common problems, understanding of shared principles, and awareness of being bound to world society have all increased. The view from the summits is of a fractious yet organized, divided yet single, blue planet.

It is a planet Lord Macartney, whose mission to China we described in Chapter 3, would hardly recognize. What were then radically new ideas, such as that of the autonomous individual possessing inherent rights, have now become taken-for-granted elements of world culture. Though Macartney knew about states and their interests, the enshrinement of nation-states, charged with vastly greater responsibilities, as core elements of world society is new. The possibility of progress was once a vision of intellectuals; by 2000, the assumption that progress can and must be achieved through rational human effort was omnipresent. Macartney attempted to bring certain Western principles to the East, but the very emphasis on universalism, on principles that equally apply to all, represents a new thrust in world culture. The actual global apparatus for deliberating about problems and the rational procedures devised for addressing them similarly mark a qualitative shift – a shift to a world that, culturally speaking, has become one. In all these respects, and many more, a canopy of world culture now spans across the particular problems and fields of various gatherings. To this thick "ontological" sediment of world culture, to use another metaphor, UN meetings have contributed greatly, along with many others. It is the sediment, in turn, that makes the view from the summit possible in the first place.

The record of the meetings shows that the theories of world culture we discussed earlier capture much of the evolution of world culture described here. World-system theory sheds light on the North–South conflict typical of several meetings, a conflict that reflected differences in, among other things, the economic position of states. On balance, as this theory would expect, the conferences established universal principles that have Western roots. However, not all disagreements fit its simple conflict model. In shaping conference outcomes, the West is not uniformly influential; the USA often departs from an apparent consensus. World polity theory captures the evident elaboration of global models and recognizes the special role of nongovernmental actors in the conference process. The ritual insistence on the state's special status also fits its expectations, but this theory does not cover division and change equally well. For Robertsonian theory, the cumulative effect of the conferences is to elaborate the things humanity has in common; in the process, participants interpret, and contribute to, universal categories from their distinct vantage points. This theory captures both the drawing-together and the difference-articulating aspects of the meetings. It has less to say about the source of the differences or the consequences of the common culture. Thus, no single theory captures the whole; jointly, however, the theories offer useful guidance in analyzing global culture work.

In this chapter, we have focused on the process of construction, though along the way we have also addressed the substance being produced. However, world culture is not just an ongoing process of deliberation and debate; the construction work is made possible by an organizational scaffolding, which we examine in the next chapter.

Appendix: Overview of Key UN World Conferences

Table 4.1:   *Two conferences on human rights*

Conference name	International Conference on Human Rights	World Conference on Human Rights
Place and date	Tehran, May 1968	Vienna, June 1993
Attendance	84 states, some IGOs, 47 NGOs	171 states, 15 UN bodies, 248 UN-recognized and 593 other NGOs
Themes	Review of progress since 1948; apartheid, race, Israel, women	Review of UN efforts; right to development; rights of women, indigenous peoples
Outcome	Proclamation (affirms universal human rights as common understanding and obligation for all); 29 resolutions (re nondiscrimination, self-determination etc.)	Declaration (reaffirms human rights as universal, objective, equal, of individuals, collective responsibility); Programme of Action (proposes UN HR Commission)
Debates	Imperialism vs. Communism; Arabs vs. Israel; human rights vs. apartheid	Particularism vs. Universalism ("East" vs. "West"); NGOs vs. official meeting

Table 4.2: *Two conferences on the human environment*

Conference name	UN Conference on the Human Environment	UN Conference on Environment and Development
Place and date	Stockholm, June 1972	Rio de Janeiro, June 1992
Attendance	113 states, 134 NGOs in official proceedings	172 states, 1,600 total NGOs, 30,000 people for UNCED + Forum (8,000 journalists)
Themes	Man-made harm creates need for protection, UN action, rational planning; link environment to underdevelopment; state rights and responsibility	Link environment to development; global partnership for sustainable development; principle/need vs. special circumstances
Outcome	Declaration ("common outlook"; improving environment is imperative goal for mankind; steps outlined; national institutions entrusted to manage resources); Action Plan (109 recommendations re human settlements, resource management, pollutants etc.)	Declaration (equitable partnership to protect "our home"; sovereign state rights and different responsibilities vs. unsustainable practices); Agenda 21 (40 chapters on problems and paths; stress on sustainable development, via trade, consensus-building; commission proposed); Forest Principles
Debates	Developed vs. developing (e.g. aid); China vs. US; state rights vs. cooperation	North/environment vs. South/development; US vs. others; sovereignty vs. obligations; words/hype vs. deeds/negotiations on agenda

Table 4.3: *Two conferences on population*

Conference name	UN World Population Conference	International Conference on Population and Development
Place and date	Bucharest, August 1974	Cairo, September 1994
Attendance	136 states; 1,400 reps at NGO meeting	181 states; 1,500 NGOs at related Forum; 20,000 delegates overall
Themes	Population control vs. development; state sovereignty	Development and family planning; role of women and reproductive health
Outcome	World Population Plan of Action (108 recommendations; population and development interrelated; policies to recognize diversity; right of couples and individuals; no new UN program)	Programme of Action (universal family planning; population integrated in sustainable development policies; women's empowerment; major reservations, e.g. by Islamic states)
Debate	G77*/new economic order vs. West/population focus	Abortion; individual vs. family emphasis; family reunification

* Group of 77, the nonaligned countries.

Table 4.4: *Two conferences on women*

Conference name	World Conference of the International Women's Year	Fourth World Conference on Women: Action for Equality, Development, and Peace
Place and date	Mexico City, June–July 1975	Beijing, September 1995
Attendance	133 states, 114 NGOs (6,000 reps at related tribune)	189 states, 2,100 NGOs (30,000 reps at related Forum); 47,000 overall
Themes	Women in development and peace; demands for discrimination convention; Decade for Women	Women's freedom in sex, health; against traditional abuse; state sovereignty and "full respect" for cultural background
Outcome	Declaration (30 principles; peace stressed); World Plan of Action (equality, role in development, peace contribution)	Declaration (women's rights are human rights; empowerment key to equality, development, peace; overcome inequality); Platform for Action (global/universal issues; 12 priority areas; targets in health, education; follow-up via many UN bodies)
Debate	Zionism; Islamic vs. others regarding equality and nondiscrimination in family	Broad vs. restricted views of reproductive health; culture, religion, family tradition vs. general principles

Chapter 5

Sustaining World Culture: The Infrastructure of Technology and Organizations

Cable Grips the Globe

On August 6, 1857, the USS *Niagara*, a naval vessel provided by the US government, eased away from the shoreline of Valentia Bay in western Ireland. Slowly the huge gears of the paying-out machine on the foredeck eased a copper wire cable into the calm sea. The cable was 1,250 miles in length and 5/8 inches in diameter, consisting of seven strands, each 0.028 inches in diameter, coated three times with gutta-percha insulating resin from Malaya, wound with hemp yarn mixed with tar, linseed oil, and wax, and wrapped in iron wire with a final coating of tar (Smith 1974 [1891]). The cable weighed about one ton per mile. A nearly identical cable burdened the HMS *Agamemnon*, a British naval vessel that was to begin paying out its serpentine cargo in Trinity Bay, Newfoundland, some 2,500 miles across the Atlantic Ocean, at depths of up to two and a half miles. After five days of mostly smooth operations, failure to release the brakes on the paying-out machine aboard the *Niagara* led to excessive tension on the cable and it snapped. Some 380 miles of cable lay useless on the ocean floor. The "heroic story" of the transatlantic cable, told by some participants and later historians (Bright and Bright 1899; Smith 1974; Gordon 2002), seemed to have come to a less than heroic end.

Undaunted, the companies, partners, engineers, and crews engaged in the Atlantic cable project made a second attempt in the summer of 1858. Despite a fierce storm that almost sank the *Agamemnon* and repeated breakages that required new splicings and several restarts, the small flotilla of cable-laying and support ships at last achieved the final connection exactly one year after the initial cable-laying attempt began. The first clear message, transmitted on August 13, proudly proclaimed: "Europe and America are united by telegraph. 'Glory to God in the highest, on earth peace, good-will toward men'" (Bright and Bright 1899 I: 336). This message was followed by an exchange of congratulatory greetings between Queen Victoria and President Buchanan. A passage in Buchanan's message deserves special notice:

> May the Atlantic Telegraph, under the blessing of Heaven, prove to be a bond of perpetual peace and friendship between the kindred nations, and an instrument destined by Divine Providence to diffuse religion, civilisation, liberty, and law throughout the world!
> In this view will not all the nations of Christendom spontaneously unite in the declaration that it shall be for ever neutral; and that its communications shall be held sacred in passing to the place of their destination, even in the midst of hostilities?   (Bright and Bright 1899 I: 337)

Only 14 years after the first successful telegraph transmission of any kind, rapid communication across a vast body of water had moved from speculative enterprise to established fact, tying the North American continent to the burgeoning European network of telegraph lines, which by this time included submarine cables linking Ireland and England, England and France, Italy and Corsica, and Holland and Britain, among others. The cable, it was hoped, would promote harmony among nations and the spread of (Christian) culture and (Western) civilization, and it was to be a neutral medium above (more aptly, below) politics.

The first cable allowed for a transmission rate of only a few words per minute and failed definitively after three months, having carried only 732 messages. Other spectacular failures, such as a cable beneath the Red Sea and a cable to India, along with the US Civil War and the difficult technical problems that emerged in the ongoing work with long underwater cables, held up the next Atlantic cable attempt until 1865. That too failed, leaving more than a thousand miles of cable on the sea bottom; however, yet another cable was successfully laid in 1866 and the lost 1865 cable was located and completed. By 1900, 15 cables of much higher capacity than the early entries were in full operation across the Atlantic, including lines to Brazil and Argentina. Only two years later, the last link running clear around the world was established with the first transpacific cable from Vancouver to Australia, which had been connected to the Asian continent (at Singapore) as early as 1871.

The successful laying of the transatlantic cable and the subsequent completion of a global telegraph link mark major milestones in the development of what we call the infrastructure of world culture. This infrastructure has two dimensions. The "hardware" of world culture comprises the technological and organizational apparatus of global transportation, media, financial, and other systems that make the operations of world culture possible. It encompasses the machines and devices that carry goods, people, and information around the world: transoceanic cables, ships, railroad rolling stock, passenger jets, satellites, televisions, cell phones, transmission towers, computers, and the like. It also includes what we might call ancillary machines, buildings, and devices that tie these carriers together and organize them into coordinated networks and systems: docks, loading cranes, control rooms and towers, switching stations, maintenance hubs, fuel depots, Internet routers, and the like. A vast array of companies, most local or national rather than global, operate all this hardware and keep the networks and systems functioning. The hardware is mainly tangible, visible things, and the key concern is making sure that things work well and keep on working. This is instrumental, practical, hands-on work, even though much of the hardware is the result of abstract theoretical work by scientists and engineers.

The second dimension of world culture's infrastructure is what we call its "software." This encompasses, first and foremost, the many global governance organizations, beyond the level of companies and networks of companies, which make rules about the hardware. For example, the International Telecommunication Union (ITU) regulates use of the electromagnetic spectrum for radio broadcasting, microwave transmission, shortwave radio frequencies, and so on. The International Chamber of Commerce (ICC) makes rules about bills of lading, insurance, and other aspects of international shipping (Berman 1988). The Universal Postal Union (UPU) governs the flow of mail and packages among national postal systems, while the International Organization of Securities Commissions (IOSCO) makes global rules about the operations of stock exchanges, and the International Air Transport Association (IATA) develops agreements regarding air safety, baggage handling, ticketing, and the like. As these examples illustrate, both intergovernmental organizations (IGOs: ITU, UPU, and IOSCO) and international nongovernmental organizations (INGOs: ICC, IATA) are global rule makers. While IGOs are the dominant governance structures in numerous important social sectors, in most sectors INGOs exercise primary global authority, albeit informally and through a logic of voluntary conformity with the rules they oversee (Boli and Thomas 1999). By and large, states are not of much importance in global governance sectors in which INGOs have a major role, and many INGOs jealously guard their independence from states.

In the software of world culture we include the users of world-cultural hardware. All kinds of people and organizations are users, of course, but of greatest interest are those who invent, define, revise, discuss, debate, elaborate, expand, propagate, and ponder world culture. To extend the metaphor we have used, the most important users of the hardware of world culture are the software "programmers" who encode world-cultural principles and definitions, develop blueprints to solve complex global problems, develop information-gathering systems, gather and analyze data to understand the many dimensions of global change, and so on. Complementing them are world-cultural implementers, who activate these principles, definitions, blueprints, and data to deal with concrete situations and issues. Most visible among the implementers are political and social activists, UN summiteers, Olympic organizers, and the like, who deliberately seek public and media attention; but the vast majority of implementers (or enactors) of world culture are ordinary people doing everyday jobs in businesses, schools, government agencies, service organizations, and so on. These users build world culture into daily life, aided by the hardware and software infrastructure that is the focus of this chapter.

Previous chapters provided glimpses of this infrastructure. We gave examples in our introduction, included some aspects of its history in Chapter 2, and alluded especially to the software dimension in the chapter on constructing world culture. Here we describe the hardware and software infrastructure in greater detail. This description also serves to reinforce a point we made in our first chapter, where we made the case for thinking about culture as concrete and structured, not simply a set of disembodied, free-floating, abstract conceptions. This chapter shows how culture is embedded in things.

Hardware: Transportation and Communication Infrastructure

We leap ahead a century from our introductory vignette. By the 1970s the technical limitations of coaxial submarine telephone cables began to loom like a giant, unclimbable wall. Advanced cables could carry more than 4,000 voice connections simultaneously and had facilitated exponential growth in international telephony for two decades, but the emergence of satellite transmission systems threatened to render land lines permanently obsolete. Enter the fiber-optic cable and room-temperature lasers, technologies that had been under development since the early 1950s and early 1960s, respectively. Despite the much greater role played by theoretical physics in their conceptualization, improvements in these technologies came primarily via the same methods that had made the telegraph cable possible in the 1850s: much trial and error, careful note-taking, repeated failures, and considerable sweat (fiber optics research labs were often stifling due to the heat used to soften or melt glass). In 1971, a fiber-optic system demonstrating the usefulness of the technologies for video communication was demonstrated for another English queen, Elizabeth II, at the Institution of Electrical Engineers' hundredth anniversary celebration. As chronicled by Hecht (1999), development then entered a frenzied period of "three generations in five years" such that, by 1983, the capacity, reliability, and durability of fiber optics were dramatically greater and telephone and cable television companies could begin implementing commercial systems.

On land, fiber-optics technology was still not obviously superior to the prevailing long-distance transmission mode of microwave relay stations. Across the oceans, however, microwave relay was not feasible and satellite technology was plagued by intractable problems like transmission delay (the quarter-second travel time required for signals to reach a satellite and return to Earth), echoing, lost connections, and the like. Originally proposed in 1969, the first intercontinental fiber-optics submarine cable projects stretched over a period of more than 10 years, with formal bids requested in late 1982 for a transatlantic cable and in early 1983 for a transpacific cable. These projects required unusual development efforts, such as experiments by biologists to understand why sharks were attracted to fiber-optics cables (sharks had ruined a line installed in the Canary Islands) when they had never been known to gnaw at coaxial cables. The first project to reach completion, known as TAT-8 (for TransAtlantic cable 8, continuing the numbering system used for coaxial cables), ran from New Jersey to both France and England after splitting at an offshore connection. Unlike the nineteenth-century experience, the cable laying itself was largely uneventful and TAT-8 was operational by December 1988. It reached its carrying capacity of 8,000 simultaneous telephone conversations (later boosted to around 40,000) almost immediately. Meanwhile, the transpacific line was in progress and went operational just a few months later. These initial long-distance successes led to many further cables that have been progressively smaller in diameter (now down to one inch or less, including insulation and steel ribbon protective cover), lighter, and of ever greater capacity.

Telegraphy and voice/video submarine cables are but two of the many technologies that have emerged since the nineteenth century to shrink time and distance by several orders of magnitude. The capacity to communicate across great distances has increased astonishingly; TAT-8 transmits 560 million bits of data per second, compared to a few bits per second for the first telegraph cable in 1858. The most recent transatlantic fiber-optics cable, TAT-14, with landing stations in the USA, England, Denmark, Germany, the Netherlands, and France, transmits 640 billion bits per second, three orders of magnitude greater than TAT-8 and equivalent to 8 million to 10 million simultaneous phone calls (though most of its load is Internet traffic). At the same time, the cost per transmission unit has fallen at roughly the same rate that cable transmission capacity has increased, so far more communication is possible at ever lower cost.

While the developed countries account for the bulk of the long-distance cable construction and traffic, the rest of the globe is increasingly becoming wired, as Glover's (2004) chronological listing of all fiber-optics cable systems demonstrates. The ARCOS 1 cable (operational in 2001) links developing countries in the Caribbean and Central America; the SAT 3/WASC system links West African countries; the SEA ME WE 3 system wends its way from northern Germany through the Mediterranean and Red Sea to India, southeast Asia, Australia, China, and Korea, directly linking more than 30 countries on all continents but the Americas over its total length of 39,000 kilometers. It is, indeed, a wired world.

Such advances have "shrunk" both space and time; Harvey (1989) calls this now-commonplace experience "time-space compression." A succession of world-spanning technical and industrial systems has made it vastly cheaper and faster to move goods, people, and information. The past two centuries have witnessed the rise and consolidation of a number of these systems: railroads, shipping, and the telegraph in the nineteenth century, followed by motor vehicles, the telephone, radio, television, air transportation, and the Internet in the twentieth century.

The expansion of these infrastructural systems is stupendous. Consider some key figures (drawn from UN 1948–98; Banks 1976; International Telecommunication Union 1991, 2003; Mitchell 1998; World Bank 2002; Internet Systems Consortium 2003):

- Rail lines: about 10,000 miles of track in 1845; 200,000 miles by 1880; 400,000 miles by 1900; 600,000 miles by 1920.
- Rail passenger travel: just over 200 million total kilometers traveled in 1845; almost 100 billion in 1900; over 1,000 billion in 1965.
- Telegraph lines: about 50,000 miles in 1845 (almost all strung in the previous decade); 168,000 miles in 1865; peak of around 1.6 million miles in 1925 – seven times the distance from the Earth to the Moon, or more than 60 times the circumference of the globe.

- Telegrams: 21 million in 1865; 440 million in 1925.
- Commercial ships: 43 million tons gross displacement in 1913; 80 million tons in 1948; 420 million tons in 1980.
- Passenger cars: half a million in 1910; 100 million by 1955; 500 million by 1995.
- Telephone subscribers: about one million in 1900; 13 million in 1935; 116 million in 1965; over 1.7 billion in 2000.
- International telephone calls: 22 million in 1960; 2.2 billion in 1980; more than 100 billion in 2000.
- Radios: several million by 1935; over 600 million in 1965; billions by the 1990s.
- Televisions: 77 million in 1950; 250 million in 1970; 1.7 billion in 2000.
- Air passengers: 74 million international passengers in 1970; 311 million domestic passengers in 1970 and 375 million by 1995; 1.3 billion international passengers in 1995.
- Air travel: 159 billion total kilometers traveled in 1970; 1.25 trillion kilometers by 1995.
- Personal computers: about 150,000 in 1980; 103 million in 1990; nearly 500 million in 2000.
- Internet servers (hosts) and users: about 200 hosts in 1980, 313,000 in 1990, and 162 million in 2002; serving a few thousand users in 1980, a few million by 1990, and an estimated 500 million to 600 million by 2001 (user counts are notoriously inexact).

Many more exponentially increasing aspects of global transportation and communication could be added, but these suffice to show the extraordinary technical explosion of the last century and a half, which has been chronicled many times. Things, people, and information flow around the world as never before, with great leaps in these flows occurring in successive waves of technical and industrial advance.

Hardware and World Culture

The mobility of people and ideas varies enormously across countries, classes, and status groups, of course. Access and affordability are highly uneven – the mere existence of these globally enveloping systems does not imply that everyone has the same opportunity to become a world-cultural user. By the same token, the mere existence of these systems and the mobility they provide do not guarantee that their users will engage in world-cultural activity, rather than national or local cultural work. Since national segments of the global infrastructure are more densely interconnected than the transnational systems, one could argue that they favor national and local culture more than transnational or global culture. Neither is global cultural work directly dependent on this infrastructure. After all, the formative period of global cultural construction – the second half of the nineteenth century, discussed in Chapter 3 – preceded, in large degree, the development of globally integrated technical infrastructure.

The hardware is thus not determinative but it is highly facilitative. It is unlikely that Europeans, North and South Americans, or south Asians would have begun to form and join INGOs in rapidly increasing numbers in the nineteenth century in the absence of several centuries of global voyaging by wind-powered vessels whose captains, crews, and cargo – including, above all, their human cargo of soldiers, merchants, missionaries, slaves, peasants, adventurers, and bureaucrats – began to make the international and the global, as modes of thinking and arenas of action, both familiar and routine. This routinization of the fundamental dimension of world culture – that individuals and groups understand what they do and how they do it as broadly applicable and useful knowledge set in a widely appropriate normative or prescriptive framework that reaches far beyond their local or nearby regions – is the most important effect of global infrastructural systems.

Routinization is in large degree "built in" to global infrastructure in that use of these systems inherently brings into play the transnational and the global in many ways. For example, the home page of a travel website includes advertisements for vacations to four or five continents; radio news programs regularly include international or foreign events; phone books and pre-paid cards present rate tables for calls to many countries around the world. Routinization also means, in light of the ubiquity of the communications technologies in particular, that some degree of world-cultural awareness and orientation, with the possibility of participation in producing, debating, or extending world culture, is experienced by a very large proportion of the world's population, despite uneven access to and use of the global infrastructure. Poor villagers with little education in remote locales may debate the merits of NAFTA, the North American Free Trade Agreement (in Mexico), urge resistance to vulgar Western films (in Iran), write to Amnesty International for help in chronicling human rights abuses (in Mindanao), and so on. The global is present in the local, almost everywhere, even when the local is only weakly tied to the global.

As a practical matter, of course, the most important effect of the hardware of world culture is its globalization of global thinking and doing in the literal sense: it spreads (transmits) world-cultural doing to ever more people ever more regularly, with increasing levels of interaction and denser networks of organizational linkages, as the reach and availability of the technical systems increase. The hardware makes it possible to operate ever more globally: to seek and find like-minded anti-dam activists or knitting enthusiasts or particle physicists or architectural consultants, to spread emotion-wrenching images worldwide to promote a cause or enlist widely scattered doctors of jurisprudence to assess soberly the legal implications of the Kyoto Protocol.

The hardware of world culture is not simply instrumental in sustaining it. Contrary to conventional understanding, this technical and mechanical hardware of world culture is itself world-cultural, in several senses. The root meaning of "technology" refers not to material devices and machines but to the knowledge that makes the invention and production of devices and machines possible. Such knowledge has long been decidedly world-cultural in that its producers have assumed that the knowledge they generate is valid and applicable everywhere. Consider the water wheel as an example. Improvements to water wheel designs made by anonymous carpenters, blacksmiths, and millers over hundreds of years were seen as transferable to places near and far, not as useful or workable only at the local mill or irrigation system. Implicitly, these practically minded improvers assumed that the physics of hydraulic flow, angular momentum, and friction that determine the efficiency of a water wheel are universal and invariant – and the diffusion of their technical innovations over time demonstrated that these implicit assumptions were valid.

We should not overstate the case, however. It makes sense to think of such practical knowledge, produced largely by trial and error, as taking on genuine world-cultural significance only when it is codified in the form of general designs, abstract principles, or production schematics – only, that is, when the practical knowledge is simplified, organized, codified, and transferred to a medium that allows for its propagation as abstract knowledge not requiring the presence of an experienced wheel builder for its use. This is the key difference between "local knowledge" (Geertz 1983) and world-cultural knowledge: while the former may also be universalistic in principle, the latter must be available in a form that permits impersonal transmission. Once a truly global infrastructure for impersonal transmission came into being, many realms of local knowledge could then become candidates for world-cultural embedding.

Thus, technical and mechanical hardware is, in essence, the embodiment of technical knowledge – i.e., a form of culture. As a result of the explosion of formal, scientized knowledge in the past two or three centuries, most of the hardware of world culture's infrastructure is itself the product of world-cultural knowledge – of chemistry, physics, materials science, mechanical and civil engineering, electronics research, and so on. The construction of world culture's infrastructure is part and parcel of the construction of world culture.

Another sense in which the hardware infrastructure is itself world-cultural is that it is dependent on and promoted by the organizational software that is crystallized in INGOs, IGOs, and global companies. Without these "control programs," which we discuss next, the hardware would accomplish very little. Just as printed circuit boards are not particularly useful physical objects (though they can make for interesting wall clocks), the massive amounts of copper wire, fiber-optic cable, and high-capacity computers that carry the Internet would be little more than curiosities to entertain future archaeologists if they were not managed by a complex array of globally connected organizations that ensure the orderly, efficient flow of information through these sinuous globe-encircling connectors. A revealing form of mutually reinforcing dependency is at work: world-cultural knowledge enables the construction of global technical and organizational infrastructure that is crucial to the expansion of world culture that, in part, focuses precisely on the technical and organizational infrastructure without which world culture would shrivel and shrink.

While we have stressed the world-cultural role and character of infrastructure, it goes without saying that the motive forces behind the development of global transportation and communication hardware are many. Capitalist competition has been a major driver, both in the development of new technologies and in the compulsion to extend them to ever larger expanses of the globe (markets). Competition among powerful states seeking global or regional domination has been important – even decisive – in many arenas (e.g., the technological race to develop radar, jet engines, and rocketry during the Second World War). Like so many other forms of massive social and technical change, the hardware of global systems is due to a confluence of factors, all pushing in the same direction, all producing compelling logics for why the telegraph, telephone, radio, television, satellite, and computer came to be seen as necessary, desirable, progressive, useful, and inevitable – here, there, and everywhere. That logic continues to dominate in world culture, almost unopposed, almost unquestioned. In that light, we can safely predict further elaboration into the foreseeable future of the hardware shell enveloping the world.

Software: International Organizations Integrating, Innovating, and Advocating

An international body eventually arose to safeguard the submarine cables whose story opened this chapter. The International Cable Protection Committee, established in 1958, is one of a rare breed of organizations that includes among its members both states and commercial companies that own or operate submarine telecommunications or power cables. As of September 2002, it had 79 members from 41 countries. Organized in "working groups" for different geographical areas, it operates programs in conjunction with fishing, mining, oil and gas, dredging, and other offshore industries to prevent damage to cables. It also sponsors programs to improve cable resistance to damage from human and natural hazards, emphasizing technical and legal information exchange and research (International Cable Protection Committee 2003). Its programs and rule making are part of what we call the software of world culture's infrastructure. Especially prominent in this software are the activities of INGOs, several of which we have encountered earlier in this book.

One of the oldest of the generally acknowledged INGOs is Anti-Slavery International, originally known as the British and Foreign Anti-Slavery Society when established in 1839. It was the outgrowth of local abolitionist societies that had formed in many British locales from the 1780s onward, led primarily by Quakers, Baptists, Methodists, and members of other nonconformist Protestant sects. Impelled by the view that slavery was not simply morally opprobrious but genuinely sinful, abolitionists in a number of countries joined hands in this new international organization to seek the end of the slave trade and slavery everywhere. In 1840 the Society sponsored the first international anti-slavery convention, with delegations from the USA and France joining their British counterparts; the convention expanded on the abolitionist movement's success in outlawing the British slave trade (1807) and slavery in Britain's colonies (1833). Over time the Society's mission broadened to include the abolition of slavery-like practices of all sorts, including the "apprenticeship" system that replaced slavery in many colonies, the mistreatment and exploitation of indigenous peoples in European empires, forced labor, and so on. Its current efforts focus on child labor, debt bondage, child prostitution, and the exploitation and abuse of domestic workers (Anti-Slavery International 2003).

A very different kind of INGO is Nordiska föreningen för befrämjande af odontologisk undervisning och forskning (Scandinavian Association for Dental Research). Founded in 1917 at a meeting in Gothenburg, Sweden, the association set itself the task of promoting the scientific and technical development of dentistry, including dental education, in contrast with its much older parent organization, Skandinavisk Tandläkarförening (Scandinavian Dentists' Association, in operation since 1866), whose main concern was promoting the profession of dentistry in the Nordic countries. The association quickly incorporated *Odontologisk Tidskrift* (*Journal of Dentistry*, published since 1893) as its official journal and launched programs to promote cooperation, information exchange, and state support of dental research (Scandinavian Association for Dental Research 2004). Following the pattern in many INGO sectors, the association eventually joined other national and regional dental groups in a global body, the International Association for Dental Research (IADR, established 1920). The IADR is the umbrella organization for virtually all dental associations in the world, holding a biennial convention that draws thousands of dentists and related professionals.

A third, more hybrid INGO is especially important for world-cultural development but unlikely to be recognized as such. Those who send or receive money from abroad may notice a SWIFT Bank Identifier Code (BIC) in the transaction documents but few give any thought to what SWIFT could be. The Society for Worldwide Interbank Financial Telecommunication is a hybrid organization; it refers to itself as a company and it operates on a for-profit basis, but in essential ways it has the structure and logic of a financial-industry INGO. SWIFT is a cooperative society whose shareholders are the international banks, investment firms, brokers, and dealers who use its services – a total of more than 7,500 institutions in almost 200 countries. It employs more than 1,600 people, has annual revenues of almost 600 million euros, and constantly works to improve efficiency, but its directors and shareholders are happy if the company just breaks even at the end of each year.

When established by some 239 banks from 15 countries in 1973, in an effort to move beyond the telex to computer technology and automated message delivery, the SWIFT vision was a system that eventually would handle about 300,000 messages per day. Once the system began operations in 1977, however, SWIFT traffic expanded far beyond expectations. Traffic exceeded more than eight million messages per day in 2003, or a total of two billion messages for the year – about four times as much traffic as ten years earlier (SWIFT 2004). To ensure that the messages sent on the system are readily and uniformly interpreted, SWIFT cooperates with ISO (the main global standardization INGO) on the development and promotion of ISO 15022, a standard for the syntax and design rules of electronic securities messages. ISO Sub-Committee 4 of Technical Committee 68 handles standards for "Securities and Related Financial Instruments" (ISO 2004); in 1999, ISO 15022 replaced the ISO 7775 standard from 1984 (revised several times until 1997). By 2003, compliance with the new standard by banks and other financial institutions was estimated at 99 percent (Parker 2003).

Why is SWIFT crucial to world culture? Because SWIFT is an essential lubricant of the world economic engine. It facilitates the clearing of inter-bank and other international transactions through its global messaging system, SWIFTNet, which is crucial to the smooth and timely operation of the entire global financial system. It makes sending payments from one country to another easy and routine. More pointedly, it makes it easy for a person in one country to pay dues or donations to INGOs or IGOs based in any other country. Thanks to SWIFTNet, an INGO based in Japan can purchase documents from an IGO in Geneva or Paris and neither party need be aware of the clearing process that ensures payment. When participants in a global conference gather in Cairo or Singapore, the currency exchange clearing transactions required to finance their airfare, lodging, meals, and souvenir purchases are of no concern – because, when the transactions reach the level of interbank credits and debits, SWIFTNet ensures (with 99.98 percent operational reliability) that the transactions will close out properly.

Evidently, SWIFT does not operate its complex messaging system in the service of world culture. SWIFT company officers and managers would be more than a little puzzled to hear that SWIFTNet is part of the infrastruc-ture of world culture, since in their vision the system is not cultural at all – it is a technically advanced assembly of hardware and software that sup-ports the global financial system. Yet SWIFT, along with a myriad other business and technical systems, is essential to the flow of information, resources, and people engaged in the making and propagating of world culture. It would take us too far afield to survey the entire range of such systems here, of course. We introduce SWIFT as an especially crucial yet largely unknown example of this range of infrastructural supports that, fully global in scope, help to ensure that world culture becomes ever more truly global.

The Primacy of INGOs in World-Cultural Activity

SWIFT represents one of three types of international organizations that are especially prominent at the global level. These are global companies (a term we use for convenience to refer to both multinational and transnational corporations), intergovernmental organizations (IGOs), and international nongovernmental organizations (INGOs). Best known are the global companies that produce high-profile consumer brands – Coca-Cola, Sony, Gucci, Rolls-Royce, Burger King, and so on. Much less well known are companies in less brand-oriented sectors – wholesale, technical, engineering, financial, mineral, agricultural, and the like. A few thousand of these global companies account for large proportions of total world economic output and even larger proportions of international trade, much of which occurs within these economic behemoths. Similarly, a relative handful of IGOs are well known – the International Monetary Fund, World Bank, World Trade Organization, and a number of United Nations bodies such as the World Health Organization, UNICEF, UNESCO, and UNAIDS – but most IGOs have minimal public presence, concerned as they are with technical, financial, infrastructural, and political global governance activities.

Multinational companies number in the tens of thousands (Gabel and Bruner 2003); truly global companies (having global reach and not identifying themselves with any particular country or locale) number in the few thousands at most. IGOs are much less numerous – a generous definition identifies about 1,600 organizations, and fewer than 250 IGOs count among their members a substantial portion of all the world's states or a sizeable number of members from every major continent (Union of International Associations 2001). Global companies have enormous resources and considerable autonomy from states; IGOs depend almost entirely on resources provided by their member states and, in theory, exist solely to facilitate collective decision making among states and to implement the policies and programs agreed upon by their members. Because states are also powerful organizations with enormous resources, however, many IGOs have strong global authority in their respective domains and they can draw on member resources as necessary to manage the issues within their purview.

INGOs are another bird altogether. With a few well-known exceptions, they are small organizations with relatively few resources – often little more than the voluntary labor of their members – and they lack the seductive allure of global companies' money or the coercive capacity of states. They are numerous (as we discuss below, using a broad definition, the contemporary world hosts tens of thousands of INGOs) but they are largely invisible, known, by and large, only to their own members. Yet INGOs are far more important with respect to world culture than either companies or IGOs. How can this be?

The key elements accounting for this seemingly paradoxical situation – that, despite their small size and lack of resources, INGOs are the essential "organizational backbone" of world culture (Boli and Thomas 1999) – are two. First, INGOs are the most diverse and ubiquitous type of global actor. For virtually every domain of human activity, be it economic, cultural, political, technical, religious, scientific, whatever, one or more INGOs is working globally or regionally in that domain, and often there are many relevant INGOs at work. The same is far from true of IGOs, which are concentrated in economic, technical, and political domains (Boli and Thomas 1999); neither is it true of global companies, which cover a broad spectrum of activities but are absent from a great many domains encompassed by the INGO world. What is more, INGO headquarters, regional offices, and memberships are much more widely dispersed among the countries and peoples of the world than is the case for IGOs and global companies, despite the strong global presence of a number of the latter.

Second, INGOs are more important to world culture because they are, by their very nature, disinterested and irresponsible. These may seem like odd terms to apply to INGOs, perhaps, but we choose them with care. The vast majority of INGOs are disinterested in the sense that they are not especially concerned about their own interests. INGOs are nonprofit organizations promoting collective benefits, public goods, the common weal, or the welfare of diffuse categories of beneficiaries (which may, but often do not, include their own members). They seek not profits or power but the vitality or success of their respective sports, branches of knowledge, professional norms, environmental causes, or medical specialties. Unlike companies, they do little to market themselves, and many reject marketing in principle; unlike states, they cannot impose or coerce, and most find the very notion of coercion abhorrent. They focus on developing principles, rules, ethical codes, technical know-how, philosophical precepts, and many other types of world-cultural abstractions without being restricted or hampered by the pragmatic economic and political exigencies that face companies and states. This is not to say that INGOs ignore such practical matters as raising money, motivating members to volunteer their time, recruiting competent paid staff and directors, and the like, but such activities are deemed regrettable necessities rather than central goals.

In addition, INGOs are irresponsible, in the following sense (Meyer 1996): they are not responsible for the principles, prescriptions, policies, or programs they present to the larger world. Neither the Rainforest Action Network, Friends of the Earth, nor the Pachamama Alliance would have to answer to the wives and children of jobless tropical lumberjacks if their efforts to preserve the rain forests succeed in reducing timber production. INGOs calling for better working conditions and expanded labor rights for cutters and seamstresses producing textiles in low-wage countries do not have to find alternative employment for workers if their jobs move to even lower-wage countries with weaker labor protection legislation (the infamous "race to the bottom" problem). Precisely because INGOs have neither economic might nor political authority, they are culturally free – that is, free from responsibility for the consequences of their words and deeds (for which they are increasingly criticized; see Bond 2000 on the "global backlash" against INGOs). Global companies are responsible to their shareholders and, in varying degrees, for their employees; states are responsible to and for their citizens in a whole host of ways. Here again, then, we find that companies and states are constrained by practical concerns and the pressures of competition far more than are INGOs. INGOs are free to advocate, promote, and propose almost willy-nilly, leaving it to states to figure out how INGO proposals might be rendered feasible and to companies to adapt to the changed conditions that INGO-inspired legislative and regulatory changes engender.

"Willy-nilly" is too pejorative and casual a term, of course. Bearing in mind that most INGOs deal with technical, scientific, economic, infrastructural, knowledge, and professional matters (detailed below), not political or social advocacy, the typical INGO's world-cultural work deals with sober, rather technical, rather staid, usually uncontroversial matters. In these domains, irresponsibility is hardly an appropriate term – and states, IGOs, and global companies are hardly relevant. Large INGOs are the principal global actors in these domains, tying together local and national associations in distinct, comprehensive global sectors that are largely self-contained, autonomous from states, and non-commercial (Boli 1999). They carry the responsibility of developing and propagating their respective bodies of knowledge, technological expertise, "know-how" (practical and applied engineering), branches of medicine, schools of thought, academic disciplines, and so on. Their business, as it were, is to expand the frontiers of knowledge, thought, expertise, and technical possibilities; to improve production methods, synthetic materials, chemical compounds, surgical techniques, and so on – matters for which only these organizations can be responsible because they bring together the most knowledgeable and most highly credentialed figures in their respective domains. States and IGOs are generally incompetent to regulate or direct these domains (attempts to do so often are seen as ignorant "meddling"), though states fund much of the research and development work that helps keep these domains going. Global companies are indirectly involved in that they also fund much of the research and development, and they often pay the expenses of employees who are engaged in INGOs (to attend conferences and workshops, work on committees, serve as officers or directors, and so on), but companies' direct INGO involvement is generally limited to the industry or trade INGOs that represent their special niches.

Advocacy and cause-oriented INGOs that target states, IGOs, or global companies are less constrained by considerations of knowledge and technique because their principal concerns are normative, but they too increasingly rely on scientific knowledge and systematic data (about human rights violations, air and water pollution, poverty, ecosystem management, and so on) in formulating their policies and demands. In addition, they have learned that uncompromising principled criticism tends to be self-defeating because it is rejected as unworkable "radicalism." Advocacy INGOs therefore have moved toward more pragmatic, often openly cooperative relationships with states, IGOs, and companies. In the end, however, states, IGOs, and companies are still mostly on the receiving end of world culture.

While most INGO sectors involve "disinterested" INGOs, one major type – industry and trade INGOs, which bring together large and small companies in a myriad economic sectors and branches – are decidedly self-interested. Industry and trade groups push for state (and, to a lesser extent, IGO) policies and programs that will benefit their products and markets. Even these groups, however, are relatively unconstrained in terms of producing and refining world culture, because the INGOs themselves are also voluntary associations (with companies as members) that are not directly concerned with profit or competition. This is why we commonly see industry and trade INGOs producing codes of ethics, standards regarding labor conditions, guides to good environmental stewardship, and the like, and taking a leadership role in trying to induce their members to abide by them.

Organizational Connections

What gives the INGO/IGO nexus an especially infrastructural character is the ever-thickening web of networks and links among these globally oriented organizations. Consider, for example, the International Law Association (ILA), mentioned in Chapter 3. Founded in 1873 as the "Association for the Reform and Codification of the Law of Nations," it brings together some 3,700 legal scholars and practitioners to promote the "study, elucidation and advancement of international law" (both public and private) in the interest of "the furthering of international understanding and goodwill" (International Law Association 2003). Over the years, the ILA has developed relationships with a wide range of organizations, communicating with and participating to varying degrees in the meetings and conferences of the latter and, in turn, bringing representatives of other INGOs and IGOs into its work. Currently it has consultative, liaison, or observer status with numerous UN agencies, such as the Economic and Social Council (ECOSOC), United Nations Educational, Scientific, and Cultural Organization (UNESCO), the Food and Agriculture Organization (FAO), the World Intellectual Property Organization (WIPO), and United Nations Conference on Trade and Development (UNCTAD). It also works directly with the Committee on the Peaceful Uses of Outer Space, the International Telecommunication Union, and other IGOs, while maintaining membership in umbrella INGOs (the International Social Science Council and the Conference of Non-Governmental Organizations in Consultative Relationship with the United Nations) and working relationships with a variety of other INGOs, such as the Deutsche Vereinigung für Internationales Recht, the International Committee on the Underwater Cultural Heritage, the International Chamber of Commerce (ICC), the International Institute of Higher Studies in Criminal Sciences, and the International Red Cross and Red Crescent Movement (Union of International Associations 2001). Note the variety of these linked organizations: their central concerns range from the law as such to culture, business, social science research, and charity and emergency relief.

This degree of formalized interaction among INGOs, and between INGOs and IGOs, is widespread and constantly increasing. The *Yearbook of International Organizations* provides systematic data about the extensiveness of this networking in statistical tables summarizing the links indicated by INGOs and IGOs. Considering only truly international organizations with members from several or many countries (*Yearbook* categories A–D), we present in Table 5.1 the extensiveness of network interconnections between and among INGOs and IGOs (Union of International Associations [UIA] 2000).

One striking finding in Table 5.1 is that IGOs form links with many more international organizations than vice versa. The average IGO is connected to almost 17 other IGOs and 16 INGOs, while the average INGO is connected to only three other INGOs and one IGO. IGOs are clearly more central nodes in these global networks; UN agencies are the most central of all. At the same time, the average IGO is much more constrained by other organizations (both IGOs and INGOs): it must manage relations,

Table 5.1:   *Connections reported by international organizations, 2000*

	Total	Average	Number of organizations
IGOs with other IGOs	4,204	16.7	251 IGOs
INGOs with other INGOs	18,460	3.2	5,825 INGOs
IGOs with INGOs	10,151	1.7	6,076 INGOs and IGOs
Of which:			
IGOs with INGOs	3,895	15.5	251 IGOs
INGOs with INGOs	6,256	1.1	5,825 INGOs
Totals	32,814	5.4	6,076 INGOs and IGOs

Note: Only INGOs and IGOs in categories A–D ("conventional" bodies) are included.
Source: *Yearbook of International Organizations* (Union of International Associations 2000).

coordinate activities, debate policies, and put up with influence attempts from an array of 33 organizations, whereas the average INGO lives in a much simpler world in which it regularly interacts with only four or five organizations. INGOs, in other words, have much freer rein in their activities; typically, if they direct their energies at IGOs at all, they concentrate on only one or two that are most relevant to their particular issues and concerns.

The UIA data also tally the number of connections mentioned in all sections of the organizations' self-descriptions, not just the sections explicitly devoted to this issue ("IGO relations" and "INGO relations"). For example, in its "History" section the World Meteorological Organization (WMO, an IGO) mentions the seminal role of the International Meteorological Organization (an INGO, founded in 1873) in the WMO's creation in 1947. Similarly, the International Council of Ophthalmology (an INGO) mentions in its "Structure" section that its governing Council includes an ex officio member from the International Agency for the Prevention of Blindness (also an INGO), though the latter organization is not among those with which it has official links. This broader measure indicates a total of 46,851 "cross-references," as the *Yearbook* calls them, among these 6,076 IGOs and INGOs – an average of 7.7 per organization. This is a more representative figure for the interconnections among international organizations, though it is still an underestimate because many informal connections among international organizations are not captured by *Yearbook* entries.

This highly interwoven character of the INGO/IGO world is a central element of global civil society. Like national civil societies, a plethora of voluntary associations both cooperate and compete with each other in defining, building, elaborating, promoting, and governing particular social sectors or domains. One important difference about global civil society, however, is the decentralized character of world society. In the absence of a world state, global authority and governance are parceled out among a great many international organizations, both IGOs and INGOs, and no single organization in any sector – not even the most powerful IGO – has the kind of authority and coercive capacity that states exercise across many sectors in their national societies. Decentralization combined with informal but well legitimated global authority is a recipe for interconnectedness, with IGOs serving as central nodes for many global networks but INGOs alone forming networks in sectors that operate autonomously from states.

INGO Expansion and Its Implications

The first INGOs emerged before 1850; early examples include the British and Foreign Anti-Slavery Society from 1839 (profiled above), the World Evangelical Alliance (1846), and the World Alliance of Young Men's Christian Associations (1855). By the 1860s and 1870s new organizations began to appear regularly across a wide range of sectors: the *Société universelle d'ophthalmologie* (1861); the International Committee of the Red Cross, International Working Men's Association (the First International), and International Geodesic Association (all in 1864); the Association for the Reform and Codification of the Law of Nations (1873); and the International Union of Marine Insurance, an early industry INGO (1874). Rapid expansion then followed: for the decade 1871–80, 22 new INGOs appeared; succeeding decades produced 38, 95, and (for 1901–10) a booming 261 INGOs. This early period of rapid globalization involved much more than the world economy. As we saw in Chapter 3, globally oriented voluntary associations concerned about universalistic knowledge, values, law, and many other cultural dimensions, proliferated as never before (see also Boli, forthcoming). Put another way, world culture was beginning to get organized.

Imperialist European powers were dominant internationally in this period, and most of the early INGOs had European origins, though they drew members from many other parts of the globe, particularly the Americas. However, from the point of view of the geographers, lawyers, industrial workers, women's rights advocates, teetotalers, cyclists, engineers, sugar producers, dentists, photographers, prisoners' relatives, mathematicians, ethicists, vintners, firefighters, Zionists, ice-skaters, insurers, explorers, surveyors, and freethinkers involved – all these groups, and many more, established INGOs in the formative period – these were not European or American concerns. Rather, nearly all of the INGOs founded before the Second World War were explicitly global, understanding the world as a single, comprehensive society embracing all of humanity (Boli and Thomas 1999). They welcomed members from all corners of the globe and hoped to engage as broad a range of individuals and societies as possible, in the hope that peace, harmony, and cooperation among all peoples could reign in world society.

As Table 5.2 shows, by 1909, when the fourth edition of the *Annuaire de la Vie Internationale* (forerunner of the *Yearbook of International Organizations*) appeared, some 374 INGOs were in operation. The First World War interrupted the INGO boom, but world-cultural organizing found renewed strength in the 1920s (801 bodies were in operation in 1931). Then the great paroxysm of the twentieth century – the Depression and the Second World War – drastically disrupted the process. Yet the second great war also opened the door, in this as in so many other arenas, to more internationalism and globalization than ever before. INGO foundings shot up dramatically after 1945, to well over a hundred organizations per year. By the end of the century, over 6,300 "conventional INGOs" (international bodies with members from many countries) and roughly 19,000 other INGOs of highly varied form and type were active in world society.

The table shows that the overall proliferation of INGOs is impressive. Leaving aside various inactive and dissolved organizations counted separately by the UIA, active INGOs increased from fewer than 400 to more than 25,000 over these 90 years, with the numbers for categories B through D increasing substantially in the past 20 years. The result is a dense population of organizations that form a complex array of networks concerned with an enormous number of activities, themes, and issues (see also Boli, forthcoming). Note in the lower part of the table that IGOs have increased greatly as well, but INGOs outnumbered IGOs by a factor of seven to twelve throughout the period.

What do these many INGOs do? As any reader thumbing through the *Yearbook of International Organizations* quickly recognizes, they do anything and everything. Virtually every sport is organized at the global level by one or more INGOs; every scientific discipline has an INGO that sponsors global or regional conferences; every medical specialty publishes a prominent journal through its worldwide INGO; every dimension of social inequality is the focus of one or many INGOs dedicated to redistributing

Table 5.2: *Number of INGOs and IGOs, 1909–2000*

	1909	1920	1931	1940	1951	1960	1972	1981	1991	2000
International Nongovernmental Organizations (INGOs)										
Total "Conventional" INGOs*	374	474	801	841	1,307	1,987	2,976	4,265	4,620	6,357
(A) Federations	–	–	–	–	–	–	–	43	39	37
(B) Universal	–	–	–	–	–	–	–	370	427	475
(C) Intercontinental	–	–	–	–	–	–	–	859	773	1,063
(D) Regional	–	–	–	–	–	–	–	2,991	3,381	4,782
Other ingos	–	–	–	–	–	13	622	5,133	11,493	11,966
Special forms	–	–	–	–	–	–	–	539	2,654	6,946
Currently active INGOs, all types*	374	474	801	841	1,307	1,987	2,976	9,937	18,767	25,269
Intergovernmental Organizations (IGOs)										
Total "Conventional" IGOs	37	–	–	–	123	154	280	337	297	243
Other IGOs	–	–	–	–	–	–	–	702	1,497	1,593
Special forms	–	–	–	–	–	–	–	–	306	709
Currently active IGOs, all types	37	–	–	–	–	–	–	1,039	2,100	2,545

Source: Union of International Associations, *Yearbook of International Organizations*, various years.

*Figures for 1909–72 are based on data using founding and dissolution dates from the 1988–9 and 1984–5.

Yearbooks. Actual totals are underestimated due to missing data. The categories of conventional INGOs reflect the breadth of membership in these bodies: "universal" implies members from at least 60 countries (or 30 countries from several continents); "intercontinental" signifies members from at least 10 countries and at least two countries on each of two continents; "regional" implies members from at least three different countries, usually in the same continent.

Table 5.3:   *Sectoral distribution of INGOs founded in three eras (percentages)*

Social sector	Founded by 1910 %	Founded 1911–45 %	Founded 1946–88 %	INGOs active in 1988 %
Industry/trade/industrial groups	11.0	14.2	17.7	17.6
Medicine/health	8.6	10.3	13.6	14.9
Sciences/math/ knowledge/space	13.8	9.5	12.2	11.6
Sports/hobby/leisure	5.4	6.6	5.7	8.0
Technical/infrastructural communications	6.5	6.7	8.2	7.5
Tertiary economic/ finance/tourism	4.2	6.0	7.9	7.2
Individual rights/welfare	5.4	8.8	5.7	6.3
World-polity oriented	10.5	11.2	7.2	6.2
Religion/family/cultural identity	10.3	9.4	6.6	6.0
Labor/professions/ public administration	12.4	7.6	5.0	6.0
Education/students	4.7	4.0	5.1	4.2
Humanities/arts/philosophy	4.9	4.0	4.2	3.9
Political ideologies/parties	2.6	1.9	0.9	0.6
Total	100.0	100.0	100.0	100.0
Number of ingos	429	854	3,673	4,449

Source: Union of International Associations, *Yearbook of International Organizations* (1985, 1988–9).

wealth or promoting economic development. In Table 5.3 we present data from Boli and Thomas (1999) showing the distribution of INGOs across 13 major categories, with INGOs active in 1988 shown in the far right column and historical comparisons for three eras (the formative period before the First World War, the interwar period, and the post-Second World War era). The categories are ranked by percentages of the total in 1988.

Table 5.3 indicates the predominance of business, scientific, medical, knowledge-related, technical, infrastructural, and sports and hobby INGOs. These first six categories accounted for about two-thirds of the active bodies in 1988, 65 percent of those formed after 1945, and almost half of those founded by 1910. Note that INGOs concerned with rights, the environment, relief, and development (e.g., Human Rights Watch, Greenpeace, CARE, the Red Cross, Oxfam, which fall in the "individual rights/welfare" and "world-polity oriented" categories) accounted for only one-eighth of the total in 1988, though somewhat more earlier (20 percent for the 1911–45 period). The great majority of INGOs – like most IGOs, which are concentrated in the first five categories – have very little in common with the INGOs in these two categories, and they almost never catch the public eye. Many of them have close relations with IGOs and deal with globally important issues: medical and health-care INGOs are involved with the World Health Organization, technical INGOs with the International Telecommunication Union, scientific and humanistic bodies with UNESCO. Yet only their respective members know much about most INGOs, and even powerful business and industry INGOs normally are below the public radar screen – except for those few that come under attack from advocacy or social-activist INGOs.

The table also shows that some sorts of activities have fared rather poorly at the transnational level. Note the declines in labor/professions/public administration, from 12 percent of early INGOs to 5 percent of those founded after the Second World War; in political INGOs, from 2.6 percent to less than 1 percent; and in religion/family/cultural identity bodies, from 10 percent to 6.6 percent. Labor organizations account for all of the decline in the first of these categories, falling from 9.3 percent to 2.2 percent of organizations across the three periods, while professional and public administration groups increased modestly. Similarly, religious and family-oriented INGOs declined proportionately while cultural-identity INGOs' proportion was roughly unchanged. Transnational political organizations (most of which have been socialist, communist, or broadly leftist in orientation) have always been rather rare.

Above, we argued that INGOs are the primary "doers" of world culture: that is, the main components of world culture's organizational software. Much more than IGOs or companies, INGOs formulate global principles, debate world issues, propagate globally applicable knowledge and technology, develop global rules, and so on. Correspondingly, we think it makes good sense to interpret Table 5.3 as a rough indicator of the content of world culture. Given that most INGOs are found in the top five or six categories of Table 5.3, we infer that most of the cultural elements that have global reach, are well established around the world, or have achieved taken-for-granted status in most societies are found in these domains: business, medicine and health, technical and scientific activities, sports and games, knowledge and infrastructure. Their global institutionalization is also indicated in another way: most of these elements are uncontroversial, evoking little public debate. The laws of physics, the usefulness of vaccines, the rules of table tennis, and the meaningfulness of the metric system, to mention but a handful of examples, are well anchored globally and largely taken for granted.

However, few of the INGOs in these categories are globally prominent. This is the INGO paradox: though relatively few in number, the highest global profile is maintained by human rights, environmental, relief, development, and related INGOs. We think this is so, above all, because such INGOs directly engage states, IGOs, and global companies, the power actors of global society. Rights and environmental INGOs habitually make demands of states and global companies, urging conformity to certain standards of conduct or promoting particular social and economic policies. Relief organizations try to make up for the failures of states to maintain internal order or international peace (relief and refugee work); development INGOs try to stimulate economic and social development where states and companies have failed to engender it (cf. Rosenau 1997). Many of these prominent INGOs even go so far as to challenge the very existence and legitimacy of states, IGOs, and global companies, arguing that states are archaic impediments to the promotion of a peaceful and just world, global companies exacerbate poverty and inequality, and IGOs are simply the servants of powerful states and companies. All this challenging and confrontation, much of it occurring as public events of sometimes spectacular character, grabs the attention of global media and news organizations. The result is high name recognition for (a small portion of) these INGOs and a prominent place on the global public agenda for the issues they bring to the fore. We will encounter several of these in later chapters but our main point here is to stress the world-cultural importance of less heralded INGOs that operate, as it were, behind the scenes.

Conclusions

This chapter fits and supports three of the main perspectives on world culture we outlined in Chapter 2. The infrastructure we have described provides the tracks along which the "flows" in Appadurai's "scapes" proceed. INGOs creatively help to foster the kind of global consciousness, centered on new conceptions of "humanity," that Robertson regards as a hallmark of world culture. The technical apparatus of world culture is instrumental in facilitating the "enactment" of world-cultural knowledge emphasized by world polity theory; the embedding of world culture in both hardware and software similarly fits this perspective. From a world-system standpoint, by contrast, one might question whether our discussion slights the importance of economic factors and, in particular, of corporations. We conclude by reflecting on this question.

While we see global (multinational) companies as less important to world-cultural development than INGOs, except in a few social domains, it is revealing to review their growth in comparison to that of INGOs. The earliest generally recognized multinational companies (MNCs) were the privately financed but state-backed trading companies of European imperial expansion: the English East India Company (1600), Dutch East India Company (1602), Hudson Bay Company (1670), and so on. With the simple definition of an MNC as a company doing business in at least two countries, around 500 MNCs were in operation by 1600. That number reached about 1,000 a century later and passed the 2,500 mark around 1850. Such slow growth – about ten companies a year, on average – continued until well into the twentieth century, with rapid acceleration only after the Second World War. In recent decades, the number has risen exponentially: more than 7,000 in 1970, 18,500 by 1988, more than 63,000 by 2000 (figures are from Jones 1996, as reported in Gabel and Bruner 2003).

The explosion of global companies after the Second World War parallels, and even outstrips, that of INGOs, but the first wave of INGO proliferation in the latter part of the nineteenth century was not matched by similar MNC expansion. As world-system theory correctly claims, the organization of the world economy has been a longer, more gradual process than the organization of world culture via INGOs. The historical sequence suggests that the internationalization of capitalism helped prepare the ground for world-cultural organizations while also generating new and greater resources that made this ground a fertile field for world-cultural interaction. However, we do not see economic internationalization or globalization as primary; many of the domains of contemporary world culture are deliberately insulated from the rules and motives of the economic realm, and the economic realm also has important cultural dimensions. Nonetheless, economic expansion and internationalization have clearly enabled ever more people in ever more places to think and act globally. The economic and technical realms have facilitated world culture's expansion, elaboration, and organization, though they have had rather little to do with its content or evolution. A case in point is the problem of national identity, which we discuss in the next chapter.

Chapter 6

Differentiating World Culture: National Identity and the Pursuit of Diversity

In Defense of Difference

In June 2001, the ministers of culture from the countries united in the Organisation Internationale de la Francophonie gathered in Benin for a major conference on cultural diversity. Globalization, the organizers declared, threatened to make the world entirely uniform (Francophonie 2001). The prime but unnamed suspect was the English language, the upstart "lingua franca" [sic] of international life. Because a single dominant culture threatened to crush all others, supporters of diversity had to unite "in defense of difference." La Francophonie had a special role to play in that regard, for it constituted a "privileged and representative site of cultural diversity," and therefore, in the words of the French foreign minister, it expressed "the rejection of cultural and linguistic uniformity" (Védrine 2001: 23). Thus the member countries vowed to pursue diversity as their particular "struggle." They would rescue the globe, culturally speaking, by finding a way out of the "desert" of uniformity without leading into the "jungle" of ghettoization (Zoavi 2001: 8). Encouraging the use of French in education, the arts, and international life thus had a noble purpose: defending French meant defending "difference." As former prime minister Jospin put it in an earlier address to a group of French teachers, "French can become one of the languages in which the resistance to uniformity in the world is expressed, the refusal of identities to fade, the encouragement of freedom to create and to express oneself in one's own culture. It is in this respect that France wants to be the motor of cultural diversity in the world" (Gordon and Meunier 2001: 59).

La Francophonie, founded in 1986, has been only one part of this "motor of diversity" (Oakes 2001: 162–3). At home, French officials have also resisted "uniformity" by defending the purity of the French language, for according to the Conseil Supérieur de la Langue Française, the High Council for the French Language created in 1999, language is "at the heart of our culture and heritage" (Gordon and Meunier 2001: 58). A 1994 law, named after former culture minister Toubon, attempts to preserve that purity by banning "franglais" from public discourse and requiring the use of French in official settings (Oakes 2001: 160–1). The law led to some 8,000 linguistic inspections and 124 successful prosecutions in 1998 (Gordon and Meunier 2001: 60). In the spirit of this law, a French ministry subsequently banned the use of terms such as "e-mail" and "start-up" (ibid.: 60). Nor is this just a heavy-handed attempt to impose linguistic standards from the top. For example, when Air France tried to require its pilots to communicate in English at Charles de Gaulle airport for the sake of safety, its employees protested and the policy was quickly suspended (ibid.: 61).

According to a long line of French officials, more than language is at stake. At a 1982 UNESCO conference, another minister, Jack Lang, famously called for "real cultural resistance, a real crusade against – let's call things by their name – this financial and intellectual imperialism that no longer grabs territory, or rarely, but grabs consciousness, ways of thinking, ways of living." This broader French resistance against the new "imperialism" has taken the form of a complex system of quotas and subsidies administered by the Ministry of Culture (Gordon and Meunier 2001: 49–52). By requiring theaters and TV channels to show a certain number of French films, among other provisions, it aims to sustain domestic film production in competition with lowbrow Hollywood fare.

Underlying such policies is not just a fear of bad taste in movies. Hollywood represents the larger threat of US-inspired cultural uniformity. As the head of the Cannes Film Festival once put it, America "is interested in exporting its way of life" (Micklethwait and Wooldridge 2000: 187). Reflecting this same fear, the former secretary of the philosopher Jean-Paul Sartre called the arrival of Euro-Disney near Paris a "cultural Chernobyl," while a less despondent wag considered it a "Trojan mouse" (Ceaser 1997: 8, 251). Though former foreign minister Hubert Védrine has displayed greater confidence in the vitality of French culture than many of his colleagues (Védrine 2001: 24, 18, 50), he, too, has lamented the ultraliberal individualism and the dominance of English that mark the US approach to globalization (ibid.: 17, 43). Against the dominance of America's hard and soft power, against the dominance in people's heads of "American globalism" (ibid.: 4, 44), he has asserted the need to protect cultures and oppose hegemony (ibid.: 24, 44). Not surprisingly, French intellectuals have also been prominent critics of cultural globalization. In the leading newspaper *Le Monde* and in numerous books on globalization, they regularly decry the influence of the "unique thinking" of neoliberalism, which they consider a typically American approach to economic affairs and a dominant "illusion" from which France must liberate itself (Touraine 1999; Passet 2000). On one attention-grabbing occasion in 1999, a vocal critic of mono-cultural globalization, self-styled peasant leader José Bové, actually ransacked a McDonald's establishment with some fellow activists, fearlessly attacking *la malbouffe*, bad food that symbolized cultural standardization according to an American model (Meunier 2000; Bové and Dufour 2001).

Although one could argue that the current worries of the French cultural elite mainly express loss of influence, reflecting the frustrations of a former major power unable to revive the diminishing appeal of its own universal aspirations, this elite's anxiety over declining difference, and its commitment to France's "cultural exception," is undeniably real. As such sentiments indicate, among many French officials and intellectuals a particular image of world culture, rooted in a long-standing national tradition, has taken hold. According to this image, world culture is the creation of the United States, the "hyperpower" that dominates not just the world economy but global consciousness as well. The USA has left its imprint on popular tastes in movies and food. Its language threatens to displace all others. Its laissez-faire economic philosophy has no regard for the values of solidarity and equality. By imposing a single world-view, it threatens to obliterate cultural differences. World culture, in short, is the product of a nefarious kind of cultural imperialism. This juggernaut must be stopped, French critics have urged, first of all in France. The French defense of difference therefore also articulates a particular view of world culture.

This view has deep roots in a tradition of French criticism of "America" (Revel 2003). After the French Revolution, many French intellectuals invidiously compared their country's grand vision to the more mundane accomplishments of the American Revolution (Ceaser 1997: Ch. 3). For different reasons, French thinkers on the left and the right have disparaged American culture – or their image thereof – ever since. As the French writer Henry de Montherlant once put it, "One nation that manages to lower intelligence, morality, human quality on nearly all the surface of the earth, such a thing has never been seen before in the existence of the planet. I accuse the United States of being in a permanent state of crime against humankind" (ibid.: 2). The founder of the newspaper *Le Monde*, Hubert Beuve-Méry, considered America's attachment to capitalism one cause of this "crime": "If they cling to a veritable cult of the idea of liberty, they don't feel the need to liberate themselves from the servitudes that their capitalism entails" (quoted in Revel 2003: 52). This French tradition has helped to make the symbol of America an "object of universal reference" in world culture (Ceaser 1997: 3).

Whether or not they blame America, many groups and national elites now view world culture as a threat. They attribute the threat to globalization, a merciless process of stirring cultures into a global "goulash" (Micklethwait and Wooldridge 2000: 197). A single world culture, they fear, will impose a particular way of life on everyone. To them, world culture resembles an ever-tightening symbolic straitjacket. As the Benin meeting recognized (Francophonie 2001), the vulnerability of the French language pales in comparison to the threat to the languages of the world's small indigenous peoples. For example, a dossier from the 2001 conference reminded the delegates that in nominally French-speaking countries such as Guinea or Niger, languages spoken by only a few thousand people are in danger of disappearing. By some estimates, it added, 10 minority languages disappear with the deaths of their last active speakers every year. Such loss of language, long documented by linguists, often signals the demise of a way of life. And, as representatives of indigenous peoples have long argued, language is only one part of the heritage of indigenous peoples that is under threat. When children of Australian aborigines were taken to be raised by white parents, or when Malaysia allowed the clear-cutting of Dayak rainforest territory on Borneo, the intrusion of the outside world undermined the very continuity of these cultures. Lacking a state to call their own, such indigenous peoples' old ways of life are at risk of disappearing along with their native habitats. Few of the small groups under siege can muster the resources of La Francophonie in defending their cultural interests. To be sure, the circumstances of indigenous groups vary greatly and not all of the harm suffered by them can be attributed to the amorphous process of globalization attacked in Benin. However, from the vantage point of such groups and their defenders, it is fair to say, globalization presents a threat similar to the one feared in France: difference itself is endangered. In this chapter, we critically address this fear of world culture as straitjacket. We do not dismiss it: world culture does indeed contain powerful homogenizing tendencies, as we have already shown in other chapters. Yet the theories we have used throughout this book entail a more complex picture of world culture as inherently diverse and diversifying. We focus on one form of difference, namely the national distinctiveness that is so much on the minds of French critics, to show how it is both built into world culture and reproduced in the way particular nations relate to world culture. Our conclusion is not that world culture simply lets hundreds of differently colored flowers bloom, to vary an old Maoist phrase. Rather, we think world culture grows through the interplay of standardizing uniformity and diversifying particularity.

Differences about Difference

What is it about globalization that makes world culture a specter to fear? One view of globalization suggests that its key feature is deterritorialization (Held et al. 1999; Scholte 2000). Increasingly, people maintain relations across time and space and derive their identities from far-flung groups. Networks and organizations span the globe; communication relies on a single language. But historically culture was made by particular groups in particular places. The world was a world of difference because each community could arrange its space according to its own design. Thus if globalization breaks the age-old link between groups and their concrete place in the world, if social life proceeds without regard to geographic constraint, then the basis for maintaining differences between groups atrophies as well. If the world becomes a single, globally organized space, then humanity may end up with only one universal culture at the expense of all particular cultures.

Closely related to this description of globalization is the idea that its main thrust is rationalization. Modern institutions, according to this view, must adopt certain structures to make their work efficient and controllable. Transnational organizations especially embody this kind of stifling standard rationality. Ritzer (1993) has memorably described it as the McDonaldization of the world. If McDonaldization were merely a matter of rationalizing institutions, this might not by itself present a great threat to diversity. However, the Ritzer thesis holds that, ultimately, standard procedures will flatten out even differences in taste, with fatty hamburgers displacing the wonders of local cuisine. Global institutions, in other words, create the workers and consumers they need – they create a world in their image.

This thesis has an affinity with the critical view of multinational corporations exemplified in our brief discussion of Sklair's work (1995) in Chapter 2. As he and others maintain, TNCs (transnational corporations) seek to quench their thirst for profits by mobilizing their superior resources to create similar practices, tastes, and lifestyles. The world culture they create is a culture of consumerism, not only adapted to but actually generating the demands of the world market. Rather than cultivating distinct traditions, individuals become uniformly attached to commodities to satisfy material desires. This amounts to a kind of ideological take-over of the world; some have dubbed it Coca-Colanization.

As we saw in the examples above, some French critics and their comrades-in-arms would generalize this last point to argue that it is really the USA – the reigning "hyperpower," to use Védrine's term – that is spreading a particular world-view. Its unrivaled economic and military power enable it to push a particular model of globalization. To critics like Védrine, this model relies on an extreme neoliberalism: a minimally regulated world market that gives free play to companies but constrains states obsessed with producing wealth but unconcerned about inequality or social costs (Gray 1998). By globalizing its peculiar blend of Adam Smith and the Wild West, America is putting a distinctly individualistic consumerist stamp on world culture – turning its own type of "modernity" into a global model (Taylor 1996). Not only do Americans publicly advocate the virtues of virulent free markets, protected by only minimal safety nets, they also have many covert agents in their cartoon characters, movie heroes, and music stars. American media products actually mediate more and more people's experience of "reality." By means of their "videology" they create a "McWorld" (Barber 1995). America's "hard" pursuit of a world that fits its own structure thus combines with the "soft" but seductive influence of its media offerings to create a world culture inhospitable to diversity.

According to a broader version of the same indictment, one more congenial to advocates for the indigenous "Fourth World" than to French foreign ministers, America is not uniquely to blame. The more general evil that stalks the world is Western cultural imperialism. The West has used its military and economic dominance to impose its values, beliefs, and institutional forms on others (cf. Tomlinson 1991). Conveniently, these values and beliefs also contain a universal message: they purport to apply and be valid everywhere. Democracy, free markets, and human rights (or, alternatively, consumerism, commodification, and rationality), all bear the ethnocentric marks of their origins. The world did not choose them. World culture, in this view, is simply the globalization of the West. Like deterritorialization, McDonaldization, Coca-Colanization, and Americanization, the cultural imperialism argument portends a single world with a single culture.

While this scenario contains important kernels of truth, it is far too stark. In many ways, globalization itself is a "motor of diversity." For example, McDonaldization, much derided by French activists, captures only part of global food trends. As Asia takes to hamburgers and Cokes, Europe and

North America adopt Eastern cuisines; though a less standardized product, sushi is as global as the golden arches (Bestor 2000). Globalization thus fosters many kinds of cultural cross-fertilization. Within particular countries, it usually expands the "menu of choice" for individuals by liberating them from the constraints of place (Cowen 2002: 129), as French consumers of jeans and jazz and Japanese electronics – as well as hamburgers and "French fries" – can attest. This applies to language as well. Through translation, particular languages and literatures increasingly build "bridgeheads" to other places, as illustrated by the success of Latin-American novelists in France. Immigration and cultural contact introduce impure innovations, a form of linguistic diversity that official French opposition to franglais ironically attempts to stifle (Revel 2003). Among global audiences, globalization thus fosters cultural experimentation. Even in the industry that most provoked French ire, the feared homogeneity brought about by American dominance is by no means absolute: Hollywood must still compete with other centers of film production, such as India's Bollywood (Tyrrell 1999); its global success depends in part on its ability to attract non-American talents and adapt to non-American tastes; and it encourages the development of home-grown niche productions (Cowen 2002: Ch. 4). As these examples suggest, the "creative destruction" of global competition also has diversifying consequences (ibid.). Even if we implausibly assume that all place-based culture is doomed, there is no reason why supposedly deterritorialized communities should be culturally uniform. Underground dance club aficionados are distinct from professional soccer players or fruit fly researchers; the proliferation of their multifarious ties stimulates new kinds of transnational diversity. While multiplying empirical examples of diversity "on the ground" would take us too far afield in examining the intricacies of the much-feared globalization process, our first response to the doomsayers is simply that the world is still a very diverse and surprising place, unlikely to be smothered in one cultural goulash.

Our second rejoinder is more closely related to the agenda of this book. As we have described world culture, some of its fundamental substance is quite abstract. McDonald's-style rationality, American neoliberalism, and Western universalism provide only very general models for social action. At least two of the theories we discussed in Chapter 2 argue that the implications of such models impel creative adaptation by particular groups in particular places. Robertson calls this glocalization, Hannerz creolization. World-cultural precepts become socially real by being incorporated in locally situated practices. Thus, Hong Kong becomes McDonaldized rather differently than Peoria (Watson 1997); neoliberal privatization proceeds differently in India than in the UK (Yergin and Stanislaw 1998); democracy takes hold differently in Mexico than in the Czech Republic. Certain kinds of pop music may be transnationally popular, but their vibrancy still depends on the way musicians make such music part of their own traditions (Taylor 1997). The upshot of the Robertson/Hannerz line of thought is that groups and societies mix and match, borrow and adapt, learn and revise. By its very generality, world culture gives an impetus toward highly varied interpretation.

What is more, world culture is not of a piece. Even the elements in the homogenization scenario are not identical: though McDonald's does serve Coke, McDonaldization and Coca-Colanization metaphorically capture different forms of homogenization. While the "America" that has left its imprint on world culture is a reality, "the West" is a vague community of values (Védrine 2001: 50). McDonald's and Coke, America and "the West" – the forces evoked by those terms are themselves quite different. However close the affinities of these components, a culture that is rationalized à la McDonald's, dependent on lowbrow consumer taste, influenced by popular culture, and infused with falsely universal aspirations is not an internally consistent whole. The components define different aspects of global reality; they vary in strength and scope. More generally, as we saw in Chapter 2, Appadurai (1996) has described the "disjunctures" between the different dimensions of world culture. World culture contains different sets of universally applicable and influential ideas that operate at different rhythms, creating multiple tensions and unpredictable intersections. For example, two of the core ideas identified with American-style cultural imperialism – namely a fully liberalized market and democratic governance – may have contradictory implications when applied globally: one encourages the unregulated pursuit of self-interest, the other stresses deliberate collective control of social affairs. World culture therefore does not, and could not, prescribe any single course of action to be followed by everyone everywhere. Indeed, the very process of globalization itself is molded by contending views of how it ought to be structured (cf. Védrine 2001: 28–30), as we will see in the next chapter. Disjuncture and contention preserve diversity.

We saw in Chapter 2 that such varied interpretations and disjunctures are a common theme in much recent scholarship. Recall Breidenbach and Zukrigl's book on the "dance of cultures" (2000), which shows with a wealth of ethnographic examples how people around the world incorporate global products and practices into their own world-views, adapt new categories such as "feminism" according to their own needs, "talk back" to the supposed sources of cultural flows, and engage in all manner of resistance. Or recall the Berger and Huntington volume on "many globalizations" (2002), which shows how a supposedly universal process takes different paths according to local cultural contexts. Both in his book on cultural globalization and even more systematically in an earlier work on cultural imperialism, Tomlinson (1991, 1999) has subjected the cultural imperialism argument to criticism, arguing against the idea that the cultural "synchronization" produced by the spread of modern institutions is a destructive imposition. As we pointed out, not all these scholars fully share our view of world culture. But we detect in their work a convergence on a basic point, namely that any emerging world culture is bound to be refracted in complex ways by the prisms of specific groups and societies and that diversity is bound to flourish through the multiple ways in which they relate to such an overarching world culture.

We can go a step further. Difference is flourishing not just in the way a nascent world culture "plays out" in practice, but also as an organizing principle of world culture. To return to the example we started with, while the tone of the francophone conference may have been defensive, it also emphatically called for recognition of diversity as a value in its own right. It advocated the mutual recognition of cultures and their right to participate on an equal basis in the "concert of nations" (Zoavi 2001). Though its cause was French, its appeal was framed in universal terms, referring specifically to the support of international organizations such as UNESCO. Indigenous peoples and movements working on their behalf similarly claim the right to maintain their particularistic heritages. The importance of "cultural survival" as such, to cite the name of one advocacy group, has become conventional wisdom. The very concept of indigeneity points to a burgeoning global respect for the heritages of minority groups. Both national and indigenous defenders of difference have vested some of their hopes in UNESCO, and that organization has become a linchpin in the globalization of diversity as a value. Thus far, it has done its share in fostering difference by issuing reports charting cultural diversity within world culture, celebrating diversity as a goal for the world community, and instituting programs to protect the world's cultural heritage (UNESCO 2000). Among state leaders, movement activists, and IGO officials, the cause of diversity thus has been gaining strength. In Western academic circles, such trends have been bolstered by the discourse of "multiculturalism," which itself has swept across the globe, assigning equal value to different cultures and promoting coexistence rather than dominance (cf. Cornwell and Stoddard 2001). However justified the fear of indigenous groups may be as a practical matter, the globalizing diversity industry indicates that world culture is more complex than the imperialist scenario allows. Diversity has been enshrined as a counterpoint to homogenization. Particularism is universalized, as Robertson has suggested. This is not to say, of course, that "mere" rhetoric will help the French build a bulwark against Hollywood blockbusters. It is to suggest, though, that world culture itself nurtures the seeds of difference.

In other words, difference is built in. This more differentiated view of world culture follows straightforwardly from the work of Robertson, who makes contrasting definitions of the global situation the hallmark of world culture, and from the work of anthropologists like Hannerz, who treat world culture as the organization of diversity. However, the same idea also appears in world-system theory, which assumes that the geographical division of labor within a single world market depends on competition among culturally distinct units within the system. By comparison with these perspectives, Meyer and his colleagues put more emphasis on the way in which similar institutions are enacted across the globe, though they also portray the world polity as internally differentiated. The scholarly pendulum is thus swinging away from the kind of anxiety that dominates much public discourse. But rather than dismissing the fears of cultural loss, our picture of world culture helps to put them in perspective: as world culture grows, some differences may fall by the wayside, others require redefinition, still others are constantly created. To summarize, while fears of a world-cultural goulash are understandable, there are at least three reasons to be skeptical of the scenario such fears assume: the globalization process, regarded as pushing homogenization, actually has varied effects; the process takes place in the context of an existing world culture to which individual groups and societies relate in varied ways; and world culture itself fosters difference through the principles it contains and the institutions it legitimates. This argument entails that fears of American hegemony, so common in French responses to world culture, are overstated. To make our case more concrete, we now turn to a particular form of difference often regarded as endangered, the kind at issue in the francophone example with which we started, namely national difference. Our argument implies that nations can flourish as distinct entities under the canopy of world culture. We support this argument by showing how, in one instance, the reproduction of national difference occurs. However, we do not aim for a Panglossian conclusion that for nations this is the best of all possible worlds. While world culture fosters national difference, it also embeds nations in a transnational framework that constrains and homogenizes them.

The Difference Nations Make

Is there still a place for nations in the world? Those who fear global uniformity believe the answer may be negative, for the reasons we discussed above. Deterritorialization implies that the control of the nation-state over its own affairs diminishes. The upshot of McDonaldization, Coca-Colanization, and Americanization is the accelerating demise of the national, as national distinctions are undermined by transnational rules, tastes, and institutions. Not surprisingly, then, influential authors foresee the end of the nation: "Too remote to manage the problems of our daily life, the nation nevertheless remains too constrained to confront the global problems that affect us" (Guéhenno 2000: 13). Another student of nationalism concludes that today's world "can no longer be contained within the limits of 'nations' and 'nation-states' as these used to be defined . . . It will see [these] primarily as retreating before, resisting, adapting to, being absorbed or dislocated by, the new supranational restructuring of the globe" (Hobsbawm 1990: 182). As the "isomorphism of people, territory, and legitimate sovereignty that constitutes the normative character of the nation-state" has eroded, the nation-state itself "has become obsolete and other formations for allegiance and identity have taken its place" (Appadurai 1996: 169, 191). Under conditions of globalization, "[t]he centrality of national cultures, national identities and their institutions is challenged" (Held et al. 1999: 328). While Appadurai and Held et al. do not infer from the nation's dire straits a picture of a homogeneous world culture, the more common diagnosis remains that a one-size-fits-all culture leaves little room for national difference.

We argue against this common diagnosis. As we have suggested, the "one-size-fits-all" view of world culture is itself misleading. Focusing on the nation allows us to elaborate our main points about world culture, namely that it produces difference in practice and contains difference in principle. Addressing the demise-of-nations scenario further enables us to refine our position by showing how the fear of uniformity rests on questionable assumptions about static national cultures confronting an oppressive, alien force. For illustrations we return to the French example we have cited before. This case is especially pertinent because France has played a major role in the history of nationalism as the "archetype" of a nation-state (Crowley 2000) and because, as we have seen, many influential figures have championed France as a nation in the global debate about difference. This championing is rich with ironies. In discussing these ironies, we aim not to convey all the ways in which nations reproduce their identity but only to focus on the extent to which the reproduction of difference revolves around the operations of world culture.

The first irony in presenting the nation as a bulwark of cultural difference is that historically the drive toward nationhood itself has often obliterated differences. In most places, nations were forged out of previously distinct regions and peoples. The unity they possessed often sprang from visions of coherence pursued by elites in control of states (Kedourie 1993) who deliberately created "imagined" communities (Anderson 1991). According to one interpretation, these visions themselves first gained plausibility in industrial societies that placed a premium on a shared high culture, fostered by formal education, that facilitated communication among large populations (Gellner 1983). Historically, then, nation is to difference what single-crop agriculture is to biodiversity. The French state, for example, has itself been relentlessly homogenizing, not least by requiring the use of standard French throughout its territory. To Bretons, the idea of French as a carrier of diversity can seem far-fetched. This implies that one assumption underlying the common scenario is implausible. Since nations are relatively recent creations, it is misleading to think of them as fully formed cultural wholes suddenly confronted by a stream of global cultural material that invades them. Though it is now conventional wisdom to think of nations as "constructed" and "imagined" rather than "primordial" (Anderson 1991), defenders of difference have an ironically primordial view of national identity, insofar as they treat it as something deeply rooted and unchanging. However, even in seemingly old nations, national identity is always in flux. In the case of France, that identity was established by turning "peasants into Frenchmen," as the title of one prominent study put it, in the late nineteenth century, when "long didactic campaigns" taught inhabitants of France to speak French and to think of themselves as French (Weber 1976: 70). The Third Republic of that period built a new nation by means of "coercive elimination" of regional diversity and languages, notably by instituting a nationalized system of free public schools (Crowley 2000: 97). Applied to France itself, the "defense of difference" advocated by the public figures discussed above risks locking into place a fairly recent version of national identity at the expense of further experimentation and the "intertemporal diversity" that might result (Cowen 2002: 135).

Another irony in the defense of national difference against a global cultural juggernaut is that critics of homogeneity appear to have so little faith in actually existing difference. It is as if uniformly hapless countries await a common fate. However, even a cursory glance across the globe shows that nations vary greatly in their understanding of what it means to be a nation. "Is there in fact any one thing called a nation?" asks one scholar (Pecora 2001: 6), explaining that "[e]ach nation-state now on earth could supply a slightly different meaning for the word 'nation,' a different official account (perhaps more than one), not only of its own origins and development, but of the idea of national identity that it supposedly embodies." In many instances, these "different accounts" were deliberately created by elites attempting to draw distinctions between their own nation and foreign counterparts, thereby charting distinct paths toward nationhood (Greenfeld 1992). Pecora's point applies to France as well, where at least two conceptions of the nation – one rooted in visions of the traditional Catholic monarchy, the other in the revolutionary vision of a secular republic – have been at odds for two centuries, perhaps to be replaced by a third vision more attuned to new social realities (Schnapper 1991). To infer from the enormous variety of national situations that a single world-view or way of life will prove uniformly devastating is simply implausible. The case for national difference against global homogeneity depends on a far too homogeneous view of national identity.

Scenarios that oppose nation to world culture portray them as somehow separate. However, far from being unrelated adversaries, world culture and national cultures evolved together. As we showed in Chapter 3, nineteenth-century world culture was in part made by and for nations. From the outset, nationalism was itself a *trans*national movement, important first in Latin America and Europe, later in Asia and Africa. The creation of nations was always accompanied by claims to universal respect of politically organized but culturally distinct communities. Of course, world culture could only become "transnational" when the form and legitimacy of nations were largely taken for granted. In this entwinement of world and national culture, France in fact played a pivotal role. France took shape as a nation-state when its revolutionary elite articulated a new creed with universal aspirations. Liberty, equality, and brotherhood have been ideological elements of world culture ever since. By organizing itself dramatically as a nation-state at the time of its revolution, France created a model for others to follow. Ironically, the world culture French intellectuals bemoan is therefore, at least in part, of their predecessors' making. By presenting this particular nation as the embodiment of universal values, France also created an influential, nonethnic or "civic" version of nationhood (Crowley 2000: 92), which competed with others such as the "ethnic" German version

(Kohn 1967). This variety in the ways nations formed and asserted them-selves has itself become entrenched in world culture. National difference has long been built into world culture.

World-system theorists would modify this point about entwinement of the global and the national. As we have seen, they regard the existence of politically and culturally distinct units as critical to the system. The worst-case scenario for world capitalism, their argument implies, is the transfor-mation of a differentiated market system into a single world empire. A more successful Napoleon might have wrecked that system. Differences are there-fore functional, but they hardly produce the kind of tolerant diversity current critics of world culture envision. Historically, differences fueled competition and conflict. The rise of nation-states amounted to the reor-ganization of previously existing regional differences into more politically organized and internally homogeneous units fit for global competition. France's rise as a nation-state was therefore less a matter of spreading a revolutionary faith than of positioning it for that competition. Yet that faith had consequences as well. For all its universalism, it also set up a hierar-chy among nations. Some countries could fully live up to France's stan-dards, others only partly so, while still other groups could not even aspire to nationhood. Nationalism, Wallerstein has noted, "first emerged as the response to the universalizing imperialism of the revolutionary power, France" (1991b: 145). This form of "popular antisystemic mobilization" subsequently "received sustenance particularly from the successive waves of struggle taking place in the semiperipheral areas of the world-economy" (ibid.: 146, 156). As the embodiment of enlightened principles, France helped to create a world culture legitimating Euro-American dominance throughout the colonial age. The irony here is that for most of two cen-turies world culture actually resembled the hegemonic kind of culture French commentators now oppose, a hegemony to which Frenchmen actively contributed. In world culture, then, not all differences are created equal. Given its involvement in establishing a hierarchical version of world culture, France's more ecumenical defense of difference today rings a bit hollow to world-system theorists.

World polity theorists amplify the point about the historical entwine-ment of the global and the national in a slightly different way. They are most impressed with the way in which the trappings of the nation have become truly global norms, applying equally to all properly constituted societies (Meyer et al. 1997). In the nineteenth century, even European nation-states' capacity to control their territory and their people was actu-ally quite limited. For a long time, nationalism was more vision than reality, but the nationalist definition of the global situation was real in its consequences. Once the model was defined, its content expanded greatly, as we have seen in earlier chapters. In some ways, of course, this reduced global pluralism. By the year 2000, more countries looked more alike. Yet the very success of the nation-state model now also provides global standards for what nations must do to reproduce themselves, and globally legitimated tools to satisfy those standards. Nation-states cannot be passive. They have work to do in upholding their identity. We have already seen examples of that work in the French case. The media policy that protects France's cultural "exception" depends on global norms authorizing state responsibility in this area. The same goes for its educational policies. France's effort to teach children across the country in the same way, striving for closely coordinated teaching in a single system designed to turn individuals into good citizens, is a particularly energetic way of discharging a global responsibility. The broader point here is that locally distinctive policy processes such as these are ways to reproduce national identities in keeping with world-cultural standards. Upholding national identity through national institutions is the world-cultural thing to do.

Robertson's globalization theory also complements our analysis. As we have seen, this theory portrays world culture as stimulating rather than suppressing difference. With regard to national culture, this works in at least two ways. National and world culture stand in a kind of dialectical relationship. To Robertson, the generalization of a partly French model of nation-states to globally legitimate status is an instance of the "universalization of the particular." But such universalization always provokes the opposite trend of "particularization of the universal," in the French case an increasingly anxious attempt to define more actively and precisely what makes France stand out as a nation among others. Nations are therefore always caught in the interplay of standardizing uniformity and diversifying particularity. Worrying about how-to-be-national is inherent in the rules of the world-cultural game. To some extent, nations have always been part of a single "game," identifying their position relative to certain universal rules and principles. Relativization, to use Robertson's term, is nothing new. However, as world culture has grown along with other forms of global integration, this burden of distinct identification has increased as well. The common notion that many French lamentations stem from a loss of former great-power status is relevant here, since this relativization especially hits home in a society that was so instrumental in building up the world-cultural edifice within which it now must find a new place. The French concern about the viability of their national identity is thus rooted in the key world-cultural process Robertson has identified. But the Robertsonian argument also suggests that the French can be sanguine about their prospects, since relativization with regard to world culture, from the historically varied standpoints of nations, will lead to a great variety of outcomes. Through relativization, world culture actually drives differentiation. By redefining their role as defenders of difference, the French are thus playing out a differentiated scenario.

Even more emphatically than Robertson, anthropologists like Hannerz stress the highly variable entwinement of world and national culture. To push their point a bit with French metaphors, national culture becomes a *bricolage* or *mélange* of world-cultural elements through creolization. This is not a case, however, of world culture bearing down on hapless nations. Creolization refers to continuous, critical interaction. When France sticks to its media quotas while also enjoying Hollywood fare, when French-speakers adopt franglais, when Disney icons rival the Eiffel Tower, when adherents of a secular universal faith discover the value of diversity, the result is a national culture less pristine than its leading intellectuals prefer but more distinctive than they are prepared to admit. Further, because creolization is a form of interaction, world culture is affected as well. In practice, it is a composite of the ways nations make sense of it. The French way of "doing" world culture contributes to the overall organization of diversity. By their actions, ironically, French critics of homogeneity disprove their point.

We have argued that world culture contains and fosters difference, but with regard to nations it has not always done so in the same way or to the same degree. Until recently, leading nation-states were more intent on spreading their influence than on guaranteeing difference. France, for instance, has had little compunction about globalizing its own culture, including the use of its own language as an international lingua franca. Would the French be as worried about uniformity if it were expressed in French? Would French politicians lead La Francophonie in defense of difference if France's once universal aspirations had been universally accepted? The irony here is that our argument, as well as the position of the French intellectuals itself, depends in part on the outcome of struggles against former French dominance in world culture. It is the success of movements asserting their right to political and cultural independence from colonizing powers – movements that themselves took different directions (Pecora 2001: 30) – that has helped to entrench the right to self-determination and distinctive identities as universal principles in a world culture less tainted by hegemony.

Conclusions

As our extended illustration shows, the global and the local/national are thoroughly intertwined in the reproduction of difference. In carrying out its identity work through public policy, as France has done in enforcing its cultural exception, the nation-state firmly rests on world-cultural principles of great legitimacy. The very task of defining the nation is a standard responsibility of the state, taken especially seriously in France, and in this sense any definition of national identity is always more-than-national. Insofar as the forces of globalization undermine a nation's settled forms of self-understanding, which is certainly true of France, the magnitude of that task increases. Where the capacity of a nation to respond is in question, the salience of national identity as a project may well be even greater, especially if, as illustrated by the strong sentiments of many French public figures cited above, the relevant cultural elite is deeply invested in it. Nations can show resilience precisely in becoming embattled, as the French example shows. In fact, the components of French identity – universalistic culture, a strong state, a quest for a world role (Meunier 2000: 116) – may make it especially suitable as a defender of difference, and its defensive actions may well enrich and expand French culture (Gordon and Meunier 2001: 43).

Of course, the degree to which a nation's identity becomes embattled and the particular way in which it shows resilience are shaped by the sediments in its cultural foundation, by its global exposure and vantage point, and by its own historical trajectory in relation to the interplay between globalizing forces and national sediments. The global–national dialectic is clearly path-dependent. We showed, for example, how France's own involvement in the history of world culture now shapes its critical posture. Other factors we can only mention here will further shape the way France deals with the "crisis" of its national identity (Crowley 2000: 93–5). Will the growing presence of Muslim immigrants and their offspring lead to a gradual loosening of national attachment or trigger strong reaffirmations of "traditional" national identity? Will European integration further erode the sovereignty and domestic control of the French state? Will the relatively low proportion of the French people who consider themselves "very proud" of their nationality, around 40 percent in 1999–2000 (Pei 2003: 32), increase or decrease? Since histories vary, depending in part on such "local" factors, no single case such as the one we have discussed can fully illuminate the dynamics of what is now a global experience. The very fact that it is difficult to generalize supports our argument against the homogenization scenario. But even if France no longer serves as a global model, the

French are not unique in the predicament they face and the response they have fashioned. The upshot of our analysis is, once again, that expectations of cultural doom or the demise of diversity are simplistic. However, our argument should not dispel such notions entirely. The world-cultural legitimation of difference depends for its efficacy on the practical identity work of distinct groups, work that is contingent on "local" factors. From a general picture of world culture, even combined with strong assumptions about globalization, we therefore cannot derive clear-cut local predictions. Because the observable diversity of world culture stems from the multiplicity of particular identity projects, however much relativized and implicated in the global circumstance, that diversity is, so to speak, always up for grabs. We also cannot say that the nation and national identity are secure as the defining form of difference in the twenty-first century. For all the current focus on the national in France, national identity may well become less salient over time. This is by no means to forecast a happy cosmopolitan future; rather, it is to suggest that national distinction may lose out in competition with other forms of collective identity, other claims on particularized loyalty. The rise of indigenous movements raises this possibility. On the horizon are more forceful claims for recognition of groups that differ in their sexual orientation and practices. World culture in principle legitimates alternative forms of particularism and therefore allows for such a pluralism of differences. We therefore need not fear homogeneity, little comfort though it may offer to defenders of any specific, uniquely cherished kind of difference, such as the French exception. In any case, a world in which a hundred differences bloom is not necessarily peaceful or pleasant. It may not sustain the kind of difference, such as the national, for which many have given their lives. When it comes to difference, contemporary world culture offers no guarantees.

Chapter 7

Transforming World Culture: The Antiglobalization Movement as Cultural Critique

In January 2001, more than 10,000 people came to Porto Alegre, Brazil, to participate in the first World Social Forum (WSF). Initiated by Bernard Cassen, founder of the French antiglobalization group ATTAC, Chico Whitaker, secretary to the Commission on Justice and Peace of the Council of Brazilian bishops, and Oded Grajew, coordinator of the Brazilian Business Association for Citizenship, the forum was staged as "an attack on planet Davos" (Lloyd 2001; Cassen 2004: 161). In Davos, corporate executives and government leaders had for many years gathered at the World Economic Forum to discuss the virtues of globalization while enjoying the pleasures of the Swiss slopes. The WSF aimed to offer a pointed contrast. Supported by the Brazilian Workers' Party, which at the time held power in Porto Alegre and the surrounding province, the Forum took place on the campus of a local Catholic university. Its delegates mostly represented nongovernmental organizations rather than companies or countries. Attracted by free admission and motivated by ideological fervor, they coped with crowds, chaos, and temperatures unfamiliar in Switzerland. A kick-off "March against Neo-Liberalism" that took attendees through the streets of the city set a different tone from the outset. While Davos celebrities included figures such as Bill Gates of Microsoft, in Porto Alegre the image of Che Guevara was everywhere and one star of the proceedings was a French peasant leader and veteran of international protest who elicited chants of "We Are All José Bové" and "Olé, Olé, Bové, Bové" (Klein 2001; Lloyd 2001).

After several days of deliberation, fueled by fiery speeches of a sort unknown in Davos, the WSF issued the "Porto Alegre Call for Mobilisation" (WSF 2001a). Speaking on behalf of a "great alliance to create a new society," it argued that, while "Davos represents the concentration of wealth, the globalization of poverty and the destruction of our earth," Porto

Alegre "represents the hope that a new world is possible, where human beings and nature are the center of our concern." Challenging "the elite and their undemocratic processes," the "social forces" gathered at the WSF had come to demonstrate "our total rejection of the neoliberal policies of globalisation." Such globalization, according to this manifesto, reinforces sexism, increases racism, and destroys the environment. Resistance requires "fighting against the hegemony of finance, the destruction of our cultures, the monopolization of knowledge, mass media and communication." In the same vein, the manifesto opposes the privatization of public services, a free trade area in the Americas, and the patenting of life. It calls for the strengthening of alliances in the common "struggle." As part of a growing movement, the WSF could be "a way to achieve peoples' sovereignty and a just world." Signatories included more than 100 labor, peace, environmental, and women's groups from across the globe. The WSF proved invigorating: as one participant, Philippine economist Walden Bello, put it, "Davos is the past, Porto Alegre the future" (Wallerstein 2001). To many participants, the WSF symbolized a true alternative world-view and therefore was the beginning of "the end of the End of History" (Klein 2001).

To maintain the momentum generated in Porto Alegre, some of the Brazilian organizers subsequently drafted a "World Social Forum Charter of Principles" (WSF 2001b). It describes the forum as an "open meeting place" to be used by all groups that are "opposed to neoliberalism and to domination of the world by capital and any form of imperialism, and are committed to building a planetary society centered on the human person." Though these groups stand together "in opposition to a process of capitalist globalization commanded by the large multinational corporations," they would not make decisions as a body, for the forum had to remain a "plural, diversified, non-confessional, non-governmental and non-party context." Describing the WSF as a "movement of ideas that prompts reflection," the Charter also urges participants to increase their capacity for "resistance to the process of dehumanization the world is undergoing." The WSF, the Charter suggests, would now become a "permanent process of seeking and building alternatives," indeed a "world process." Its guiding inspiration would be the motto formulated at the first Forum, which rapidly became the defining slogan of the antiglobalization movement: "Another World Is Possible." The success of the second Forum in 2002, which attracted some 50,000 activists, confirmed its appeal (Ponniah and Fisher 2003: 5).

If the annual World Social Forum is a peak event in the antiglobalization movement, the Zapatista uprising in Chiapas, Mexico, is its most

exemplary instance. On January 1, 1994, the Zapatista National Liberation Army (EZLN) occupied six towns and numerous ranches in southern
Mexico (though it failed in its plan to seize a military base and proceed to
the state capital of the region [Carrigan 2001: 430]). The EZLN aimed to
recapture land for dispossessed indigenous people and to achieve autonomy
for a long-oppressed region, directly challenging the legitimacy of the
Mexican government. Yet the uprising also had a broader purpose,
symbolized by the date of the action: on that first day of 1994, the North
American Free-Trade Agreement (NAFTA) went into effect. To the
Zapatistas, opening Mexico to market competition from the north would
usher in a new era of oppression, leading to insecurity and poverty for
indigenous groups. Their actions provoked a violent response from the
Mexican army, which attacked indigenous communities suspected of supporting the EZLN. After hostilities in which more than 100 people were
killed, a cease-fire was declared on January 12. In the following years, negotiations between the EZLN and the government alternated with army
and paramilitary violence that reversed most Zapatista gains (Hansen and
Civil 2001: 448–51). In 1996, the San Andres Accords appeared to meet
Zapatista demands for land reform, autonomy, and cultural rights, but
Mexico's president rejected the agreement, producing a stalemate that
prevented the EZLN from reaching its specific goals.

The EZLN's local struggle resonated globally. As an indigenous group
claiming the right to maintain its culture and habitat, it attracted support
from many other groups facing similar predicaments. By broadcasting its
message over the Internet, it became a node in a network of citizen advocacy groups around the world. Deliberately linking its own cause to global
trends, acting locally while thinking globally, it constituted a form of "grassroots globalization" (Karliner 1997). In addition to armed action, it staged
meetings of sympathizers in the jungles of southern Mexico, which became
platforms for disseminating its message. Instrumental in making the EZLN's
global case was its masked leader, Subcomandante Marcos. With poetic
flair, in tune with emerging critiques of globalization, Marcos effectively
globalized the Zapatista cause. In remarks at the first "Intercontinental
Encuentro for Humanity and against Neoliberalism," alluding to divisions
within Mexico, he said that neoliberalism "turns each country into many
countries" and leads to "national societies being militarized" (Marcos
2001: 117–18). He associated neoliberalism with patriarchy, discrimination, and marginalization (ibid.: 124). At its worst, he implied, the advance
of neoliberalism leads to a "world war," in which "on the one side is neoliberalism, with all its repressive power and all its machinery of death; on the

other side is the human being" (ibid.: 118). Marcos encouraged the international gathering of comrades to adopt the position of the Zapatistas toward this global menace: "Enough is enough." From southern Mexico, an "echo" could go forth "of the local and particular, which reverberates in an echo of . . . the intercontinental and galactic," an echo of the "rebel voice transforming itself and renewing itself in other voices" (ibid.: 122). Such echoes can produce a united resistance pursuing, in the words of the Zapatista slogan, "Democracy! Liberty! Justice!" on behalf of a more "plural, different, inclusive, tolerant" humanity (ibid.: 127, 123). While advocating equal justice for all within Mexico, Marcos thus also articulated a larger vision of "a world where there is room for many worlds, a world that can be one and diverse" (ibid.: xxi).

The WSF and the Zapatista uprising illustrate the growth of a global counterculture – a term that captures the overall movement's self-understanding as a force of resistance against a dominant global ideology. As the examples show, this counterculture opposes the "neoliberal" ideas, values, and models that make up the ruling world culture. By its opposition, the antiglobalization movement that articulates the counterculture demonstrates some of the fissures that characterize contemporary world culture as a whole. To remedy the evils of neoliberalism, the counterculture also advocates what it takes to be a new set of principles, a vision of "another world." This ambition to reshape world culture shows that "antiglobalization" does not adequately describe the critics' intent; rather than undermine globalization as such, most aim to channel it in different directions. As a broad, diverse "movement of ideas," it also displays an alternative approach to cultural creativity, based on "grassroots" citizen initiatives. By their activism, they show that the meaning and future of world culture are heavily contested. To put it mildly, world culture is continually under debate.

While trying to capture the self-understanding of globalization critics, we also see their contributions to this debate as deeply embedded in the culture they claim to contest. The very attack on capitalism, translated as "neoliberalism," is hardly new. The values invoked in this critique, such as the dignity of the individual and equality of wealth and power, have a venerable history. World culture has prepared the way for the global consciousness so evident in Porto Alegre. "Counterhegemonic" organizations themselves gain leverage from the "global spread of certain basic norms" (Evans 2000: 231; 2004). In some respects, to be sure, critics introduce new ideas. Some of the worlds they imagine indeed require radical transformation, as we will illustrate. But like the participants in an older counterculture that once tried to loosen the uptight bourgeois morality prevalent in some Western countries, globalization's critics owe more to the culture they ostensibly oppose than they have cared to admit. We therefore view the debate about world culture as primarily a form of immanent critique, a process in which various groups mobilize terms and ideas from an already available repertoire to fashion partially new attacks on partially new targets.

In this chapter, we show the fissures, contention, and critical reflexivity inherent in world culture by analyzing the content and sources of the counterculture promoted by the so-called antiglobalization movement. We first describe more precisely the counterculture's goals. Drawing in part on the perspectives we have used before, we then examine how world culture fosters this countercultural reaction and what the reaction adds to world culture. We conclude with some critical reflections derived from our own perspective on world culture. Throughout this chapter, we treat critiques of globalization as alternative views of the world and therefore as constituent parts of world culture. We selectively use the discourse of globalization, not detailed analysis of globalization itself, as an extended example to make our points about world culture. As our summary of WSF statements shows, that discourse does not revolve exclusively around cultural issues. Yet when activists in Porto Alegre bemoan inequality, corporate power, or environmental devastation, or when Subcomandante Marcos laments the consequences of neoliberalism, we see them invoking broad cognitive schemas and deep values. In all sorts of global debates at the beginning of the twenty-first century, world culture is always also at stake.

"Opposed to Neoliberalism"

The antiglobalization movement opposes neoliberalism. As our examples suggest, that term has many meanings. For critics of globalization, it is an all-purpose conceptual grab bag. A wide range of groups invoke neoliberalism to confront a wide range of evils. It serves as a rallying cry at Zapatista meetings, as an epithet to be hurled at IMF (International Monetary Fund) and World Bank officials in street demonstrations, and as a theme in academic attacks on globalization. Yet at the core of the critiques lies one common idea, namely, that globalization proceeds according to a single set of rules and principles, that the world is being shaped according to one particular world-view. Neoliberalism therefore describes a widespread image of world culture as a dominant ideological project.

Neoliberalism stands for the pursuit of classic liberal ends by new global means. Nineteenth-century liberals argued that government should leave individuals free to pursue their economic interests and that market competition and free trade were the keys to economic progress. Neoliberalism is the effort to apply this philosophy on a broader scale, an effort that received a strong impetus in the 1980s from the conservative governments of Margaret Thatcher in Britain and Ronald Reagan in the USA. Their policies reflected the idea that market competition serves the public good and that government's economic role should be limited. As applied today, neoliberalism specifically encompasses privatization of government-owned companies, liberalization of domestic markets by easing regulations, more open international competition by lowering tariffs, and expanded international investment by loosening restraints on capital mobility (cf. IFG 2002: 19). By comparison with nineteenth-century liberalism, critics contend, neoliberalism is more relentlessly global in subjecting all countries to similar rules, more radical in rejecting any political control of economic processes, and more dominant in sweeping aside any alternative arrangements (Gray 1998). This body of thought – sometimes described as the "Washington Consensus" driven by the Bretton Woods institutions, sometimes (by French intellectuals) as the "pensée unique" (Passet 2000) – is taking over the world.

Neoliberalism is more than a set of ideas and policies, however. As critics insist, it is also institutionalized. NAFTA, reviled by the Zapatistas, is an instance of neoliberalism in action. European countries practiced neoliberalism when they sold off public utilities. The International Monetary Fund applied neoliberal principles in urging the transition of former communist countries to capitalist economies. The IMF and the World Bank are agents of neoliberalism when they require "structural adjustment" of Third World government budgets, including the tightening of social safety nets, as a condition for extending loans. The World Trade Organization is neoliberal in preventing labor or environmental standards from infringing on free trade. Pharmaceutical companies reflect the neoliberal mindset when they give priority to their profits and intellectual property rights in response to demands for cheaper AIDS drugs for poor countries. In short, neoliberalism is pervasive. Far from advancing freedom, critics argue, it builds an "iron cage," especially through the operation of international financial institutions (Bello 2001).

The concern of the antiglobalization movement goes still further. At heart, what critics object to is the general neoliberal idea that the world is or ought to be dominated by market relations (Gray 1998). They oppose "rule of the market, by the market" (Notes from Nowhere 2003: 25). By elevating the market as the model of all social relations, neoliberalism undermines the ability of states to organize societies in different ways. If market exchange is the norm, democratic deliberation about collective priorities is bound to suffer. The world as market leaves no room for collective control of economic processes. As the pursuit of profit takes priority, social relations become instrumental, fraying communal ties and even family cohesion. Neoliberalism disrespects social order itself, thus fostering a kind of anarchy. The market model further deforms nature by turning it into a mere resource and devalues things by making them into commodities. It demeans people by treating them as factors of production or bodies desiring only boundless consumption. In principle, therefore, neoliberalism has profoundly negative political, social, ecological, and individual consequences.

The antiglobalization movement attacks not just this market model of the world but also its philosophical rationale. The neoliberal world-view is individualistic in assuming that individuals possess intrinsic autonomy, that they are capable of choice, and that exercising choice is inherently good. The neoliberal world is a world of and for individuals. It is also a world in which success is measured by material gain, whether in the incomes of individuals, the portfolios of investors, the profits of corporations, or the GDP of countries. Neoliberalism is also universalist: the same ideas and principles are valid everywhere and all human beings share basic rights and goals. It is Promethean in envisioning a world made according to human will and desire. It assumes that by mastering nature, humans can shape their own lives. In the eyes of its critics, neoliberalism is the continuation of Enlightenment thought by global means.

Yet neoliberalism is also a great deception; it is an ideology, a Global Project (Esteva and Prakash 1998). Though ostensibly concerned with individual freedom, it actually serves to justify the interests of large corporations. World culture, in this image, defines the world situation to the advantage of the strong, solidifying existing inequalities (Bourdieu 2001). Neoliberal tenets do not prevail through persuasion; they are imposed by powerful countries and organizations. They represent a political agenda. Neoliberalism is itself an instrument of rule, preventing people from deciding for themselves how to live. Stifling cultural competition, it imposes a global party line.

The source of this ideology, according to most globalization critics, is the USA. Many of the intellectuals pushing the neoliberal agenda are American. American society glorifies the free market and disdains the state.

American culture, critics argue, is hyper-individualistic. America also embodies the belief that its own principles are universally valid. Its faith in its own notion of a universal civilization has been inextricably linked to the worldwide reach of American corporate dominance (Gray 1998: 216), and the chief beneficiaries of neoliberalism are American corporations (Bello 2001: xii). As the sole remaining superpower, it is able to impose its vision on everyone else; neoliberalism is one of the spoils of American victory in the Cold War (Touraine 1999: 27). Neoliberal globalization is America's attempt to remake the world in its own image, a form of neo-Darwinist colonization (Bourdieu 2001: 27ff., 97). In short, neoliberal world culture is a tool of empire. Not surprisingly, when the United States responded to the attacks of September 11, 2001, with a "war on terror," its critics viewed it as a "new Nero" (Bernard 2003) that burned the world while advancing its own delusional ideas. In response, they aimed to "build a global opposition capable of inflicting defeats on Washington's neo-imperialist ambitions as well as its neoliberal goals" (Mertes 2004: xi)

As this summary shows, the antiglobalization movement is cultural insofar as it opposes contemporary world culture, which it construes as an American-imposed capitalist dystopia. To build another world, it also proposes an alternative kind of culture.

"Another World"

The WSF, one observer noted, "affirmed the birth of a new culture" (Houtart 2001: vi). This fits the self-perception of WSF participants as engaged in a "movement of ideas." As the range of his writings illustrates (Marcos 2001), Subcomandante Marcos similarly views the Zapatistas as the vanguard of a new intellectual movement. One purpose of this movement, diverse though it may be, is to construct a vision of "another world." Articulated in the work of movement organizations and intellectual fellow travelers, this vision encompasses both specific principles for reform and a grand design for a new world order.

To counter the nefarious effects of neoliberal globalization, movement activists have proposed a number of reforms (Houtart 2001: 57; Broad 2002: Parts III and IV). They aim to replace free trade with fair trade, which respects the rights of workers and takes into account the impact of trade on the environment. To safeguard domestic markets, states should have the ability to set necessary tariffs and standards. To control the movement of capital, antiglobalizers advocate a "Tobin tax," to be levied on short-term cross-border financial transactions that risk destabilizing a country's economy. They argue that corporations must be subjected to both state regulation and new corporate codes of conduct. Essential public services, such as water and power, should remain or be brought under government control. The IMF and World Bank should more liberally forgive developing countries' debts and loosen conditions for future loans. The common thrust in most of these reforms is to contain the market, to rein in capitalism.

The counterculture thus puts the economy in a subordinate place. Rather than glorifying the market, it champions social needs and social cohesion (Gray 1998). In this view, social life should not revolve around the drive for profits, communities should be spared the disruptions of market competition, and groups should be able to shield their identities from economic assault. Reflecting a long tradition of critical responses to capitalism, the counterculture also calls for thorough democratization of the world. Its unifying goal is "to bring about sufficient democratic control over states, markets, and corporations to permit people and the planet to survive and begin to shape a viable future" (Brecher et al. 2002: 67). This control should not be limited to formal, national elections, but comprise a more "radical democracy" that operates at all levels and involves extensive deliberation by all parties affected by decisions (Esteva and Prakash 1998: 158; cf. IFG 2002: 56). One chief aim of such radical democratic control would be holding corporations and intergovernmental organizations accountable for their actions. The new culture also posits that justice demands greater equality of global wealth and power (Brecher et al. 2002: 73). Among other things, this involves redistribution of resources toward the global South and establishment of a "globalized welfare system" (Aguiton et al. 2001: 63). The WSF further promotes the "reinvention of democracy" as a continuous process subjecting all spheres of society to "a radical, participatory and living democratic process" (Ponniah and Fisher 2003: 13). Community, democracy, and equality are watchwords of the anticapitalist counterculture.

Just as neoliberalism has a philosophical rationale, the culture envisioned by its critics embodies a distinct world-view. In stressing the virtues of community and the need for equality, it aims to balance collective needs against the claims of individuals. A case in point is ATTAC's version of "associational statism," which links state intervention in the economy to a free-flowing participatory politics (Ancelovici 2002: 451). Among the most radical proponents of the new culture, even human rights are suspect, since they might be the Trojan horse of destructive individualism (Esteva and

Prakash 1998: 117). By contrast with the materialist old culture, the counterculture voices special concern for the planet as a whole and for the intrinsic worth of nature, calling for limits to the pursuit of material well-being. The world shares a common obligation to protect the common human heritage and the global commons (IFG 2002: 61–4). While the antiglobalization movement opposes neoliberalism as a false universalism, the alternative world envisioned will center on "truly universal goals" (Bourdieu 2001: 108). Even this more modest universalism is qualified by a balancing emphasis on the value of cultural diversity. The world does and must contain "many worlds," as Marcos put it; it should take the form of a "pluriverse" (Esteva and Prakash 1998). The new culture thus stands for a pluralist ecological collectivism. At the same time, it denies that there is any truth that must be universally acknowledged. This anti-universal universalism is also an anti-ideological ideology, since it rejects the very role of ideas as instruments of rule in the service of powerful interests. To most advocates, this constitutes a genuinely global alternative to ongoing globalization. For a radical few, the vision implies a new "paradigm" that contributes to the demolition of the current system (Khor in IFG 2001: 13–14), leading to a "deglobalized" world in which local communities exert local control over their resources and cultures (Bello 2001: 223). Only deglobalization, such radicals argue, can bring about "another world."

A "Great Alliance"

Both its critical thrust and its alternative vision mark the antiglobalization movement's distinctive approach to world culture. The way in which it carries out the "world process" of resistance is further evidence of its intent to transform world culture.

The antiglobalization movement is diverse. The 1999 "battle of Seattle" against the WTO (World Trade Organization) mobilized student groups like the Coalition for Campus Organizing and the United Students against Sweatshops; unions such as the AFL-CIO and the United Steelworkers of America; environmental groups ranging from the Sierra Club to Friends of the Earth; activist networks like Global Exchange and the Third World Network; as well as the anarchists of the Ruckus Society (Smith 2002: 212). The following year in Prague, Polish punks, German squatters, British Earth First!ers, Czech anarchists, and Indian activists joined forces to demonstrate against the IMF and World Bank (Notes from Nowhere 2003: 63). Gathered in Porto Alegre were representatives of French and Brazilian labor groups, numerous human rights organizations, several chapters of ATTAC, Third World development groups, Diverse Women for Diversity and the World Rainforest Movement, among many others. The Zapatistas similarly drew a wide range of sympathizers to their jungle headquarters. Nor is the struggle limited to such highly visible events. It is carried on as well in the more mundane work of nongovernmental organizations such as the British-based anti-poverty group Oxfam and the international anti-debt coalition Jubilee 2000. Larger organizations have become associated with the cause as well, as illustrated by statements by Pope John Paul II and the World Council of Churches on the dangers of neoliberal globalization (Lechner 2005). As this range of participants and supporters suggests, self-professed critics of globalization are motivated by different faiths, work on different issues, and pursue different goals. There is no single agenda, principle, or platform to which all must subscribe. Prominent participants, such as WSF organizers, have explicitly denied any intent to impose a program from above. To some extent, the "movement of movements" (Mertes 2004) thus displays in practice the diversity it advocates as a principle.

The content of the antiglobalization vision is further reflected in the structure of the movement. The movement has leaders but no governing body. It is a loosely linked network of self-organizing autonomous groups (Brecher et al. 2002: Ch. 7), mostly made up of "citizen movements" (IFG 2001: 1) and "citizen initiatives" (Broad 2002). Individual initiatives, such as Jubilee 2000, anti-IMF demonstrations, or the WSF itself, consist of loosely coordinated coalitions of willing participants. As the Zapatista model illustrates, "grassroots" mobilization is the preferred mode of action. Even while they participate in globally oriented events, groups seek to maintain "local" control over their own identities. Specific ideas orienting the movement, such as the stress on cultural diversity and indigenous rights, preferably emerge "from below." In the way it operates, the movement thus reinforces its message about the kind of anti-ideological, more pluralistic world culture it envisions.

Though it disparages ideology and vaunts diversity, the great alliance against globalization has a unifying thrust. For all the variety of causes they represent and despite the disparate domestic contexts in which they often operate (Ancelovici 2002), most antiglobalization "global justice" groups (Evans 2005) are part of the global political left by virtue of their joint opposition to neoliberal capitalism and their advocacy of a more egalitarian world. In the self-understanding of many participants, they are carrying out what Karl Polanyi (1985) called the "double movement" – the inevitable reaction of society against the destabilizing consequences of unbridled market competition. This reaction is itself framed by specific cultural assumptions (Ancelovici 2002), above all the notion that the movement represents the reassertion of social control over an uncontrolled economic juggernaut, both in advocating specific forms of regulation and in fostering a commitment to another way of life. By their resistance, critics aim to build a culture of containment that reorders the spheres of global life. They thus try to offer living proof that "another world is possible."

Transforming World Culture

What accounts for the growing resonance of the counterculture we have described? Part of our answer is historical: the antiglobalization movement is responding to the intensification of globalizing trends in recent decades, some of which helped to generate the symbolic resources the movement now uses. The theoretical perspectives we have applied throughout this book supplement this point by arguing that world culture inevitably fosters debate and conflict, a tendency currently expressed most clearly by globalization critics. At the same time, some of these perspectives also suggest that existing world-cultural frames shape even seemingly radical forms of opposition, blunting their transformative impact.

Many characteristics of the counterculture we have described are not new. The idea that industrial capitalism is a brutal system, that market competition undermines stability, and that the pursuit of wealth also aggravates inequality has accompanied every phase of the Great Transformation that started in the West. By the same token, the antiglobalization movement is not the first to envision a utopian "other" world in which communities flourish and equality prevails. Such themes have been especially prominent in the socialist tradition. In some respects, therefore, the new counterculture represents the continuation of socialism by other means. This was reflected in the fact that the WSF was hosted by the Brazilian Workers' Party. Some intellectual supporters have explicitly called for a "renewed vision of socialism" as a key goal for the antiglobalization movement (Houtart 2001: 59). To be sure, the counterculture is not simply a continuation. For example, its critique of neoliberalism does not rely exclusively on old socialist arguments about exploitation and class inequality. Its vision of another world appeals to principles of democracy, ecology, and diversity not found or stressed in earlier periods. The overall movement operates less hierarchically and is more broadly inclusive than socialist parties and their intellectual vanguards of old (Wallerstein 2004: 270–1), yet the antiglobalization movement also revives and reconstructs an older critical discourse whose resonance stems in part from the historical setting in which the movement operates.

After the end of the Cold War, after the "earthquake that brought down the Soviet bloc [and] set China on course for a pragmatic integration with the capitalist market," a "new world-political landscape for the Left" appeared (Sader 2004: 248). In the movement to recover "the legacy of the historical Left" (ibid.: 260), socialist ideas stepped further away from orthodoxies enforced by communist regimes. Even groups linked to traditional socialism, such as Italy's Refounded Communists, applauded the "break with the 20th century and its truths and myths," putting their faith in the antiglobalization movement as the only basis for a "left alternative" (Bertinotti 2003). Such participants in the movement envision the WSF as a platform for "reconstructing the Left on the basis of the movements, going beyond every alliance with the existing structures of political and economic power," pushing beyond mere social democracy to "the democracy of the multitude" (Hardt and Negri 2003: xix). Anticapitalist ideas and values could thus mutate without being tied to the legitimation of old regimes, and such mutations included combinations with new intellectual currents, illustrated in the indigenous people's struggle in Mexico. At the same time, the end of the Cold War also created a widespread perception that the end of geopolitical conflict spelled the victory of a particular set of ideas, unleashing neoliberalism as a dominant ideology. "Globalization" came to be used increasingly to describe global change in the mold of this ideology. As "globalization" made old problems appear more urgent on a global scale, critics of capitalism were free to adapt old ideas to the new world situation.

World-system theorists are not surprised by the rise of this counterculture. According to the Marxist tradition that informs their work, any culture is the expression of dominant interests. As we saw in Chapter 2, culture as ideology necessarily suppresses the interests of excluded groups. Since the latter always have a stake in opposing what oppresses them, resistance is normal. World culture, construed as ideology, expresses and undergirds the superior position of a global class (Sklair 1995). It has made normative a particular view of state and economy, of gender, race, and nation. Its seemingly progressive scenario of ever-expanding rationality and universalism legitimates a structure of inequality, but its false promises are bound to stir discontent. Precisely because it is ideology, world culture in its current incarnation necessarily provokes resistance. Challenges to hegemony make culture an ideological battleground (Wallerstein 1991b). Since world culture is both the target and the arena of struggle, hegemony is bound to be transformed. Such transformation is the task of antisystemic movements.

Following this line of reasoning, world-system theory can account for several features of the antiglobalization movement and its counterculture that we have described thus far. For example, since neoliberalism is the key set of justifications for global capitalism, it must become the focus of resistance (Wallerstein 2004: 271). Since different groups and regions occupy different positions within the world-system and therefore perceive its problems differently, opposition will take the form of a variety of antisystemic movements rather than primarily class-based resistance. The theory makes no firm predictions about the advent of a classless society after a final crisis of capitalism, though some of its proponents hold out hope for "what used to be called socialism" (ibid.: 273). It suggests that the shape of a post-capitalist future must be worked out through open debate in a transitional period of ideological uncertainty, when divided global elites themselves lose faith in the existing system (ibid.: 271–2). Such critical creativity is in fact displayed in the instances we have summarized. In a more normative vein, some world-system theorists have also offered speculations about "global democracy" that could serve to guide radical reform as capitalism "spirals" into socialism, showing an ideological affinity with other globalization critics (Boswell and Chase-Dunn 2000). In its view of culture as hegemony and of antisystemic movements as diverse resistance, and in its openness to critical alternatives, the world-system theory account of the counterculture closely fits with the way WSF participants view themselves. Not surprisingly, Immanuel Wallerstein participated in the second WSF in 2002. Moreover, world-system theory also closely parallels, in academic terms, the revisionist adaptation of the socialist heritage that animates a significant part of the antiglobalization movement.

Globalization theory in Robertson's sense calls into question several ideas shared by antiglobalization activists and world-system interpreters. For example, Robertson denies that world culture consists of a single dominant ideology or is shaped by a single model, and he questions the notion that the economy is the single most important driving force in the process. Yet in some respects globalization theory complements world-system theory. Globalization creates a new global condition that raises questions about how to turn this into a meaningful order. While there are some common standards brought to bear on this task, such as principles that reflect the value of "humankind," different societies and individuals approach it from distinct standpoints as their identities are "relativized" in the process. World culture contains a number of alternative models of world order or definitions of the global situation. These models serve as ideal schemas for channeling the globalization process, assigning a particular role and value to the world economy as part of a larger whole. World culture is thus the symbolic arena in which participants in globalization critically reflect on the direction of the process and its desirable outcomes.

In some respects, Robertsonian expectations about cultural conflict converge with those of world-system theory. The antiglobalization movement confirms that world culture contains ongoing contention about the effects of globalization and its variegated elements fit the idea that relativization entails different perspectives on global order. The focus on neoliberalism, in Robertson's view, is not so much a direct response to actual hegemony as a reflection of the way in which globalization turns the value of the world economy into a problem. What purpose should economic activity serve, and what place should it have in world affairs? What is the merit of material progress, and how should its benefits be distributed? Anti-neoliberal answers are not the only answers possible. Globalization theory also sheds light on the content of the counterculture by arguing that these answers fit certain broad types of world-view, depending on whether they give primacy to communal ties or more impersonal societal ties. Much of the counterculture articulates a *Gemeinschaft*-style picture of world order as the unity of distinct communities, in opposition to the *Gesellschaft* of market domination.

The anthropological perspectives we have applied previously further complement these views of the counterculture. The core idea we distilled from them, namely that world culture consists of the organization of diversity, already implies that contention rather than consensus must be the normal state of affairs. As the "ideoscape" globalizes, aided by advancement in the "technoscape" and movement in the "ethnoscape," so must distinct cultural challenges. In the global "ecumene," different forms of life come to be valued by different groups as they filter globalization processes according to their local circumstances; world culture is marked by exchanges among these forms. As we saw in Chapter 2, these forms of life are inevitably "creolized" to some degree. Even as anthropologists ascribe special significance to the ongoing vitality of the local, they also recognize that globalization necessarily challenges the viability of any single place or community and the overall continuity of diversity. Interpreted from this standpoint, the counterculture creatively draws on the infrastructure of the ideoscape to spread a new message, advocating an ecumenical version of world society in which local identity gains new recognition, global allegiances blend seamlessly with grassroots commitments, and the problem of diversity is turned into an explicit symbolic principle.

The first three perspectives on the counterculture assume that world culture fosters contention. The antiglobalization counterculture therefore broadly fits their expectations, even if these vary in detail. However, the counterculture appears to pose a problem for world polity theory, too. After all, it posits that world culture contains a template of models to be followed, a cognitive script that commands significant agreement across the globe and is enacted in similar ways. This seems to leave little room for fundamental conflict or antisystemic movements. Yet the world polity is not entirely harmonious. It contains principles, such as liberty and equality, that are in tension with each other. Some of its precepts, such as respect for human rights, are so general that any attempt at implementation is bound to fall short. The very decentralization of the world polity prevents enforcement of a single "party line," providing opportunities for the crystallization of new ideas. Some of the typical carriers of world-cultural principles, especially nongovernmental organizations, are authorized by those very principles to pursue their own goals as they see fit, which leads to continual expansion of the world-cultural script. Overall, what world polity theory tells us is not that contention and challenge are impossible but rather that they are likely to occur within the framework of existing world culture.

Applied to the antiglobalization movement, this suggests that its counterculture relies on key elements of world-cultural scripts while exploiting the tensions within them, insisting on adequate enactment, and opposing the appearance of a "party line." Thus, two WSF participants propose the following as "values of a new civilization": liberty, equality, and fraternity, democracy, respect for the environment, and socialism as an alternative (Löwy and Betto 2003). Other antiglobalizers similarly vaunt familiar values: "Autonomy is our means and our end . . . Autonomy is freedom and connectedness . . . an irrepressible desire that stalls every attempt to crush the will to freedom" (Notes from Nowhere 2003: 107). Appeals to human rights and affirmations of equality, characteristic of much of the movement, also adapt world-cultural content for new purposes. The structure of the movement, notably the self-authorizing, self-organizing work of grassroots citizen groups, is not a form of deviance but instead rather typical of much world-cultural activity. At least part of the counterculture is already "trickling up" into existing institutions, as illustrated by shifts in lending policies by the World Bank to give priority to alleviating poverty, promoting women's issues, and protecting the environment. The counterculture may still contribute to a subtle transformation of world culture, but its self-understanding overaccentuates the radical and therefore downplays the continuities in its critique.

This interpretation complements the earlier ones by stressing the constraints built into world culture. In doing so, however, it may underestimate critical new elements in parts of the counterculture. By contrast with the celebration of the individual in conventional world culture, some of its critics elevate local community and global solidarity as major principles. On behalf of "social majorities," they envision a good life liberated from the "Global Project," "defined in local, rooted terms" and marked by "incommensurable truths or perceptions regarding the nature of Nature, or Reality" (Esteva and Prakash 1998: 193–4). Opposing the reformist tendencies at the WSF, which they consider "too happy, too celebratory, and not conflictual enough," they disdain "any national solutions" and seek a more disruptive "democratic globalization" (Hardt 2004: 232–3). As their critique of neoliberalism and their stress on environmental concerns suggest, they are also skeptical of the rationalist belief in secular progress. That belief is an instance of the destructive, outdated "humanism" that has ruined the planet (Gray 2002). By advocating "deglobalization" – "decentralization, greater pluralism, more checks and balances" (Bello 2004: 60) – at least some groups convey a desire for truly radical change in the world polity itself. Even without achieving political power across the globe or taking control of major international organizations, the antiglobalization movement has made its mark on world culture by inserting its critique and its vision of "another world."

Conclusions

We have argued that the antiglobalization movement makes strong claims about world culture and thereby aims to transform it. Our main purpose in this chapter has been to understand the thrust of the counterculture and its potential transformative impact on overall world culture, yet in this book we have also presented a picture of world culture that differs from the one that prevails within the antiglobalization movement. The difference illustrates the kind of contention this chapter has described. However, because our work enters contested terrain and we are not simply neutral observers, we also want to say more explicitly how we respond to the actual claims of the counterculture.

In the first part of this chapter we tried to sketch a coherent picture of the counterculture, but the scope and diversity of the movement defy such simplification. Some inconsistency is evident in details, such as the Porto Alegre Call for Mobilisation's opposition to the importation of cheap agricultural products (to protect the livelihoods of "local" farmers), a stance it justifies as a method of aiding the poor (who as consumers would normally benefit from cheaper food). A more important example is the tension between the preservation of "local" identity and control, on the one hand, and advocacy of global governance in a single "planetary" society, on the other. While parts of the antiglobalization movement address the issue head-on, as illustrated by the International Forum on Globalization's call for a division of labor across levels, known as "subsidiarity" (IFG 2002: Ch. 4), the movement displays great differences on this and other issues.

Related to the problem of coherence is that of plausibility. For example, while globalization critics are rhetorically effective in denouncing neo-liberalism, few have confronted the trade-offs involved in pursuing the alternatives they propose. An ecological-collectivist approach to the world economy that also strives to improve the plight of the poor – the "renewed vision of socialism" some aspire to – becomes more plausible if it also takes seriously the historical costs of state efforts to achieve equality through regulation and redistribution, a concern more evident among academic critics of globalization (Rodrik 1997) than among movement representatives. Of course, social movements often have priorities other than logical consistency or empirical plausibility; their goal is not to interpret the world but to change it. Yet the content of the interpretation matters. Because we observe intrinsic difficulties that are likely to hamper it, our expectations about the transformative impact of the world process celebrated in Porto Alegre are more modest than those of most attendees.

Most participants in the antiglobalization movement portray world culture as a single juggernaut, an ideological project that serves the interests of specific groups and organizations. As our review of alternative interpretations of the counterculture has reiterated, the picture of world culture we sketch in this book is more complex. We have shown through many examples, from the Olympic Games in Chapter 1 to the issue of national identity in the last chapter, that world culture operates in many different spheres. It encompasses global forms of knowledge and rules of action that inform a range of transnational activity, from the mundane cultural infrastructure of civil aviation to highly charged ideological debate about the environment. World culture is also diverse in its content. To be sure, some key principles that have become globalized, such as individualism, rationality, and faith in progress, originated in Western culture, yet even such ideas of Western provenance can hardly be summarized as part of a single market-oriented "neoliberal" conception of the world, which is at best one variation on very general themes. World culture also has acquired a certain autonomy. In each of the cases we have analyzed, no single group or country is in charge. Many groups, not just corporations, now take a strong interest in elaborating global ground rules in specific fields. The very complexity of world culture, itself the result of a mixture of historical influences, makes even partial control by any powerful entity problematic. As a result, world culture as such is not simply a form of ideology in the sense of a set of ruling ideas that support the interests of a ruling class or dominant structure. Among its beneficiaries are not just the corporate elites often targeted by globalization critics but also state officials in developing countries, international civil servants at the UN, and tourists traveling abroad, to mention only some relevant groups. However useful it may be for certain political purposes, it is a selective misrepresentation to render world culture as a single, neoliberal, ideological project.

In keeping with the self-understanding of many participants in the antiglobalization movement, and to convey the WSF spirit, we have described its vision as a "counterculture." Yet, to extend the world polity argument from the previous section, the counterculture is also deeply embedded in the world culture it aims to transform. Like many oppositional movements, it is in thrall to what it opposes. For the socialist strand of the movement, this is again nothing new, since nineteenth-century socialism already relied heavily on "bourgeois" ideas about freedom and progress, and twentieth-century socialist states adopted "bourgeois" institutional forms like the bureaucratic state devoted to economic development. Today, seemingly new ideas, such as the celebration of diversity, derive legitimacy from already deeply engrained world-cultural commitments to societal particularity of the kind we discussed in the last chapter. Several widely supported antiglobalization arguments, such as the idea that free trade must yield to fair trade and that capital mobility must be restrained, presuppose a commitment to extending state authority and thus reinforce a key component of existing world culture. The very assumption driving the antiglobalization movement, namely that debate about general principles and agitation for reform are inherently good, itself derives from the way world culture is constituted. While there are several radical arguments in the antiglobalization movement that truly would transform world culture as we know it, the antiglobalization movement's primary impact on world culture is that of a variation on long-standing themes, some of which will become part of the available global repertoire for thinking about social issues, some of which will be institutionalized in international organizations or particular societies. With regard to such institutionalization, one case in point is the election of Luiz Inácio Lula da Silva, leader of the party that hosted the WSF, as president of Brazil in 2002. Overall, the counterculture's record therefore fits our view of world culture better than its own image.

There is a romantic quality to parts of the antiglobalization movement. Activists communing with Zapatista rebels in the jungle or enjoying a march against neoliberalism in Porto Alegre experience an intense form of solidarity common to many movements. More specific to the countercultural vision, as we have seen, is the anti-universalist idea that world society should be a deglobalized "pluriverse," one world of "many worlds," a community of communities. For some advocates, though certainly not all, this requires reversing globalization and "blowing up" existing world culture. Our view of world culture leads us to be skeptical of such a radical attempt. Because world society operates on a truly global scale, and because world culture encompasses many significant sectors of social life, trying to return to an untainted, undisturbed communal life becomes a costly illusion. World culture allows no romantic escape from living globally. Rather than deglobalization, we expect continued debate about alternative forms of globalization and continued contention about the shape of world order. The chief impact of globalization critics on world culture is to foster such global debate, a debate that itself refutes the ideological view of world culture all too common among counterculture advocates. On balance, then, the counterculture is more interesting as an indicator of the actual state of world culture than it is adequate as a guide to its desirable – or at least likely – transformation.

Chapter 8

Expanding World Culture:
Pentecostalism as a Global Movement

Situated on an island in Seoul, South Korea, the Yoido Full Gospel Church occupies an impressive campus-like complex. The church needs the extensive facilities, for it is the largest congregation in the world. Since he started his pastoral career in 1958, minister David Yonggi Cho has assembled a flock of more than half a million members. His management of this vast enterprise is a marvel of sociological ingenuity. To give members a personal tie to an otherwise impersonal organization, Cho has divided them into small groups. To keep control over the church and its many subsidiary programs, he has adopted the formal, top-down structure of Korean conglomerates. Simply meeting the logistical challenge of organizing Sunday worship is a feat in itself, accomplished by providing seven services in a large auditorium and adjacent chapels, where Cho appears either in person or on video. The church is more than a successful exercise in applied sociology, however. It claims a particular religious mission. Like other Protestant ministers, Cho teaches that the Bible is literally true, that Jesus died for our sins, and that his kingdom will come. Yet such standard teaching hardly explains his phenomenal success, which Cho would attribute to his special message, the *full* gospel. More than a set of theological tenets, it involves above all a strong faith in the power of the Holy Spirit as an active force that bestows the blessings of health and prosperity on all true believers (Anderson 2004). The point of worship at Yoido is to call forth that Spirit. During services, it descends through music and dance, through incantatory prayers, and through the hands of ministers who heal the sick and drive out evil spirits (Cox 1995: 222–3).

Yoido Full Gospel, in other words, is a charismatic church, rooted firmly in the Pentecostal tradition. As this Korean church shows, Pentecostalism has come a long way since its origins in the 1906 Azusa Street revival held by a group of poor blacks and whites in Los Angeles. In fact, by the end of the twentieth century, Pentecostalism had become the most rapidly growing branch of Christianity, counting between 150 million and 400 million adherents according to scholarly estimates (Barrett et al. 2001: 4; César 2001; Martin 2002: 1), which made Pentecostal/charismatic churches the largest single Christian category after the Roman Catholic Church. Especially due to growth in Asia, Africa, and Latin America, it is fast becoming "the dominant expression of Christianity" (Anderson 1999a: 19). Though Yoido Full Gospel itself emerged from the postwar "second wave" of charismatic evangelizing, it has also contributed to the more recent "third wave" of worldwide expansion throughout a variety of Christian churches (cf. Burgess et al. 1988: 810–11). Long part of the Assemblies of God that originated in the USA, it is now an independent megachurch, sending scores of missionaries abroad and using the Internet to spread the gospel. As the quintessential evangelical entrepreneur, pastor Cho has become an international religious celebrity, "arguably the most influential minister in [his] denomination globally" (Anderson 2004: 116).

Members of the International Central Gospel Church (ICGC) in Accra, Ghana, founded by Mensa Otabil in 1984, would recognize Yoido's faithful as spiritual kin. Here, too, the Sunday worship services are professionally staged yet highly personal, using music to grab and inspire believers from the outset. This church also organizes its thousands of members in cell groups. Its message is the "faith gospel," a version of Yoido's full gospel, stressing divine power as the basis for worldly success. The ICGC is committed to "the holistic preaching and demonstration of God's plans and purposes for all mankind as revealed in the Holy Scriptures" (www.centralgospel.com 2003). Like Cho, minister Otabil publishes extensively and is part of an international evangelical network (Gifford 1994). The ICGC is not a church of the dispossessed, for it attracts a relatively young, middle-class audience, which it assists in finding suitable marriage partners. It conducts services in English rather than indigenous languages. Though the church focuses less on casting out demons than similar African churches, Otabil has a distinctive message that directly addresses his parishioners: faith is the road to black racial pride and self-liberation – a message that "breaks the shackles of mental slavery." The very name of his church expresses his aspiration to make his gospel of ambition an international cause. Through evangelizing in West Africa and in the Ghanaian diaspora in the West, Otabil's followers are doing just that (Van Dijk 2001).

Even in Sweden, one of the most secular countries in the world, some nationally prominent churches resemble their counterparts in Korea and

Ghana. The Word of Life Church in Uppsala, founded by Ulf Ekman, has built a large congregation around a "health and wealth" full-gospel message that both Cho and Otabil would heartily endorse. Though its modestly innovative preaching antagonizes nearby traditional Pentecostal congregations, its worship style dramatically enacts its members' faith in charismatic fashion – speaking in tongues and rituals of healing – investing the Word with an emotional power uncommon among Scandinavian congregations (Coleman 2000). Having been trained in the USA, Ekman maintains close ties with kindred American preachers. As in Seoul, Word of Life's success is measured not only by the number of souls saved, but also by its material possessions, the reach of its broadcasting and publishing efforts, and the worldwide prominence of its minister.

These three churches have much in common. Their leaders are strong, charismatic, entrepreneurial figures who have become highly visible. As these organizations grew, they formalized their structures and outreach programs. On the one hand, they are in tune with their local audiences, adapting their Christian message to fit the cultures that surround them, while on the other hand, they also cultivate worldwide ties, spreading the Word by increasingly sophisticated means. They share a style of worship, filling believers with the Spirit in emotionally engaging services. Their message combines familiar evangelical tenets with a special emphasis on the Spirit's power to overcome earthly adversity. To some extent, each deviates from classic Pentecostal tradition – for example, the dancing in Seoul would have scandalized Pentecostal founders, and the desire for earthly blessings risks overtaking the biblical message. Yet as successful, innovative neo-Pentecostal churches, still rooted in a century-old tradition, they represent the vanguard of a global movement.

Of course, a wave of religious activity so large and so widely dispersed is bound to be diverse. At the more traditional end of the spectrum, we find congregations like the Assembly of God in Campo Alegre, Brazil. It is smaller and more modestly housed; it lacks the fancy production values of its Ghanaian and Korean counterparts; it attracts fewer young and upwardly mobile members. Only some 200 members attend services. Yet they are moved by the same spirit, which is evident in the intense, repetitive singing during regular services, the "avalanche of prayers" and praise that is bound to flow, and the formulaic testimonies attesting to miraculous transformations in the lives of individual believers (Ireland 1991: Ch. 4). At prayer meetings and house services another staple of Pentecostal practice, speaking in tongues, is even more common. Across Latin America, there are thousands of Campo Alegres.

At the innovative end of the spectrum, indicative of the variety of forms taken by the third wave, is the so-called Toronto Blessing, an ecstatic form of worship at a Toronto church so infused with the Spirit that in the late 1990s it stimulated tens of thousands to travel long distances to share the experience (Richter 1997). Conveniently located for its far-flung audience, Toronto Airport Vineyard Church became known for the unorthodox ways in which the Spirit moved attendees of the Blessing – uncontrollable laughter, animal-like barking, falling, and weeping – that ultimately led to expulsion from the Vineyard network of churches and a new official name for the local congregation, Toronto Airport Christian Fellowship. Dispensing with biblical exegesis, the Blessing distilled charismatic practice to a few essential elements and thereby achieved global renown.

Our purpose in this chapter is to describe and explain the movement encompassing these forms of charismatic religiosity as a case of world-cultural expansion. After summarizing the key features of Pentecostalism as a global cultural domain, we account for its diffusion and its contribution to overall world culture. Our point is not to suggest that Pentecostals grew in order to expand world culture. That happened as an unintended consequence. Yet in view of our overall perspective it is not surprising that a movement apparently centered on satisfying immediate spiritual needs now also leaves a distinctly global imprint. World culture often expands, unwittingly as it were, through the actions of people addressing issues that originally may not have had an obvious global dimension. We argue that Pentecostalism illustrates a larger point about the growth of world culture more generally. Cultural creativity is likely to come from movements that in some way oppose established institutions, build on the infrastructure of globalization, give form to the new connections between individuals and the world at large, and distinctively mix the universal and particular. It comes from groups that take advantage of the open cultural spaces created by globalization, that use the very autonomy of world culture as a sphere of action. In relation to world culture, Pentecostalism has operated as a kind of sect engaged in transformation from within.

Pentecostalism as World Culture

For all their variety, Pentecostal churches are building and elaborating a new dimension of world culture. What are its essential features? Pentecostal culture is created, from the bottom up, as it were (Cox 1999: 392–3), by millions of the "culturally despised" (Martin 2002: 167) who walked out

of established churches (Martin 1990) to join independent, locally administered churches, usually led by authoritative male pastors (Anderson
1999a: 25, 28). Because much of the creative work is done in developing
countries, the West no longer "calls the tune" (Hollenweger 1999: 35). As
a result, Pentecostalism has no dominant center. While not beholden to any
single organization, Pentecostal churches maintain many transnational connections. As we have already seen, the large congregations in the vanguard
self-consciously develop ties across the globe, but even in Campo Alegre
foreign preachers come to speak and believers are well aware of being part
of a worldwide church. Another case in point is Brazil's Universal Church
of the Kingdom of God, which "projects itself as the agent and focal point
of world evangelization" in trying to make a global faith "universal"
(Kramer 2002: 40). The Pentecostal sphere is thus one of multiple, ever-
evolving networks (Dempster et al. 1999: 206) that increasingly strive to
evangelize and bear global witness (ibid.: 16). It offers a model of a global
organizational culture.

Pentecostals claim to have a universal message. They believe that Jesus
is Lord and Savior and the Bible the literal word of God for all of humanity. They think a new Pentecost is afoot, in which the Holy Spirit brings
millions the good news of salvation in the hereafter and real blessings in
the here and now. To express their faith, they have adopted a unifying style
of worship that makes use of the biblical text but also relies on believers'
physical involvement (Coleman 2000: 6, Ch. 5). Pentecostal culture is
always embodied in the way people move, sing, shout, and shake. Spread
via transnational networks but enacted by independent groups of believers,
faith and practice are eminently "translateable" (Freston 1997) from place
to place, from one language to another. They allow for creative interpretation. The dispersed authority characteristic of Pentecostal culture favors
flexible adaptation as well. Hence, Pentecostal culture is marked more by
a distinct family resemblance or set of affinities (Martin 2002) than by devotion of all adherents to a fixed creed or catechism. Rather than conform-
ing to a model made in America, it displays the diversity of variable
receptions of multiple influences (Coleman 2002). Finally, the culture is not
just "religious" in the spiritual sense. It also inculcates in adherents a
version of the "Protestant ethic" and imbues believers with attitudes largely
favorable to such global institutions as markets and democracy, which has
helped to make Pentecostalism one of the "four faces" of global culture
(Berger 1997).

Strictly speaking, Pentecostalism is not quite a "face" of "global"
culture. Its reach does not extend to much of China, India, or the Muslim

world. Pentecostalism remains one vision of the sacred among others. However, Berger is right to imply that it has begun to insinuate itself into world culture. Pentecostalism is, in fact, a prime instance of a movement expanding world culture. To existing world culture, with secular knowledge and values at its core, Pentecostalism adds a partially new vision of the world that derives its meaning from the work of the Holy Spirit. Whereas much of world culture, as we have described it thus far, has a distinctly cognitive cast, Pentecostalism universalizes a form of nonrational faith and emotional practice, thus giving shared form to inner experience. In building its networks of independent congregations, it adopts features of existing global institutions while putting them to creative uses. In word and deed, it meaningfully links the most personal concerns of individual believers to the future of the world as a whole. Carrying an ancient but revived tradition to new lands, it innovatively indigenizes the universal message, a process fostered by the content and structure of the faith itself. This face of global culture – transcendently rooted yet experiential, institutionally dynamic and operating across levels, globally ambitious yet always particularized – presents a counterpoint to the more rational and cognitive features of world culture that we have described thus far. This "biblical" and "experiential" global culture, which embraces "the whole person and the whole world," is therefore also "oppositional" (Poewe 1994: xii).

Pentecostalism is not only a counterpoint, however; it also incorporates much of contemporary world culture. Centered as it is on personal concerns, it celebrates the individual. Though fundamentalist in some of its beliefs, it also represents the breaking free of individuals from ascriptive bonds, a kind of "expressive revolution" (Martin 2002: 168–9). Individuals break free through conversion, a distinctive form of the "individual struggling to achieve selfhood" (Marshall-Fratani 1998: 285), and this symbolic link to world culture is not surprising in view of the latter's Christian antecedents. The nonrational aspects of Pentecostal worship do not preclude rationality in its organizational structures or operations, as world culture prescribes. To describe it as an oppositional or antisystemic movement would be too simple, since it comfortably accepts or even actively endorses many world institutions. As a movement, it builds on the very infrastructure that also serves more secular purposes; its decentralized network structure seems particularly fit for the global age. In keeping with the world around it, "Pentecostalism belongs by nature to open markets beyond all sponsorship . . . [and] remains incurably pluralistic" (Martin 2002: 171). Pentecostalism does not wholly transform world culture; it adds a layer to it, a set of symbolic options for linking individuals to the world (Droogers 2001: 55).

As the Spirit Moves

According to one plausible account, Pentecostalism is essentially an American export (Brouwer et al. 1996). Based primarily in the USA, it is marketed by American church leaders to grateful consumers in developing countries. Backed by the superior resources of American church networks, Pentecostalism preaches an American gospel of otherworldly salvation through Jesus combined with innerworldly salvation through the American way of life. Pentecostalism therefore is a form of cultural imperialism, spreading an already dominant view of the world. This interpretation is plausible for at least two reasons: Americans often have helped to trigger Pentecostal growth, and the world-view of many Pentecostals does resonate with that of many American evangelicals. However, the very evidence Brouwer et al. review suggests that the reality of Pentecostalism is more complex. It is not simply a set of branches on an American stem; the Spirit has planted seeds in many ways in many places, and many of those seeds germinated on their own. The condition of the local soil often proved far more important than any fertilizing done by Americans. How, then, did Pentecostalism grow?

To begin with, it grew in countries that were prepared for it in the sense that they had long-established Christian traditions prior to the first arrival of Pentecostalism. Pentecostal preachers could gain a hearing by speaking a language and offering a message many already knew. In South Korea, Methodist and Presbyterian missionaries had been active since the late nineteenth century, building churches and other institutions long before eight Pentecostal churches organized the Korean Assemblies of God in 1952 (Brouwer et al. 1996: 106ff.). Ghana similarly was Protestant mission territory before the establishment of indigenous churches of Pentecostal bent in 1914 (Asamoah-Gyadu 1998: 51). Brazil, which now has the largest Pentecostal community in the world, had experienced several waves of religious globalization, Catholic and Protestant, before the first Pentecostal churches were started by missionaries of European origin soon after the Azusa Street revival (Freston 1993: 68). Pentecostalism may be new, but it rarely starts from scratch. A movement on the cusp of a new wave of globalization, it is also propelled by the lingering effects of earlier waves.

In many cases, Pentecostalism grew by local effort. While some pastors studied in the USA and some churches received direct American support, most Pentecostal leaders are strong, charismatic figures employing indigenous staff. In Korea, pastor Cho is only the most prominent example of this leadership cadre. Minister Otabil in Ghana competes for attention with other highly articulate leaders (Gifford 1994). In Brazil, indigenous leaders not only built new churches but developed several new denominational networks, such as Edir Macedo's Universal Church of the Kingdom of God (Lehmann 1996: 122–3). Both within their own churches and in the larger networks they operate, the leaders develop a clear hierarchy. Invariably, the native-born are in charge. And that decentralized local authority, as we suggested earlier, may well be part of Pentecostalism's sociological genius. It succeeds because of its always-local nature. In Africa, as elsewhere, it has become self-governing, self-supporting, and self-propagating (Anderson 1999b: 402).

Pentecostalism grew without hierarchical direction or central sponsorship (Martin 2002). From the outset, Pentecostals followed no single American model. Even the Brazilian Assemblies of God, their familiar name notwithstanding, "tend to polities, styles, and customs that bear little resemblance to any of the major US Pentecostal denominations" (Stewart-Gambino and Wilson 1997: 229). Precisely because Pentecostalism recognizes no central authority, it also has proliferated in many unexpected directions. In nearly all countries, traditional Pentecostalism has gone through a wave of neo-Pentecostal revivalism. In Brazil, the Assemblies of God, including the congregation in Campo Alegre, still claim more than half of all Pentecostals, but rival groups like the Four-Square Gospel Church and Brazil for Christ are on the rise (Lehmann 1996: 118). In Ghana, Otabil and his colleagues have been part of this second wave since the 1970s, taking it in directions that differed from established Pentecostal and African Independent churches (Hackett 1998). As a result of new waves of revivalism, not to mention the entrepreneurial work of hundreds of individual pastors, Pentecostalism is therefore highly varied. This very diversity makes it even more difficult to see it as an export product. Religiously speaking, many countries have adapted originally American imports in creative ways (Coleman 2000: 227) or engaged in "import substitution." As it diversified, Pentecostalism also gained independence.

Pentecostalism grew by meeting local needs. As a Korean slogan put it, Pentecostals try to "find need and meet need" (cited in Martin 2002: 170). More broadly, as several observers have noted, Pentecostalism does well in periods of societal crisis (Meyer 1998). About the nature of the "needs" being met there is considerable disagreement, notably among experts on Latin America, who have proffered anomie, urban transformation, and (class) conflict as likely causes (Droogers 1998). In view of the sheer scope of Pentecostalism today, we doubt that any one general "cause" will provide an adequate explanation for its growth. But our examples from Seoul, Accra, and Campo Alegre do suggest one common denominator – that for many, especially lower-class people in developing countries, joining a Pentecostal church is a way to become modern, to open a "window to the world" (Van Dijk 1997). Another common denominator is that Pentecostalism everywhere attracts women much more than men. This is not because it treats women equally: patriarchy is alive and well in Pentecostal circles. But Pentecostalism does have much to offer. The nature of Pentecostal worship, allowing for the "feminine" work of the Spirit and contact with a "feminized" Jesus (Martin 2002: 103–4), is part of the appeal. The moral discipline the faith demands of men brings stability to their families and personal relationships, and the church invariably gives women aid and comfort in difficult circumstances. As an "antidote to machismo," it paradoxically "reforms gender roles in a way that enhances female status" (Brusco 1993: 144).

Finally, Pentecostalism grew within and against local cultures. Most churches preach explicitly against any lingering faith in local tradition. Their purpose is to transform popular culture (Hackett 1998); the choice is between God and gods. Converts must break with the past (Meyer 1998); members must see themselves as individuals detached from their ancestors (Van Dijk 1997). However, as our South Korean example shows, at least some of David Yonggi Cho's work, based on a "contextual" theology that both opposes and responds to shamanism, also fits closely with the practices of Korean shamans, as he bestows worldly blessings through his healing touch (Anderson 2004). Rather than reject tradition, Pentecostalism in Brazil and Latin America generally "redeploys" popular religion, resulting in a "bricolage" of styles and beliefs (Bastian 1994). In Ghana, minister Otabil's struggle against demons demonstrates keen awareness of local tradition; his Africanist rhetoric also distinctly appeals to his local audience. Overt professions to the contrary notwithstanding, Pentecostals in Ghana in fact are Africanizing a world religion, mixing opposition with actual closeness to local tradition (Van Dijk 1997; Meyer 1998). Of course, there is ample precedent for such mixing in the Christian tradition. The point is that today Pentecostalism is better at it than any of its counterparts. Its capacity for indigenization gives it an edge in global diffusion.

In retrospect, it is easy to identify factors that account for successful diffusion, but we should bear in mind that Pentecostalism has not yet reached all corners of the globe. Most of the places it has yet to penetrate have religious or ideological monopolies that effectively resist the free-wheeling competition stimulated by Pentecostal entry into cultural markets. There are few Pentecostals in China, hardly any in Saudi Arabia. Pentecostalism, in other words, flourishes in contexts that are already somewhat pluralistic, in which Pentecostal-style voluntarism (Martin 1990, 2002) is already minimally legitimate. There is only one serious exception to this rule, namely the limited appeal of Pentecostalism in most of Europe. In secularist Europe, parts of which are "inoculated" against Pentecostalism by earlier waves of Evangelicalism, only a minority of people at the margins is available for mobilization (Martin 2002: 67–8).

Even if it has not yet gone fully global, Pentecostalism has always had global aspirations, though few converts or congregations committed to a global cause can focus their full attention on it. It has had a universal thrust in striving for similarly emotive worship practices and a global community of believers (Van Dijk 1997). With skill and enthusiasm, Pentecostals have used modern media to spread their message, "delocalizing" it in the process (Marshall-Fratani 1998). However, its near-global growth was not the result of design; rather, it happened by unintended accretion. In hindsight, we can see why, but Pentecostal growth really is surprising: no one would have predicted it in 1906 or even 1956. Only by the 1960s did observers recognize its great potential (Stewart-Gambino and Wilson 1997: 232). By the beginning of the twenty-first century, we can see a clear pattern. It now makes sense to see Pentecostalism as a new layer within world culture, but the very surprise it represents also tells us to be cautious in predicting where world-cultural creativity is likely to come from, since movements that change world culture can grow in unexpected ways.

Its eventual diffusion turned Pentecostalism into a global force. We now turn to interpreting the significance of this force for world culture.

Expanding World Culture

In previous chapters we sketched several ways in which world culture might expand. When we described the construction of world culture, we suggested that this process is ongoing. World culture is expanding all the time, with more layers being added in ever-increasing global activities. As the infrastructure of world culture grows, this creative activity has become more regular and routine. World culture attracts specialists who make such work their explicit business. While we have argued that world culture has a coherence of its own, we also identified ways in which it undergoes differentiation. Such flourishing pluralism, congenial to Pentecostals, also counts as expansion. In the previous chapter, we analyzed the contention inherent in world culture, the clash of alternative visions of the globe. In open global debate, such visions of global futures proliferate. Expansion, in short, can come about in many ways.

Growth does not occur in a cultural vacuum. The established framework, once constructed, constrains what could plausibly count as new global knowledge or new global values. For instance, at UN conferences some ways of thinking about development or women's rights fell by the wayside. When it comes to differentiation, not all identities can be asserted with equal force. In the debate about global futures, some visions gain much more support than others. Of course, this is not due simply to conservatism inherent in the elements of world culture; constraints backed by the vested interests of many groups and countries, such as the ideological monopolies that block Pentecostal diffusion, help determine which ideas and identities succeed and which fail. World culture in our sense now has a history, and the weight of this history limits what new possibilities can be globally imagined. Many people now make world-cultural claims but not all those claims can take hold. What, then, makes for successful creativity? How can an individual or group break through, achieving recognition and support for new, globally available, universally applicable ways of thinking and feeling? It would be simplistic to suggest that there is only a single way to accomplish this, but our theoretical perspectives help to explain what should be done to "break through." Pentecostalism illustrates the patterns we identify.

World-system theory, as the previous chapter already suggested, has a straightforward answer to our question about the sources of successful creativity: any creative movement must be antisystemic. It must challenge the assumptions that underlie the dominant capitalist system, it must show that "another world is possible," and it must give voice to the voiceless. Cultural expansion stems from ideological resistance. When world-system theorists envision such expansion, they think of labor or environmental groups that attack the exploitation of workers or nature and lay the groundwork for a more just and democratic world order (Boswell and Chase-Dunn 2000: Ch. 6). By exploiting the actual contradictions of a highly unequal world-system, such groups actively help it to spiral upward toward a more rational form of socialism. This view of cultural creativity depends on a materialist description of the world-system and on materialist expectations about how it is most likely to change. While we do not share the materialist view of world order or its single-minded focus on antisystemic movements, we do think the antisystemic model has some virtues. It recognizes, for example, that resistance has a cultural component. We claim more emphatically that culture often serves as a springboard for rebellion. Contra traditional Marxists, world-system theorists also recognize that "resistance" is not limited to class-based movements. We emphasize that it can also flow from all those groups that are in some sense defined as inferior and whose world-views put them at odds with the underpinnings of world capitalism. Though we do not see world culture as the ideology of the "transnational capitalist class," we do agree with world-system theorists that at least some movements challenge it precisely because they see it as hegemonic. One lesson we take from this is that innovators often are outsiders, not resigned to perpetuate the pieties of world culture as it has crystallized.

In Seoul, Accra, and Uppsala, there are no self-professed revolutionaries in the pews. Pentecostalism is not exclusively a religion of the poor or oppressed. The faith gospel it preaches hardly counts as a ringing indictment of capitalism. Not surprisingly, some scholars think Pentecostals fit all too well into an authoritarian kind of capitalism, since they adopt the requisite discipline and value the material pay-offs (Brouwer et al. 1996). For Wallersteinians, this brand of religion produces too many whiffs of opium that are bound to suppress the pain of real discontents. Pentecostalism, in short, is hardly an antisystemic juggernaut. Yet Pentecostalism does provide a counterpoint to existing world culture. It is always "potentially in tension with the establishment" (Poewe 1994: xii). To varying degrees, Pentecostals criticize world culture as merely created by humans, a collection of false gods not worth serving. They insist on the transcendent roots of true values. Though they find their place in the rationalized institutions fostered by world culture, they also celebrate the nonrational in their own practices. Against the universality of core world-cultural principles, Pentecostals insist on the right to live their faith locally as they see fit. They ultimately reject the world as it exists; it must be cleansed of sin before Christ's Second Coming. In a fragmented world, they aim to restore a sense of personal wholeness (Droogers 1994: 34). However, this rejection is far from total. Individual salvation by faith and moral discipline, hallmarks of the Pentecostal world-view, are themselves deeply modern notions. Pentecostal faith counsels respect for authority, moderating any social critique. The Spirit enables people to live within, rather than urging them to transform, rationalized institutions. The faith builds on the broader Christian tradition that itself fostered some major world-cultural tenets. In short, Pentecostalism relates to world culture in the manner of the successful sect: creating tension while maintaining ties.

Those ties are partly institutional. Sects flourish when they find a way to fit into an existing institutional structure. As institutionalist theory suggests, world culture consists of models that provide general scripts to be enacted. These models exert pressure toward isomorphism. The more institutions grow along similar lines, the more legitimate they seem. Expanding world culture by exploring genuinely new possibilities becomes more difficult; cultures are fundamentally conservative. This gives us a good handle on the barriers to expansion, but it does not seem to leave much room for creativity. However, the institutionalist picture does suggest several avenues for expansion. Scripts may be incomplete or inconsistent, thus presenting opportunities for innovators to fill in the gaps. World culture also has no single authoritative center; instead, authority is decentralized. It is carried in part by numerous nongovernmental organizations, mostly made up of individuals voluntarily united behind common goals. The "sect" that builds on existing institutions but also fills a gap, operates globally but stays decentralized, and bundles the efforts of many individuals in a nimble network of NGOs, is thus likely to have an impact. The creative trick, from this point of view, is for innovators to adopt a familiar form while putting it to new uses.

Pentecostals constitute the ultimate religious INGO. Theirs is a religion of voluntary converts and entrepreneurial leaders. They have neither Pope nor Mecca. They are at home everywhere but bound to no single place. Avoiding entanglements with state responsibility, they have adopted a network structure that loosely binds independent congregations. This organizational form replicates that of proliferating secular organizations. Being thus embedded in existing world culture gives them both legitimacy and flexibility. Pentecostals use secular techniques and technology – conferences, marketing, and up-to-date communications are all part of their arsenal – but they pour new content into familiar forms, they adapt globally available means to ends that lie outside existing institutions. Their network structure is intended to maximize conversions. Their voluntarism has an intensely emotional quality, enabling them to involve participants more dramatically than most other INGOs. This distinctive practice carries a distinctive faith in the Spirit; its antisystemic features reflect an anti-institutional thrust. In principle, the Spirit is always moving, and staid organizations can stifle it. In the final analysis, therefore, Pentecostals exist outside the regular channels of authority and find meaning in new structures. The true church is always being built. Indeed, expansion is itself "essential to the Pentecostal movement" (Droogers 1994: 35). Their script is to have no script but Scripture. That, too, is part of its sectarian relationship to world culture: creating workable organizations while avoiding entrapment in existing institutions, building legitimate spiritual homes while staying on the move. To the channels of established world culture, Pentecostalism is flow.

Pentecostalism also represents sectarian innovation because it offers a different vision of how to "go global." Such visions, Robertsonian theory implies, should be the prime target of would-be innovators, since world culture is characterized by a set of contending visions of how the globe should be organized. Elements of world culture give meaningful form to the relationships of the units that make up the globe. Those relationships are always shifting, undergoing relativization. While a new vision or worldview can come from anywhere, Robertson suggests that it is most likely to take hold if it creatively addresses the problem of relativization. How should states be part of world society? What does it mean for the individual to be part of one humanity? What is the relationship between "our" culture and world culture? Globalization raises problems of meaning that are not settled once and for all; existing world culture contains multiple, provisional answers. Innovation therefore can come from any movement claiming to provide new answers, but these will take hold only if they help to reconstitute the identities of individuals through connections to the evolving institutions that surround them.

Pentecostalism has no single ideological program, but Pentecostals do share beliefs and practices that directly address the problem of relativization. The highly personal nature of Pentecostal conversion and immersion makes it globally significant. Becoming Pentecostal often means being lifted out of one's community of origin, forming new ties. It detaches people while recommitting them. In relation to the state, it provides a way for adherents to live as loyal citizens while reserving their ultimate loyalty for principles that transcend the state – to adopt a "postnational" identity (Marshall-Fratani 1998: 311). In relation to world society, it mobilizes adherents as elements of a self-consciously global movement aiming to conquer the world for Jesus. Though set apart by virtue of their faith, Pentecostals also establish a committed connection with humanity, all of God's creatures who are also potential believers. Pentecostalism thus works across several levels, tying individuals to community, state, and the world at large in a distinctive way. It is locally grounded, yet universally ambitious.

In the way it links the local and the global, Pentecostalism also displays a particular mode of glocalization or hybridization, as Hannerz would have it. Consciousness of the world intensifies, but what that means depends on where one stands, on the local historical experience, on the particular tradition that helps to mediate it. Universal values or principles are rarely adopted in the abstract, since they first must pass through the lens of local context and culture. Insofar as world culture becomes a set of reference points, groups relate to them very differently. Add to this the ongoing, intersecting flows of ideas, styles, and symbols that constitute the syncretic mix of any local culture, and world culture is bound to accumulate a variety of changing repertoires. World culture does not exist in some ethereal realm. On the ground, it gives meaningful form to the real life-world of real people, but in highly diverse ways. Hence, Pentecostalism also illustrates the anthropological interpretation of world culture as the organization of diversity. Expanding world culture in a significant way does not simply mean mixing yet another set of musical styles or adding yet another argument about why Eastern views of human rights differ from the standard Western models. Significant expansion is likely to come from movements that themselves offer a new way to organize diversity.

Pentecostalism is one such movement. As a sectarian challenger, is not beholden to the institutional interests of a universal church. In form and content, it is highly adaptable. As we saw above, Pentecostalism can become truly indigenized; by comparison with other faiths centered on a fixed creed, it lends itself especially well to indigenization (Martin 1990: 231, 282). Its doctrine is inherently flexible (Martin 1990: 182), not least because it elevates living practices and spiritual experience over the demands of formal belief and law. Its message is eminently "translateable" (Freston 1997: 97); people who are "free in the spirit" can more easily go their local ways (Anderson 1999b: 392). Ultimately, individuals are the judges of their own faith; this is the freedom that Pentecostals foster. But the very similarities among the churches with which we started this chapter indicate that Pentecostalism is not simply a loose collection of spiritual consumers. All Pentecostals are part of a larger but, one might say, latent church. They serve one God. They respond to one world. To think of them as all doing their own spiritual thing, as a collection of localisms, would be to underestimate the extent to which the movement also organizes Christians in a new, globally comprehensive way. Pentecostalism legitimates diversity to the point that the boundaries of denominations and kindred traditions blur, but it does have a common core.

In its pursuit of spiritual variety, Pentecostalism exploits a global cultural free space. This space is created by what we call the partial autonomy of culture. Though practically intertwined with world institutions and local practices, world culture occupies a sphere of its own. Though cultural elements are embedded in the system of states or the world economy, as we illustrated in Chapter 1, world culture also stands apart as a feature of global life. The independent organization and institutionalization of world culture explicitly encourages further experimentation. To be sure, world culture has a content that constrains what people can legitimately think and do; it is affected by the vested interests of people and institutions who wish to make their views prevail, and in that sense the space of world culture is not entirely free. Yet there is no single cultural power that sets a single direction. World culture is both differentiated from the hustle and bustle of other sectors of global life and internally open to the creative efforts of meaning suppliers seeking niches. Differentiation and pluralism, paradoxically shielded by the lack of a controlling hegemon, foster experimentation.

Pentecostalism is a "cultural" religion operating in this free space (Martin 1990: 268, 294). Of course, Pentecostals can hardly do whatever they want wherever they want. Protection for cultural experimentation is by no means universal. For Muslim clerics and Chinese officials, for example, Pentecostals constitute a threat. Yet their remarkable spread shows that the world makes room for new visions. The Pentecostal vision relates believers to state and market, as disciplined workers and proper citizens, but it claims no power over either domain. Its focus is on the spiritual needs of individuals and of the world as a whole. Its practices, as we have seen, revolve around producing certain kinds of experiences. In these respects, Pentecostalism claims a kind of independence: freedom from domination by church or state, freedom of and for faith. It thereby enacts the differentiation that helps to create the world-cultural free space. Pentecostalism also envisions a world in which individuals can seek their true purpose through voluntary association. It tolerates, indeed encourages, diversity in these searches. It asserts the very importance of the "sectarian" approach to the world that it represents. It thereby also enacts the pluralism we find characteristic of overall world culture. The Pentecostal message implies that world culture ought to be constituted in such a way as to allow for further sectarian challenges to flourish freely. By their very practice, Pentecostals strengthen the case for the need to universalize protection for cultural experimentation, religious and otherwise.

Conclusions

Pentecostalism adds new layers to world culture. For millions, it provides a new way of being in the world. In content and practice, it offers a counterpoint to the rationalist thrust of dominant world culture. It gives form to diversity. It nudges existing world culture in a particular direction with its sectarian insistence on the value of cultural free space itself. This is not to say, of course, that the whole world is about to be converted. Yet even short of wholesale conversion, the Pentecostal spirit already has left its mark on world culture.

What has made Pentecostalism so successful as a world-cultural movement? Without rehearsing all the complex reasons, we want to stress two themes in our discussion. First, in the manner of a sect reforming an established church, Pentecostalism transforms world culture from within. As we have seen, it shares much with existing world culture. It celebrates the world-cultural commitment to the individual as value and agent. As a diverse, entrepreneurial faith, it practices the liberty world culture defines. The Pentecostal version of the equality before God of all believers, including women, powerfully symbolizes world culture's secular egalitarianism. Wholesale disruption of world culture by a more radically oppositional force may not be impossible, but such a force would have to overcome the formidable accumulated weight of world-cultural principles. Second, Pentecostalism lacks the certitude often associated with sects. It is organizationally flexible, giving ample opportunity to inspiring ministers to build independent congregations and globe-spanning networks according to their own designs. It is ambiguous in its beliefs, joining the expressiveness of Spirit-filled worship with the fundamentalist faith in the inerrant sacred text, acceptance of pastoral authority with the primacy of personal religious experience, opposition to the sinful world with moral discipline in adapting to it (Droogers 2001: 48). While Pentecostals share a strong core faith, flexibility and ambiguity make for diversity. Again, a more single-minded movement bent on imposing uniformity may not be unthinkable, but it would have far greater difficulty asserting itself against an open world culture and its organization of diversity. In short, Pentecostalism's success stems as much from its "fit" with the globalized world, enabling it to reach a variety of potential believers and bridge the local and global dimensions of their lives (Droogers 2001: 54–8), as from dedicated opposition.

Pentecostals may well call this fit into question. In fundamental respects, after all, they are critical of global reality, according to their own model of the ideal world society (Droogers 2001: 54). They contest nation-states' claims to allegiance (Marshall-Fratani 1998; Coleman 2002: Ch. 9). Their sense of individuality, derived from a distinct spiritual experience and faith community, is more "expansive" than conventional secular models allow (Coleman 2000: 205–7; Van Dijk 2001). They strive to overcome sin and suffering. They expect the coming of the Kingdom of God on earth. They envision a more united global community of believers. The world as it exists is a reality to be transcended. By articulating this critical stance, Pentecostals add yet another layer to world culture, insofar as their vision becomes one of many that seek to construct an image of world order.

As we show in the next chapter, other religious movements create images far more radically at odds with existing world culture.

Chapter 9

Opposing World Culture: Islamism and the Clash of Civilizations

On February 1, 1979, millions of Iranians greeted Ayatollah Ruhollah Khomeini in Tehran upon his triumphant return from exile as the undisputed leader of Iran's Islamic Revolution. His success came as a shock. In less than a year, small, violently repressed demonstrations in provincial towns had snowballed into a mass movement, forcing the Shah, the self-styled "king of kings," to leave the country (Esposito 1990: 25). To American officials, the thought of such a popular revolution leading to the establishment of a theocratic state in Iran had been "so unlikely as to be absurd" (Arjomand 1988: 3). To foreign audiences, Khomeini's very appearance – his robe, turban, beard, and stern visage – represented a rather different image of Iran than the Westernizing version to which they had grown accustomed. Even Iranians had reason to be surprised. Few of the groups united in the Revolution, including leftist intellectuals, middle-class women, traditional merchants, and urban migrants, had consciously aimed for an Islamic alternative to the Shah; none expected its rapid success (Arjomand 1988: 106ff.). For all involved, it had been "unthinkable" (Kurzman 2004). Echoing the public shock, scholars interpreted this unintended consequence of an unexpectedly strong movement led by an unlikely figure as a "cataclysm" on a par with the French and Russian revolutions (Arjomand 1988: 3).

Ayatollah Khomeini, by contrast, expressed little surprise at his triumph. Even when his prospects had seemed dim years earlier, he had never doubted his eventual success (Kurzman 2004). Having long opposed the Shah, he viewed his triumph as the culmination of his life's work (Taheri 1986). When the Shah introduced land reform and women's right to vote in the early 1960s, threatening the status of the Shiite clergy, Khomeini's vocal resistance led the government to expel him to Iraq. As a strident critic of the regime and fervent defender of clerical status, Khomeini gained influence beyond his modest rank in the *ulama* hierarchy. In exile, Khomeini developed a new theory of government, justifying rule by an Islamic jurist and demanding the strict application of Islamic law (Khomeini and Algar 1985; Abrahamian 1993). As public discontent with the Shah increased in the 1970s, Khomeini's religious critique began to resonate with a larger audience. Untainted by dealings with the government and ascetic in his personal demeanor, he acquired a charismatic aura. When the opposition movement finally exploded in 1978, Khomeini became its leader.

Khomeini's personality and vision shaped the Islamic Revolution. By adapting Shiite tradition for specific political purposes, he gave the process its ideological direction, uniting an otherwise diverse opposition. The appeal to Islam justified the movement's sacrifices and its leader's authority. After the Revolution's victory, Khomeini turned his version of Islam from inspiring vision and tool of resistance into a program of action and a design for a new society. Discarding a short-lived secular government, he soon consolidated clerical rule to institute an Islamic Republic. According to its Constitution, the Republic creates an order cleansed of godless government, free of foreign ideas, and based only on belief in the one God, Allah. It restricts sovereignty and legislation to Him, requires submission to His command, and demands faith in the principles of Shiite Islam. Most strikingly, it also establishes the ultimate leadership of the pious jurist who takes the place of the imams of Shiite tradition in perpetuating the revolution (Arjomand 1993: 92 ff.). Preserving and obeying the Republic would henceforth be a "divine duty," Khomeini stated shortly after its founding (Arjomand 1988: 183). The Republic enforced such obedience through numerous institutions, from the clerical Council of Guardians of the Constitution and the security services to the newly Islamicized courts and media. Not surprisingly, Imam Khomeini himself held the new position of supreme religious leader until his death in 1989.

To many Iranian participants, the outcome of the Revolution constituted yet another shock. Instead of women's empowerment, the Republic brought veiling. Instead of creating democracy, it jailed secular opponents and persecuted religious minorities. As the moderate prime minister of Khomeini's first government, Mehdi Bazargan, put it, " We prayed for the rain of mercy and received floods" (quoted in Ajami 1993: 4). To outsiders, perhaps more shocking than the mere establishment of a seemingly traditionalist regime in a previously Westernizing country, was the Republic's intention to export the Revolution. Khomeini's agenda was to unite Muslims in a common struggle against West and East (Esposito 1990: 32), both by offering the Iranian Republic as an example and by active propagation of its principles.

The taking of hostages at the American embassy in Tehran in late 1979 dramatically illustrated this revolutionary ambition. Iran, it seemed, was poised to become a battering ram in a global cultural conflict.

The founding of the Islamic Republic was only the most successful instance of a much broader movement in many Muslim countries. While the Republic and Khomeini's own thinking were shaped by Shiite traditions, the world-view they put forth resonated with self-professed traditionalists across majority-Sunni areas as well (Esposito 1990: 32). From Jamaat-i-Islami in Pakistan to the Islamic Salvation Front in Algeria, from the Muslim Brotherhood in Egypt to the Taliban in Afghanistan, in the late twentieth century numerous Sunni groups advocated a similar vision of Islam returned to its roots and restored to greatness. Variously described as "militant," "radical," or "fundamentalist" (Sivan 1985; Tibi 2002), such Islamist forces have sought to create a unified Islamic community (*umma*), governed according to Islamic law (*sharia*), free from the corrupting power and ideas of infidels (*kafrs*), achieved through active struggle (*jihad*), and sustained by the sacrifice of believers striving for martyrdom (*shahada*) (Esposito 1990: 32).

The very strength of that movement, demonstrated best in Iran, challenges the case we make in this book. In the face of Islamist opposition, how can we maintain that the culture we have described really is a *world* culture? If Islamist militants successfully press an alien world-view, doesn't the resulting global cultural conflict undermine any possible growth of world culture? Isn't the lesson to be drawn from the Iranian case that the world remains hopelessly split into warring religious or cultural camps?

The short answer to the last two questions is: no. We read the implications of Islamist militance and developments in Iran very differently. In this chapter, we argue that the rise of Islamic fundamentalism does not spell the end of world culture. We first analyze the actual world-view of Islamists to understand why and in what ways they oppose world culture. We then examine the argument that growing Islamist militance shows that the world will dissolve into a "clash of civilizations," questioning the notion that solid civilizational blocs respond to the rise of world culture in uniform ways. We also stress the many countervailing factors, within Muslim societies and beyond, that favor the continued expansion and consolidation of world culture. Throughout, we refer to Iran to support our argument, not because one kind of fundamentalist experiment enables us to generalize about all of Islam but because the Iranian experience refutes the most dire predictions about Islamism's world-cultural consequences.

The Islamist Opposition

Why do Islamists oppose existing world culture? As they see it, world culture is a secular abomination that undermines the unity of the faith, corrodes cohesive Islamic societies, and imposes an alien world order. If Islam is to flourish, this world culture must be resisted and transformed, by violence if necessary. Fundamentalists have strong arguments for this view, which is rooted in a particular reading of Islamic texts and history. This reading has crystallized into a fundamentalist discourse that spans the Muslim world. Prominent contributors include the Egyptian Hassan al-Banna, founder of the Muslim Brotherhood in 1928, and his successor Sayyid Qutb (1906–66), Sayyid Abul Ala Maududi (1903–79) in India and Pakistan, and Sudan's Hasan al-Turabi. Their collective ideas have resonated widely.

To Islamist critics, the rise of world culture, instigated by Western powers, equals the decline of Islam. Once upon a time, Islam represented the pinnacle of cultural achievement and Muslim power had no equal, but the tide turned against Muslims at least from the time when the Ottoman siege of Vienna failed in 1683. Following nefarious Western plans laid "three or four centuries ago," if not since the Crusades, the "foul claws of imperialism have clutched at the heart of the lands of the people of the Quran" (Khomeini and Algar 1985: 38, 195). Thus, Napoleon "clutched" at Egypt in 1799, and Britain soon followed. After the First World War, Britain and France took over fragments of the Ottoman Empire. With the support of America, Jews have more recently "clutched" at Islamic holy ground, especially in Jerusalem. However, Muslim military defeat and political subjugation only reflect a deeper problem. Imperialism is "but a mask for the crusading spirit" (Qutb 1981: 167), that is, for the growing dominance of non-Muslim culture. The West attacked "with sword as well as with pen" (Maudoodi 1991: 14). The West won when its view of the world prevailed, its philosophy and science outpaced Muslim achievement, and its principles displaced those of Islamic tradition, ultimately leading to the "intellectual subjugation" of Muslims (Maudoodi 1991: Ch. 1). This has had painful consequences. In the world the West has made, Muslim lands are divided, Muslims are surrounded by an alien culture, Muslims have "lost the leadership of mankind to the West," and they "find the foundations of the Islamic civilization shaken" (Murad 1984: 25; Maudoodi 1991: 14). From the Islamist standpoint, therefore, the history of world culture is a history of their defeat. The Islamists' quintessential purpose is to reverse this history by leading Muslims to victory. Their motto is that "[i]t is essential for mankind to have new leadership" (Qutb 1981: 7). This new leadership must cleanse the world of the evil culture that has enveloped it and restore the noble tradition of Islam.

But why is world culture evil in the minds of Muslim opponents? The chief problem, of course, is that it is secular. The Shah's secularizing policies that so scandalized Khomeini were only one instance of a larger problem, long felt across the Islamic world, namely the intrusion of "modern" ideas into Muslim culture – what Khomeini and others called "Westoxication." Television shows and movies, nationalism and communism, women's education and bureaucratic governance, nation-states and Western economics call into question the validity of tradition and the authority of revelation (cf. Sivan 1985: 3–4). To all Muslim conservatives, these intrusions are dangerous most obviously because they are secular. They are the mark of a world in *jahiliyyah*, living in ignorance of divine guidance (Qutb 1981: 11). They comprise an "independent earthly human" system (Moussalli 1999), created by unbelievers. In this civilization, there is "no room for any fear of an all-powerful God, nor any quest for any revelation from God or Prophetic guidance" (Maudoodi 1991: 13). To stem the secularist onslaught, Islamists reassert the self-evident truth of Islam (Moussalli 1999: 25). By contrast with secular culture, they say, Islam "builds a higher system of morality by virtue of which mankind can realise its greatest potential" (Maudoodi 1984: 99). Citing the precedent of earlier revivalists such as Muhammad Abd al-Wahhab (1703–91), whose strict "Wahhabism" subsequently shaped the religious culture of Saudi Arabia, they call on believers to go back "directly" to the Qur'an and the Sunna, the sayings of the Prophet (Algar 2001: 10, 31). In restoring Islam as a civilization, human beings must not exercise the individual reason that created modern world culture but act as vessels of revelation commanded to obey God (Moussalli 1999: 23, 25). Changing "the *Jahili* system at its very roots" will leave Muslims with "a sense of triumph over error and nonsense" (Qutb 1981: 21, 143). The "faith triumphant" (Qutb 1981: Ch. XI) will replace secular world culture with a new civilization, in which "nationalism is belief, homeland is Dar al-Islam, the ruler is God, and the constitution is the Qur'an" (Qutb cited in Lawrence 1989: 216).

Secular world culture corrodes the culture of faith. Its key innovation, Islamists charge, is the idea that people can run governments, build businesses, pursue research, study at school, administer justice, and enjoy art without direct divine guidance. World culture legitimates the separation of "church" and "state" and hence fosters a variety of public institutions independent of religious tradition and control. It universalizes Europe's "division between religion and the world" (Qutb 2000: 23), an idea deliberately advanced by the "imperialists" (Khomeini and Algar 1985: 38). This creates the "hideous schizophrenia" of life carved up into "different slices" (Berman 2003: 77, 80). Against the variety and division of world culture, fundamentalists assert that their faith is "essentially a unity": "Islam chose to unite earth and heaven in a single system, present both in the heart of the individual and the actuality of society" and "it reckons all the activities of life as comprehending worship in themselves" (Qutb 2000: 26–8). Hence, "there can be no separation between the faith and the world, between theology and social practice" (ibid.: 30). This follows, they claim, from the chief tenet of the faith, namely that there is no God [deity] except God. *Tawhid*, this central oneness, "penetrates through the whole system of life" (Qutb 1981: 32). Because God is one and God is all, "nothing can be left out of His Lordship" (Murad 1984: 30). Because "nothing can be left out," the only proper Islamic society is an Islamic state applying Islamic law. In such a state, "[p]olitics is part of religion. Caesar and what belongs to Caesar is for God Almighty alone" (al-Banna cited in Lawrence 1989: 215–16). Such a state "cannot evidently restrict the scope of its activities. Its approach is universal and all-embracing . . . In such a state no one can regard any field of his affairs as personal and private" (Maudoodi cited in Arjomand 1993: 113). It is also an ideological state: "the state in Islam is based on an ideology and its objective is to establish that ideology" (ibid.: 113). By contrast with ever-changing world culture, this "ideology" holds that Islamic civilization is based on "eternal and unchangeable" principles:

> the worship of God alone, the foundation of human relationships on the belief in the Oneness of God, the supremacy of the humanity of man over material things, the development of human values and the control of animalistic desires, respect for the family, the assumption of being the representative of God on earth according to His guidance and instruction, and in all affairs of this viceregency the rule of God's law [*sharia*] and the way of life prescribed by Him.   (Qutb 1981: 104)

"God's law" is more than a formal set of rules and procedures. It encompasses every aspect of society, from forms of dress and hygiene to divorce and economic activity. It comprises "everything legislated by God for ordering man's life; it includes the principles of belief, principles of administration and justice, principles of morality and human relationships, and principles of knowledge" (Qutb 1981: 107). Thus, the *sharia* is a blueprint for a "complete social system" (Khomeini and Algar 1985: 43). Iran's Islamic Republic was intended to be just such a system. Since "[a] body of laws alone is not sufficient for a society to be reformed," the system had to be led by the supreme Islamic scholar who could properly combine religious and political authority (Khomeini and Algar 1985: 40, 341–2). In keeping with the fundamentalist principle that "nothing can be left out," his Republic pursued the Islamization of society. Only this could remedy the "hideous schizophrenia" of modernity.

In addition to tearing apart the fabric of a godly society, world culture threatens it with dangerous ideas. Consumerism tempts individuals to focus on satisfying their material interests rather than abide by religious obligations, but the return to Islam will help them resist, as demonstrated by the unique success of Islam in eradicating alcohol consumption (Maudoodi 1991: 55–6). Individualism leads people to act on sexual impulses, including homosexual desires, without moral censure, but a truly "progressive" society will "control the animal desires" to safeguard the "peace and stability of the family" (Qutb 1981: 98–9). By claiming a "monopoly of knowledge" (Murad 1984: 32), science celebrates human over divine power and creates a "poisonous" hostility toward religion (Qutb 1981: 116), but Muslims can pursue knowledge of nature as long as it serves the higher purpose of recognizing God's greatness. Modern educational institutions are devoted only to disseminating secular knowledge, yet in an Islamic state, "the concept of Islam should dominate in the teaching of each and every science and art" (Maudoodi 1991: 174). Nation-states and popular sovereignty, treated as idols in world culture (Murad 1984: 33), have led to division and strife; Islam offers a superior alternative in the unity of the Muslim community and in forms of popular consultation (*shura*) that substitute for illusory democracy. A free-market economy leads to boundless greed and divisive competition as societies pursue wealth for its own sake; Islam, by contrast, subjects economic activity to religious rules, including a prohibition on charging interest (Qutb 2000: Ch. 6). To paraphrase the medieval Muslim philosopher al-Ghazzali, world culture has shattered the glass of Muslim civilization. Through the Islamization of society, fundamentalist opponents aim to melt the shards into a single whole again.

Islamists envision more than mere restoration, however. They intend to save humankind (Moussalli 1999: 57) by rooting out the evil of secular world culture. As Khomeini put it after his victory, "we must strive to export our Revolution" (Khomeini and Algar 1985: 286). In their "revolt against the dominant world order," fundamentalists aim to create a new kind of world civilization (Tibi 2002: 15, 84). Islam, after all, is a "universal religion" (Qutb 2000: 199), centered on the "universal declaration of the freedom of man on the earth from every authority except God's authority" (Qutb 1981: 69). This call to freedom is not confined by geographic or racial boundaries but is valid for all humanity (Qutb 1981: 74).

In fact, only Islam advances the true unity of humanity (Qutb 1983: 74–6). As a unique way of life "harmonious with human nature," Islam is the "only system" capable of replacing the dying civilization created by the West, the only one eligible for the "new leadership" humankind needs (Qutb 1981: 7–8). If the direction of the world "train" is to be changed, Islamists say, "some believers in God should rise to [the] occasion and wrest the locomotive's control from the atheists" (Maudoodi 1991: 16). Their true place "is not at the tail of the caravan, but where we may grasp the leading rein" (Qutb 2000: 318). Thus will they lead the "caravan" out of the cultural desert toward the oasis of a new caliphate, a new era of Muslim rule (Tibi 2002: 146).

Reaching this destination will require struggle. According to Islamists, God commands Muslims to engage in *jihad* as an active, public struggle "striving to make [Islam's] system of life dominant in the world" (Qutb 1981: 76). At a minimum, this is a struggle to defend the honor of Islam against the imperialists and their main supporters, the Jews (Khomeini and Algar 1985: 276). But fundamentalists are not interested in defense alone. As Khomeini's calculated success illustrates, their struggle is profoundly ambitious: since the "fundamental Islamic principles are revolutionary" (Qutb 1983: 72), it follows that "[t]he objective of the Islamic movement, in this world, is a revolution in leadership" (Maudoodi 1984: 71). It must use "physical power" to abolish "the organizations and authorities of the *Jahili* system" and it must attack established institutions and traditions "to release human beings from their poisonous influences" (Qutb 1981: 55, 75). Such physical power must be applied by a vanguard (Qutb 1981: 12), an elite group of dedicated believers willing to make the ultimate sacrifice for their community by becoming martyrs (Sivan 1985: 187–8). Yet, however violent its means, the purpose of *jihad* is not destruction. Rather, it is

> to establish God's authority in the earth; to arrange human affairs according to the true guidance provided by God; to abolish all the Satanic forces and Satanic systems of life; to end the lordship of one man over others, since all men are creatures of God and no one has the authority to make them his servants or to make arbitrary laws for them . . . to secure complete freedom for every man throughout the world.   (Qutb 1981: 70)

In this way, *jihad* achieves a "universal change" by establishing "peace of conscience, domestic peace, national peace and international peace," all founded on "universal justice" (Qutb 1983: 72).

In practice, the pursuit of "national peace and international peace" has not been Islamists' most apparent purpose. For decades, militants violently targeted mostly local symbols of oppression and decadence. In Iran, of course, the Shah embodied secular evil. In Saudi Arabia, radicals attacked the Grand Mosque shortly after Khomeini's return to Tehran. Egyptian President Anwar Sadat was assassinated by fundamentalists in 1981. In the 1990s, Algerian militants intensified their struggle against their country's military government. Over time, however, *jihad* went global. Exiled by Middle Eastern governments, Islamists established networks outside their home countries. Modern technology, banking, and transportation enabled them to organize many followers across many countries. They drew resources from the economic system they despised, as illustrated by Saudi financing of radical religious schools (*madrasas*) in Pakistan and radical mosques in Europe. By the late twentieth century, Islamists were a genuinely global force, advancing the global project envisioned by their leading intellectuals.

As their global scope began to match their global ambitions, the most aggressive militants increasingly focused on the linchpin of world culture and the chief oppressor of Muslims: the United States, the "Great Satan." The struggle for an Islamic world order became a struggle against America. The hostage-taking at the American embassy in Tehran was a prelude to more violent actions – the bombing of US Marine barracks in Beirut in 1983, the 1993 attack on the World Trade Center in New York, subsequent attacks on American military and diplomatic facilities, and finally the brazen terrorist attack by operatives of al-Qaeda on New York City and Washington, DC, in 2001. According to an al-Qaeda spokesman, this action was a historic strike against "the head of heresy in our modern world" and its "infidel democratic regime that is based upon separation of religion and state," a regime that "seeks to impose on the world a religion that is not Allah's" by its own use of "terror, arrogant policy, and suppression against the [world's] nations" (Geith 2002). Since America "is immersed in the blood of Muslims," Abu Geith said, the people killed in New York City "were no more than a fair exchange" for its victims. The ultimate religious demand, namely "that the entire earth must be subject to the religion of Allah," justified any means. His words echoed those of al-Qaeda's leader, Osama bin Laden, in an interview a few years earlier, when he explained that "[t]he call to wage war against America was made because America spear-headed the crusade against the Islamic nation," and that, as long as the "present injustice" continues, the battle will move "inevitably to American soil," a battle in which the military and civilians "are all targets" (Bin Laden 1998).

As the extreme manifestation of Muslim militance, the events of 2001 produced an even greater sense of shock and "cataclysm" than the Iranian

Revolution. They showed that some militant Muslims were so implacably opposed to the culture of infidels, so embittered at American power, that they were willing to pay any price to attack the Great Satan. They showed that the Great Satan itself was vulnerable to a determined ideological foe fighting on behalf of a new world order inspired by a religious vision. They seemed to confirm dire predictions about radical Islam as a force of global division. Years earlier, in fact, students of fundamentalism had argued that the Islamist revival heralded a "clash of civilizations" (Lewis 1990). This clash had now reached American soil. By the symbolic message it conveyed, global terror thus lent support to a particular argument about the state and direction of world culture, namely that the world is divided into irreconcilable cultural blocs mired in deepening conflict that fatally undermines any overarching world culture. Because it challenges our own perspective on world culture, we will examine the most persuasive version of this argument in greater detail. We then respond to it critically by arguing that it misreads the implications of Islamism.

The "Clash of Civilizations"

In 1993, Samuel Huntington published one of the most influential essays ever written by a political scientist. "World politics," he argued, "is entering a new phase" (Huntington 1993: 22). In this phase, "[t]he great divisions among humankind and the dominating source of conflict will be cultural . . . The clash of civilizations will dominate global politics" (ibid.: 22). Though Huntington hedged his bet with a question mark in his title, "The Clash of Civilizations?", his essay erased any doubt about where he stood. Civilizational consciousness was bound to increase, and as a result the "conflict between groups in different civilizations will be more frequent, more sustained and more violent" (48). The main axis of confrontation will be relations between "the West and the Rest." Though Huntington suggested measures to contain the clash, he concluded that "[f]or the relevant future, there will be no universal civilization, but instead a world of different civilizations, each of which," he added hopefully, "will have to learn to coexist with the others" (49). For now, as he put it in a subsequent book, we live in a "multipolar, multicivilizational world" (1997: 21). Across this world run civilizational fault lines, each liable to erupt in violence as the cultural plates collide. The most dramatic collisions, Huntington feared, would occur along Islam's "bloody borders," from Nigeria to Chechnya to Kashmir (ibid.: 254 ff.).

Why should civilizational battles come to dominate the world scene? Huntington begins his argument with the end of the Cold War. For decades after the Second World War, the ideological conflict between communism and liberal democracy, embodied in a struggle between two superpowers, divided countries into three "worlds," each defined by its relationship to the two chief contenders for ideological supremacy (1993: 23). With the demise of the Soviet Union, "[t]hose divisions are no longer relevant" (ibid.: 23). The declining significance of ideology as a source of conflict enables other kinds of conflict to come to the fore. Though nation-states "will remain the most powerful actors in world affairs" (22), Huntington argues that the new conflicts will not simply reprise old-fashioned struggles about wealth and power. Nation-states now command less allegiance from their citizens and exercise less control over their affairs, making it more difficult for them to mobilize people and resources to advance their interests. Increasingly, nation-states are shaped by cultural identities and enmeshed in distinct civilizational blocs (1997: 21). As ideology and nationalism recede, the cause of civilizations takes over. This applies especially to Islam. The demise of communism and the failure of nationalism led Muslims to recover pride in their religious heritage as a source of meaning and suste-nance. In the absence of a common foe, the old, "deeply conflictual relation between Islam and Christianity" resumed in a new form (ibid.: 209–11). For the West, the underlying problem "is not Islamic fundamen-talism. It is Islam, a different civilization whose people are convinced of the superiority of their culture and are obsessed with the inferiority of their culture" (217).

Civilizations are so important in global conflict because they are "basic" – they comprise deep-rooted values and institutions that provide different answers to life's great questions (1993: 25). Civilizations are also the "broadest" and "most comprehensive" cultural entities, binding smaller subcultures to a shared world-view (1997: 42–3). Though they may adapt and change, civilizations endure by virtue of powerful "structuring ideas" that shape the identity of individuals and communities over centuries (ibid.: 45). Typically, "[r]eligion is a central defining characteristic of civilizations" (47). Recognizing that their boundaries are rarely clear-cut, Huntington identifies a limited number of "true" civilizations: the Western, Latin-American, Islamic, Sinic, Hindu, Orthodox, Buddhist, and, with some caveats, African and Japanese (26–7, 45–7). These civilizations become caught up in conflict, among groups along their fault lines and among their leading states (1993: 29), because the values they contain matter so much to so many. When the stakes are highest and groups face their greatest troubles, Huntington implies, they are most likely to fall back on what is most "basic, enduring, and comprehensive." This is precisely what happened in the "Islamic resurgence": faced with the traumas of modernization, in states that left basic needs unmet, Muslims found identity and loyalty in religious community (1997: 98). In many instances, lacking effective states capable of creating actual "cohesion," all Muslims had to fall back on was radicalized religious "consciousness" (ibid.: 174 ff.).

Civilizational clash intensifies because there is no universal civilization to contain it. Huntington acknowledges that civilizations may share certain basic values, such as "murder is evil," or typical accomplishments, such as literacy (1997: 56–7), but he thinks these are only a thin veneer covering a wide variety of actual cultures. When Westerners assume that there is a universal civilization that contains their values – "beliefs in individualism, market economies, and political democracy" (ibid.: 57) – they mistake the elite "Davos culture" of business people and diplomats for a truly global culture. Similarly, the fizz and fun of a universal pop culture hardly penetrate people's deepest desires and global media do not produce global agreement (58–9). English may serve as a convenient lingua franca, but "different Englishes" and indigenous competition make it far from universal (59–63). In fact, the very concept of a universal civilization is a "distinctive product of Western civilization" (68). Rather than lauding this concept, Huntington thinks it is a false, immoral, and dangerous form of wishful thinking (310). It is dangerous because it provokes violent reaction and it is immoral because it seeks to establish values through power. Not surprisingly, "[w]hat is universalism to the West is imperialism to the rest" (184). The Western faith is false because it is based on the idle hopes that the demise of communism will lead to the universal embrace of Western liberalism (68) and that increased interaction will produce a peaceful common culture (69). Modernization may create some commonality across societies as they adopt new economic institutions and rely on new technical knowledge, but even this does not create "homogeneity" because the non-West tries to become modern without becoming Western (69 ff.). To Huntington, Islam most dramatically refutes the Western dream of universality. Islam resists domination, resents imposition, and avoids convergence. Most Muslim countries have actually witnessed increasing resistance to the "imperialist" and "godless" West, and even liberal Muslims now stress the differences between "them" and "us" (213–14). Instead of being bridged, the cracks along the fault line are getting wider.

The behavior of the West fuels the clash. On the one hand, the West has had "an overwhelming impact" on others (302) through industrialization, modernization, and the spread of Western ideas. As Westerners made their way into the world, they uprooted local traditions, claimed control over territory, and exploited the resources of others. As noted, they aggressively asserted the universal validity of their ideas. Over time, the West's arrogant action provoked rebellious reactions. Today, "[a] West at the peak of its power confronts non-Wests that increasingly have the desire, the will and the resources to shape the world in non-Western ways" (1993: 26). Paradoxically, Western decline also fuels the clash. The West commands a steadily smaller proportion of the world's wealth, weapons, and people (1997: 82 ff.). The United States risks being "de-Westernized" as multi-culturalism dilutes its commitment to the Western tradition (ibid.: 305–7). The West thus loses power and confidence. Soon, "[t]he age of Western dominance will be over" (91). But as the West fades, others surge; its very weakness provokes reaction. The "rest" smells blood. Thus Huntington's diagnosis echoes the analysis of Islamists who have called for decisive action against an evil but vulnerable West. Escalating Islamist terror seems to represent what Huntington fears and Islamists desire – a growing clash of civilizations.

As our summary makes clear, Huntington offers the academic mirror image of the Islamist world-view. Both perceive a world made up of irrec-oncilable blocs, both regard religion as the basic source of identity, both blame the West for the troubles of others, both deride the pretension of a universal culture, both see the rest rising up against the West, and both foresee intensifying struggles in a multipolar world. Unlike Islamists, Hunt-ington wants the West to survive and civilizations to coexist, but even his recommendations, such as urging the West to have greater faith in Western values, parallel those of Islamists, who advocate the same approach on their side of the divide. By comparison with the all-consuming clash, Hunting-ton gives the possible "remaking of world order" short shrift in any case. For our purposes, the key implication of his argument is that world culture as we have described it in this book is either an insignificant façade or an arrogant but idle hope. We reject this implication. Huntington's view of world culture is mistaken about world affairs, the challenge of Islamism, and the strengths of "universal" civilization.

World Culture vs. the Clash of Civilizations

Huntington is a remarkably poor guide to world events. He describes the Bosnian conflict of the 1990s as "a war of civilizations" (1997: 288), but both in Bosnia and in Kosovo the United States decisively intervened on behalf of Muslims across the supposed civilizational divide, a move Huntington confusingly ascribes to both American "civilizational realpolitik" and "idealism, moralism, humanitarian instincts, naiveté, and ignorance concerning the Balkans" (ibid.: 289–90). Similarly, he views the Gulf War of 1990–1 as part of an "intercivilizational quasi war" (216), a version that might have fit Saddam Hussein's propaganda but would have surprised both Kuwait and Arab states such as Saudi Arabia and Egypt that fought on the American side. Contrary to Huntington's claim that US intervention in the affairs of others is inherently dangerous (312), its defeat of the Taliban in 2001 removed one source of terrorist danger, was welcomed by many Afghans and, like other US actions, provoked none of the "kin-country rallying" his views predict. Huntington envisions a grand Confucian–Islamic alliance of the "rest" against the West (1993: 45), but he recognizes that Chinese enthusiasm has been "muted" (1997: 240), an understatement that fails to take into account the internal "bloody border" with Islam in western China. Within civilizations, as well, Huntington's expectations do not hold up, as illustrated by "orthodox" Bulgaria's effort to ally with the USA and join the European Union, spurning its supposed "kin" in Russia. In fact, many recent geopolitical conflicts, particularly involving Islamic regions, do not fit the clash thesis at all. Even on his home court of world politics, Huntington's argument loses.

This failure affects his argument about Islam. According to Huntington, the problem for the West is "Islam" as such, not simply "fundamentalism." It is the problem of a whole civilization consistently oppressed, divorced from its heritage, seeking collective redemption, and therefore violently arrayed against the West and others. As its "bloody borders" show, the clash of civilizations is "Islam vs. the rest" more than "the West vs. the rest." However, even our brief sample of world events above indicates that Huntington consistently underestimates the strength of cross-civilizational ties, as Muslims in Bosnia, Kosovo, Kuwait, and Afghanistan can attest. He downplays the virulence of intra-civilizational struggles, such as the Iran–Iraq war, the Gulf War, and the Algerian civil war, which have cost more Muslim lives than the supposed clash of civilizations. The absence of "kin-country rallying" on behalf of the Taliban or al-Qaeda, or for that matter behind Khomeini and his Islamic Revolution, further shows the importance of fault lines within Islam, which thus far have limited the appeal of violent groups claiming to act on behalf of Islam as a whole. Such fault lines have appeared even within countries, as reformist opposition to the conservative policies of Khomeini's successors in Iran illustrates. In fact, the very thought that Islam and Islamism are identical, and that therefore Islamist terror is a "civilizational" struggle, is anathema to many Muslims. By equating the two Huntington adopts a mirror image of the Islamist version of Islam – but this image, all too common among commentators on Islam, is distorted.

His misreading of Islam shows the weakness of his overall argument about civilizations (Ajami 1993). To Huntington, civilizations are tight bundles of beliefs and values, not loose grab bags. He mistakes an abstract category for existential reality; civilizations are neatly organized wholes only in the eye of the academic beholder. Real civilizations are composites, cobbled together from long histories and complex exchanges with others: Iran, for example, combines an Islamic and Persian heritage, both influenced by Western imports. Nor is a civilization the unshakable bedrock Huntington makes it out to be. Because civilizations are complex, they provide no certain answers to new problems. They may inform and give meaning to social life, but this always requires creative work. The claim that civilization is a bedrock, and therefore requires ultimate loyalty, is itself an ideological claim. In Iran, for example, the return to Islam was itself innovative, using *sharia* for new purposes and establishing a new form of religious rule, while at the same time the claim that the Revolution defended a whole civilization served a clear ideological purpose. Huntington argues that such ultimate loyalty will intensify as civilizations clash, but this assumes that encounters must take the form of hostile confrontation, and that, like the East and West in Kipling's phrase, "the twain shall never meet." In practice, the twain have often already met, in beneficial exchanges as much as in destructive clashes, as "Westernizing" Iranian opposition to the Islamic Republic illustrates. Because civilizations do not operate as solid wholes, it is also difficult to draw neat and meaningful boundary lines, as Huntington attempts to do. For example, what distinguishes "Latin-American" from "Western," or "Japanese" from "Sinic" civilization? What does a fault line between "Western" and "orthodox" mean if individual Bulgarians happily try to be both? How meaningful, then, is the concept of "civilization" itself? The case for the clash, therefore, is flawed. The historical differences among cultural regions, though real and enduring in some cases, do not entail the dramatic division of the world into battling blocs.

Huntington recognizes that "the existence of civilizations in the plural" has been quite compatible with "the spread of civilization in the singular" and that, for all their differences, "modern societies have much in common" (1997: 57, 68). Yet, as we have seen, he proceeds to dismiss what he calls "universal" civilization as neither universal nor much of a civilization. He offers three arguments. His "different Englishes" argument suggests that any cultural variations undermine universality, but of course, the same applies within civilizations. If a single spoken language is the mark of a civilization, the Chinese civilization Huntington touts does not in fact exist. Huntington adds that the common experience of modernity cannot produce world culture because societies do not "necessarily merge into homogeneity" (ibid.: 69). Since the civilizations he identifies are themselves by no means homogeneous, it is unreasonable to require such merging for world culture. Huntington further suggests that trade and communications do not generate a common culture because they fail to produce "peace or common feeling" (67). Such harmony would be a tall order for any civilization. Applied seriously, the same criterion would mean that all civilizations that have witnessed internal struggle would not be worthy of the name. Since Europe has had more than its share of internal struggle, the very existence of "the West" as a coherent entity becomes questionable. Ironically, then, Huntington's criticisms of universal civilization actually call into question his own model of civilizations. To escape the conundrum, we offer a straightforward alternative: global variety and conflict are not incompatible with the emergence of a common world culture. Indeed, they are inevitable components of that emergence.

Finally, Huntington's contradictory assessment of the West further weakens his case. On the one hand, he argues that civilizational identities are basic and becoming more salient, yet on the other hand Europe and the USA appear to be losing their attachment to traditional Western values – in America's case because of the popularity of "multiculturalism" and, most recently, because of the influx of immigrants from Latin America (Huntington 2004). "The West" sees itself as having "unparalleled" dominance but at the same time its hegemony is objectively declining. Huntington laments the "sheer chaos" in many places in the 1990s yet argues that intervention by the West was nevertheless "most dangerous." He urges the West to return to its civilizational roots and "believe in itself" yet chides it for holding on to imperial and immoral universalism. He thinks the risk to the West is that "multicultural" America, favoring group rights over individual rights, will pull away from Europe, but he fails to inquire into equally "group"-oriented European deviations from the presumed Western individualist tradition. From such a confused diagnosis the ailing Western patient can draw no comfort. The West's predicament illustrates a larger confusion about what Huntington expects from civilizations. He suggests both that civilizations naturally advance their own values and that peace in a multicivilizational world depends on their search for commonality. What, then, is a self-respecting civilization to do?

Huntington misinterprets world events, misjudges Islam, misunderstands civilizations, and misprizes world culture. We have criticized him on these points partly because his perspective has been so influential. By refuting his argument, we strengthen the case for our own approach to world culture. To the extent that Islamists share the vision of a clash of civilizations, criticizing Huntington also means challenging the Islamists' self-understanding. In one respect, to be sure, both they and Huntington are right: Islamic fundamentalists do indeed oppose some aspects of world culture in abstract thought and violent action. But we deny that the Islamists represent all of Islam. Their vision of the future is not the most likely path of a whole civilization. Though greatly intensified geopolitical tension or an unexpectedly effective al-Qaeda-style terrorist campaign may yet produce a global implosion through a fiery clash of civilizations, from our vantage point such a result appears implausible. In fact, fundamentalism operates within world culture. The forces of world culture apply to it as well. While culture by itself is never a secure bulwark against violence, world culture constrains what terrorist violence can accomplish. Instead of a clash of civilizations, our argument therefore suggests a very different kind of engagement of Islam with the world. Islam is not fated to clash with "the rest" and world culture will not succumb to *jihad*.

Fundamentalism and World Culture

When Khomeini's forces seized control of Iran, they wasted no time in turning their victory to advantage in a global propaganda war. Iran had to serve as a symbol of the "faith triumphant." The Great Satan had to be taken down a notch. As the Islamic Republic took hold at home, the revolution had to be exported to remake world order abroad. In word and deed, Khomeini thus tried to make a global statement. It was precisely this kind of statement that led Robertson to rethink the direction of globalization (Robertson and Chirico 1985; Robertson 1992). As he saw it, the process produced both a common frame of reference from which to view the global circumstance and multiple responses to an increasingly common global experience. Fundamentalists like Khomeini offered one contentious response from one distinct standpoint. At first blush, one could argue that Robertson supported a clash of civilizations thesis long before Huntington by stressing that world culture takes shape through vigorous contestation regarding global problems everyone experiences, interpreted from different viewpoints. However, for Robertson the clash scenario is too simple. For all its oppositional rhetoric, even Iran operated within a common world-cultural frame of reference. Within this frame, Robertson thought, the very assertion of such a "particular" view, asserting the value of one's own culture as globally significant, itself became increasingly legitimate. By pressing one version of "globality," fundamentalists were also playing a global game.

At the same time, Robertson argued that the game was more complex than the fundamentalists, in Iran and elsewhere, realized. Though Khomeini's stance was ostensibly wholly opposed to any "Western" rules, and the hostage-taking at the American embassy deliberately violated long-standing international law, the Islamic Republic sought a kind of global legitimacy for the distinct "voice" of Muslims, staking a claim to a position and world-view it demanded others to respect. In doing so, Khomeini saw himself as spokesperson for the grievances of all Muslims, yet his revolution resonated with few Sunnis abroad. Iran stood out as an exception even among Muslim countries, its official stance toward the world shaped by its own tradition and problems. In fact, when Sunni fundamentalists seized control of Afghanistan next door, relations with Iran were actually hostile. The absence of even rhetorical kin-country bandwagoning showed that there was no single Islamic or fundamentalist response to the cultural effects of globalization. This fits Robertson's argument that relativization has variable effects even within seemingly cohesive civilizations. World culture, in his view, constitutes a kind of contest about how best to make sense of the global condition, but many individuals and groups are bound to participate. In claiming to speak for a whole civilization, fundamentalists add to the complexity of the contest. World culture fosters a consciousness of a single world, but due to multifarious confrontations it is not easily reduced to the *tawhid* or oneness Islamists celebrate.

The diversity of Islam reinforces Robertson's argument about the complexity of world culture. In fact, Islam is diverse in diverse ways. It is traditionally divided into Sunni, Shiite, and Sufi-mystical branches. For all their emphasis on a common text, Muslims vary in the degree to which they follow a particular scriptural tradition. The textual canon itself has been subjected to different forms of interpretation, as illustrated by the numerous schools of Islamic jurisprudence. Especially after the formation of nation-states, Islam's bearing on public life varied greatly – pervasive in places like Saudi Arabia, more diffuse in countries like Indonesia. Not surprisingly, Muslim intellectuals drawing on such varied sources and local traditions have responded to the encounter with modernity in very different ways, with liberals and reformists challenging Islamists. Even among Islamists themselves there is no consensus. They argue, for example, about the precise demands of Islamic law, the desirability of the Caliphate as historical model, and the wisdom of having clerics serve as rulers (cf. Moussalli 1999: 82, 107). The Khomeini version of Islamism is just that – one version that selects from the diverse diversities a particular combination of answers to questions many other Muslims answer differently.

This version of Islam came about through the interaction of "local" tradition, represented by clerical leaders of the revolution, and global forces specifically impinging on Iran. In this respect it follows a pattern of creolization very similar to that which Hannerz finds elsewhere. It took hold the way it did because, as a fairly developed society, Iran was already situated at a particular disjuncture of Appadurai's "scapes." The anthropological reading of world culture as the organization of diversity points to an "ecumene" of ever-changing, no-longer-quite-local cultures rather than a confrontation of mutually closed blocs. Iran's Islamic Republic has not escaped contamination by world culture. It represents the glocalization of fundamentalism. This contaminating glocalization was apparent in the very founding of the Islamic Republic. After all, a republic is a form of government not found in the Qur'an, but well established globally as a preferred state model, in this case adapted to serve a new religious cause. Iran continued to function as a nation-state with all the symbolism and all the organizations one would expect, while subordinating these to the demands of Shiite Islam. It drew its strength from the revolution that brought it to power, and this revolution followed in the non-Islamic footsteps of others who established the idea of the total transformation of society as a global tradition (Eisenstadt 1999; Berman 2003: 42). The politicization of Islam in Iran was an innovation (Tibi 2002), amounting to an Islamic version of the "invention of tradition" (Kurzman 2003: 17) that characterized many previous groups and nations establishing themselves as legitimate global actors. As the Iranian case shows, Islamists are not really fundamentalist in any case, if by that we mean that they in fact return to firm foundations.

Insofar as they attain power, the active remaking of society by adapting global institutions to local circumstances deeply involves fundamentalists in the institutionalization process Meyer and his colleagues have stressed. From this perspective, it was not surprising that one of the first acts of the new Republic was to promulgate a constitution, and a French-inspired one at that (Mayer 1993: 118) – an act without Qur'anic justification. As an ostensibly fundamentalist regime continues in power, Meyer would add, it

takes on all the responsibilities the world polity assigns to non-Islamic counterparts, creating pressures not easily met by purely "Islamic" solutions.
Such pressures are illustrated by Iran's struggles to create a national identity that is also "Islamic" through its education system and media, even as
public demands for women's higher education and for imported popular
entertainment also increase (Tehranian 1993: 367). To meet such demands,
the Islamic Republic has expanded educational opportunities for girls,
whose enrollment at all levels of education nearly matches that of boys
(UNESCO 2003). In striving to maintain its military stature, the Republic
has had to cultivate its scientific establishment. Though hardly liberal by
Western standards, it has also preserved at least the trappings of democracy. Wholesale rejection of world culture would distress Iranian soccer
fans, who expect their national team to do well in international competition and have used celebrations of Iranian successes in the World Cup
tournament to "slacken" the control of the state (Sanadjian 2002: 156).
Of course, this does not imply that fundamentalists must "give in" to
world culture. In the case of Iran, as Meyer's argument recognizes, the
country's still-limited economic, technological, and political ties, reflected
in its low ranking on an index measuring the extent of a country's globalization (Kearney 2004), mitigate outside normative pressure. Beyond Iran,
specific groups will continue radical resistance, acting on their Islamist
world-view. The experience of Afghanistan in the late 1990s shows that
world-cultural pressure can be resisted by fundamentalists in power, as the
Taliban blankly prohibited the education of girls and the use of modern
media. But these are exceptions that affirm the global institutional rule.
There are not many places left where Taliban-style isolation is even con-
ceivable. Elsewhere, the pressure to take part in world culture, to adopt and
adapt, is far greater. Once fundamentalists take to the global stage, they are
more likely to advance the acculturation of Islam than the Islamization of
world culture.

Stressing complexity, diversity, and acculturation, world-system theorists
might object, downplays the oppositional stance of Islamists. They resist
the imperialism that has tainted world culture, they oppose the corruption
of their societies by capitalist forces, and they recognize neoliberalism for
the menace it is (Lubeck 2000; Pasha 2000). Islamists therefore are among
the most militant "antisystemic" warriors and in some ways seem akin to
the antiglobalization movement we discussed in Chapter 7. Their *jihad* is
also a struggle against the capitalist world-system. The more the system
expands, the more it produces discontent among Muslim victims, the more
their resistance gains support, and the more integrated the *umma* becomes

as a result, undermining the culture of the world-system. Scholars sympathetic to this view applied it to the Iranian revolution in the 1980s. The Shah had been a puppet of Western interests, they argued, and the revolution had more to do with restoring local control over vital resources than with the grand design of religious fanatics. In this reading, Islamization was not the purpose of the revolution but an ideological means to an end, namely effective disruption of world-systemic incorporation of the Middle East. However, this materialist interpretation of Iran, and of fundamentalism generally, does not carry us very far. For one thing, Khomeini's religious vision was more than a means, and the same goes for the Islamists whose views we summarized above. Their God is God, not oil. Their Satan is a whole godless culture, not just the IMF. There were no Islamist organizations among the antiglobalization activists in Porto Alegre (though the European branch of the World Social Forum made common cause with some Muslim activists [Caldwell 2003]). Because Islamists define their struggle in different terms, it also has different, distinctly religious consequences, as the fusion of religious and public spheres in the Islamic Republic confirms.

More important for our purposes, the antisystemic interpretation of Islamism ignores the reaction such resistance provokes. By its own Marxist standards, it obscures the dialectical process in which cultural contradictions play out. Instead of triggering a clash of civilizations pitting Islam against the West, the Islamists' most dramatic actions actually provoke a cross-civilizational response by the international community. This response has taken different forms, including direct counterattacks, illustrated by the defeat of the Taliban by US-led forces in 2001; revived integration of Muslim countries into the world-system, as urged by UN experts in an indictment of Arab human development efforts (UNDP 2002) and a call for "building a knowledge society" (UNDP 2003); expressions of solidarity with victims of Islamist repression, triggered most visibly in 1989 when Ayatollah Khomeini issued a *fatwa* against Salman Rushdie for insulting the Prophet in his book *The Satanic Verses*; and a wave of systematic intellectual critiques (Scruton 2002; Berman 2003). Islamist opposition to world culture stimulates renewed awareness of universal interests and values among the "rest."

"Global" efforts at preempting a true clash are matched by "internal" Muslim opposition to the Islamist transformation of Islam. In conjunction with repression and co-optation by individual governments, the gathering forces of this opposition are now engaged in a battle for the soul of Islam. Broadly speaking, the opposition advocates more liberal interpretations of

Islamic law that would legitimate modernizing reform (Kurzman 1998); an "Islamic Reformation" that allows civil freedom and equal participation in a nonreligious public sphere (An-Na'im 1990); an Islamic version of "cross-cultural morality" that bolsters universal human rights (Tibi 2002); a revival of common concern for "human dignity" to complement such rights (Muzaffar 2002); and support for the doctrine of *taqarub* or rapprochement between Muslims and non-Muslims (Doran 2004). By contrast with Islamists, their Muslim critics stress the value of open debate, citing the saying of Muhammad, "The difference of opinion in my community is a divine mercy" (Bulliet 2002). They typically point to the role of human interpretation in bringing sacred precepts to bear on contemporary society, including the "dynamic creative and negotiative process" of developing doctrine on core issues, such as justifications for the use of violence (Abou El Fadl 2001: 336). In different ways, such critics also seek to adapt at least some "mobile ideas" in world culture to achieve a "creative synthesis," for example in the form of a new kind of "Islamic democracy" (Feldman 2003: 36). Disenchanted with failed Islamic regimes and drawing on their own increasing international ties, they pursue an "Islamic rights discourse" that shows "no sign of abating" (Kurzman 2002: 151–2).

Muslim opposition to Islamism is not limited to intellectuals on the margins of Islamic discourse. Explicitly rejecting the notion of a "clash of civilizations," Turkish prime minister Recep Tayyip Erdogan, leader of the nominally Islamist Justice and Development Party and a former professional soccer player, has proposed a form of "conservative democracy" committed to "universal values" supported by "principles such as human rights" and to building a secular state "impartial" toward all religions (Erdogan 2004), thus carrying out a "quiet revolution" of expanding civil and political freedoms to bring his country closer to the European Union (Kinzer 2003). In Iraq, the interim constitution adopted in 2004 to manage the transition to a new form of government after the overthrow of Saddam Hussein, endorsed Islam as the official religion of the state and a source of legislation, but also guaranteed the rights of all individuals to freedom of religious belief and practice, prohibited discrimination on the basis of gender, provided equality before the courts, and incorporated mechanisms to prevent any religious faction from dominating the government (Iraq Interim Governing Council 2004). Without prejudging the outcome and durability of Turkish or Iraqi reforms, we think the active opposition to the Islamist vision in both countries demonstrates, at a minimum, that there is no single Islamic approach to world culture. Anti-Islamist Muslim intellectuals and activists, together with many public officials, are joining a global debate about the direction of world culture and seeking to find their own versions of the models it contains.

Such trends within Islam, combined with other world-cultural processes we have described, make it unlikely that violent Islamism will gain ground in a widening conflagration. In the immediate aftermath of the terrorist attacks of 2001, militant Islam loomed as a powerful and sinister force perversely seeking to use the tools of globalization to destroy the existing global system. The willingness of young Muslims to die for their cause seemed to confirm the appeal of radical beliefs to large groups of disaffected men. Many sought "root causes" in the failure of economically stagnant and politically oppressive states in the Middle East. Subsequent bombings, from Bali in 2002 to Madrid in 2004, served notice that a wide network of militants might coalesce into a global force, yet these attacks have not rallied the faithful behind the Islamist cause in an escalating civilizational clash. As strategic moves in a global conflict they have been less than strikingly successful. While America and other affected countries launched a counteroffensive, the struggle within many Islamic countries also intensified. Without trying to predict the precise course of the struggle, we suggest that, in addition to many other factors, the cultural dimension we have discussed here also greatly constrains the pursuit of political or religious aims by means of large-scale terrorism. World culture can hardly provide immunity from terrorist attacks but would-be terrorists are up against more than military foes. It may be going too far to say that violence is a "death trap" for Islamists, but our argument supports the notion that Islamic terror is more a "desperate symbol of isolation . . . and decline" than a "sign of its strength and irrepressible might" (Kepel 2002: 375).

Let us return to the Iranian case. Arguing against the harsh imposition of Islamic law, many Iranians over the years have clamored for the relaxation of fundamentalist rule, a demand expressed in the election of a reformist president, Mohammad Khatami, in 1997, and affirmed in his overwhelming re-election in 2001. At the risk of harsh punishment by the fundamentalist elite, some Iranian intellectuals, such as the former Islamic revolutionary Haghem Aghajari, have called for an "Islamic Reformation" that would bring greater democracy and civil freedoms (Friedman 2002). Though at best moderately successful at home, President Khatami, himself a prominent cleric, made an effort to engage in global dialogue abroad. For example, in a conversation with the German theologian Hans Küng and another scholar, published on the eve of the September 11 attacks on the USA, he took a stance that might have made Khomeini shudder. Khatami argued that "one can have newer understanding of the Qur'an and religion" and that in Islam, too, "many outlooks change," notably with regard to women's rights. Holding out hope for common standards that might bind Christians and Muslims, he looked forward to "a world that has commonalities, co-existence, but that also has differences and variety," in which people "strive to ensure that there is no conflict between these differences" (Khatami 2001).

To the disappointment of his reform-minded supporters, power remained concentrated in the hands of conservative clerics during Khatami's tenure. His views therefore did not mark the end of Iran's Islamist experiment. Yet as harbingers of change, they show that Khomeini's triumphant return to Tehran did not signal a world-historical change after all. Unable to export its revolution, Iran has experienced wrenching internal change. As an instrument of fundamentalist transformation, as a battering ram in global cultural conflict, it has lost much of its power. The Iranian experience thus supports our larger point that Islamists' deeply felt hostility to world culture is unlikely to trigger the clash of civilizations they envision. The complexity, diversity, and institutionalizing pressure of world culture immunize it against a true cataclysm. The opposition Islamists provoke, especially from other Muslims, builds bridges across fault lines and draws Islam into world culture. Lacking a sense of irony, Islamists are unlikely to appreciate this unintended strengthening of world culture. But by their own creative efforts, through constructive engagement rather than destructive *jihad*, many of their fellow Muslims will actively contribute to it.

Chapter 10

Instituting World Culture: The International Criminal Court and Global Governance

On March 11, 2003, the 18 recently elected judges of the International Criminal Court (ICC) took their oath of office at a ceremony in a medieval hall in The Hague before Queen Beatrix of the Netherlands and representatives of 89 nations. With all appropriate pomp, the event inaugurated a new institution, the first permanent international criminal tribunal. UN Secretary General Kofi Annan hailed its establishment, warning that henceforth anyone tempted to engage in the "most unspeakable" crimes "must be deterred by the knowledge that they will one day individually be called to account." The newly elected President of the Court, Philippe Kirsch of Canada, stressed that it would be an independent and impartial institution, devoted to protecting the weak and advancing the rule of law. Neither the memory of the acrimonious negotiations during the development of the court nor the prospect that few cases might actually be brought before it dampened the attendees' spirits. At least for the moment, they set aside such mundane concerns to relish the sheer symbolism of the occasion, a historic breakthrough in international law.

The ICC was new but hardly without precedent. After the Second World War, the Nuremberg Tribunal had tried German leaders for war crimes, creating a new, international, and legally structured way to deal with heinous state conduct in the process. Subsequent United Nations conventions had prohibited certain international crimes, such as genocide. Since the 1940s, groups like the UN's International Law Commission had also considered ways of making Nuremberg-style bodies permanent. Such efforts languished during the Cold War. Only in the 1990s did the international community reinvigorate its common efforts to deal with the "most unspeakable" crimes by establishing special tribunals to investigate and judge atrocities committed in the wars in the former Yugoslavia and Rwanda. Spurred in part by their work, the UN General Assembly acted on new recommendations by the International Law Commission to resume serious consideration of an international criminal court that would replace such special courts with a permanent institution. That rethinking soon led to a major conference in Rome to devise a statute for what would become the ICC.

The Rome conference in the summer of 1998 was a tumultuous affair (Weschler 2000). In five weeks, more than 100 state delegations had to hammer out agreements on dozens of issues. They faced discord on matters of principle and procedure. Setting up a new legal entity from scratch required specialized negotiations in many small groups. The ultimate treaty to create the new court had to accommodate states with very different interests and legal traditions. As one delegate put it, "the treaty needs to be 'weak' enough, unthreatening enough, to have its jurisdiction accepted without being so weak and unthreatening that it would prove useless" (ibid.: 90). The outcome was uncertain until the very end. However, under the leadership of Kirsch, the Canadian diplomat in charge, a treaty finally did take shape. On July 17, the conference's jubilant last day, 120 delegations supported the treaty with enthusiasm and a sense of relief. By April 2002, 60 countries had ratified the treaty. On July 1 of that year the ICC was officially born, setting the stage for the election of its judges.

The remarks by Annan and Kirsch at the inauguration in The Hague echoed the Statute's ringing Preamble (Cassese et al. 2002, Vol. III): "*Conscious* that all peoples are united by common bonds, their cultures pieced together in a shared heritage, and concerned that this delicate mosaic may be shattered at any time, *Mindful* that during this century millions of children women and men have been victims of unimaginable atrocities that deeply shock the conscience of humanity, *Recognizing* that such grave crimes threaten the peace, security and well-being of the world . . ." To punish and deter such crimes, says Article 5 of the Statute, the ICC shall have jurisdiction with respect to the four most important offenses: genocide, crimes against humanity, war crimes, and the crime of aggression (with the proviso that the latter had yet to be defined). State parties or the Security Council may refer cases to the Court, and the Statute also explicitly authorizes the Court's own prosecutor to instigate investigations after receiving permission in either the state where the relevant offense occurred or the home state of the accused. In principle, every individual is liable for his or her conduct before the Court, regardless of official capacity, though the Court will not take a case that has already been examined and tried in good faith within a particular state. Thus, its jurisdiction is "complementary." Applying rules and rights from various legal systems, the Statute grants defendants elaborate protections; for example, they can be held responsible only for acts committed with intent and knowledge. The Court may impose sentences of up to 30 years in prison; life imprisonment, though not the death penalty, is permitted only in extreme cases. Finally, the Statute outlines the organization of the Court in detail but leaves some important work, such as defining the elements of crimes, to further deliberations.

Beyond its particular provisions, the Statute is important for the aspiration it embodies: the principle that an independent international institution, properly constituted by and for the world community, should impartially dispense justice by holding every individual accountable to universal norms regarding globally defined crimes. Although it genuflects to the sovereignty of states – for example, by prohibiting armed intervention and granting the ICC only complementary jurisdiction – the Statute also strikingly restricts that sovereignty by subjecting state behavior to universal norms (Brand 2002). While it deprives states of the ability to claim immunity for their nationals, it endows individuals, as a matter of international law, "with both significant rights and important obligations" (Bederman 2002: 218). Not long ago, international law applied only to relations among states; the ICC dramatically expands its scope. By promising to undertake globally authorized action according to globally accepted norms against globally defined evils, the ICC significantly advances the evolution of "world law" (Berman 1995).

The ICC's future business may be uniquely grim, but its founding fits a larger pattern. More and more problems in "international" life are defined in global terms, addressed according to global standards, and handled by globally responsible institutions. Even without a full-fledged world government, global governance is steadily expanding (Prakash and Hart 1999; Nye and Donahue 2000; Held and McGrew 2002). Issues of trade and public health, accounting and the environment, sports and medicine, food and communication are now subject to organized and authoritative collective action at the global level. World culture provides the framework within which groups become aware of such issues *as* global concerns. World culture grounds collective action in broadly legitimated norms and standards. It offers templates for global action and sets directions for global policy. At the same time, new institutions such as the ICC also add weight to world culture. As large groups address common problems, world culture grows by accretion. Analyzing the case of the ICC as part of this larger pattern helps us to round out our case for world culture. If world culture is as long-standing, deeply rooted, firmly structured, and practically influential as we have claimed, it should greatly affect the nature and operations of governance. If world culture is as deeply embedded in a wide range of activities as we have suggested, we should find cultural growth-by-accretion even in areas not ostensibly focused on building world culture. That is what we aim to show by example in this chapter.

The example is a challenging test for our argument. After all, the ICC potentially constrains the actions of sovereign states, traditionally the key players in the international arena. It aims to apply shared norms to problems that have historically been addressed by force, if at all. As a step toward global governance, this process of bringing elements of world culture to bear on heinous offenses by subjecting state officials to a higher authority legitimated in global terms, even against the manifest interests of particular states, is inherently more contentious than similar steps in other areas, such as sports, aviation, or health. Yet even the "hard" case of the ICC shows how world culture is being instituted.

Examining the link between world culture and global governance enables us to confront a major objection to the argument of this book. The disappointment of one person attending the inauguration at The Hague gives us a clue. David Scheffer, former US ambassador to the ICC negotiations under the Clinton administration, resented the fact that, in spite of his hard work, the USA had decided not to support the ICC; he thought his country made a terrible mistake by refusing to join. If the most powerful country in the world stands aside, as it has done with regard to many other global efforts, can we really say that the founding of the ICC is an exercise in "world" culture? If the USA strongly disagrees with this venture, can we reasonably say that it subscribes to the same world-view as those who support the ICC? Put another way, does American deviance indicate a fatal division in world culture? The question is a bit ironic in that world culture is often characterized as being too American, too beholden to America's imperial design, too corrupted by false American values. However, it is fair to turn the question around. We answer it by arguing that, political opposition to particular agreements notwithstanding, America, too, is deeply enmeshed in – and ever more on the receiving end of – world culture. However much it still longs to be the unmoved mover of the world, America is no impenetrable cultural fortress. The way it is enmeshed, as even its official opposition to the ICC illustrates, reinforces a point we have made repeatedly, namely that much of world culture is necessarily contested, though world culture also frames the form that contention about global issues takes. As the ICC case shows, world culture provides a limited set of legitimate tools for arguments about the desirable shape of world governance.

The opposition of the United States is not the only reason for skepticism about the ICC. The ceremonial inauguration of its judges in The Hague may have been deliberately loaded with symbolism, but was it perhaps merely symbolic? Even after the subsequent appointment of a prosecutor, will the ICC be only a chimerical institution preparing for imaginary legal action? How many people will it punish, how many crimes will it actually deter? Such questions further challenge our view of world culture. If we see the ICC as world culture in action, how much does it really matter? If the ICC will not become effective for many years, what does that tell us about the practical impact of world culture? We acknowledge that its impact is inevitably contingent on other, noncultural factors. Yet its growth has consequences, a point we reinforce in this chapter. The high hopes at The Hague notwithstanding, global harmony will not be among those consequences. After all, the very premise of the Court is that brutal conflicts will continue. At the same time, its presence is likely to affect the course of such conflicts and alter the expectations of even the most hardened leaders, not least because they now must take into account new potential costs of their actions. It also demonstrates the momentum of world culture. Instituted in ever more spheres, world culture channels the way the world deals with its problems. The power of its symbolic organization does not suffice to prevent atrocities, but this power is now a necessary condition for addressing them effectively.

World Culture and the ICC

The ICC is deeply embedded in world culture. It bears the mark of many features of world culture we have discussed in this book – its roots in the nineteenth century, its content and structure, its key actors, and its typical tensions.

The very site of the ICC ceremony, The Hague, symbolizes the Court's nineteenth-century roots. The city hosted two peace conferences in 1898 and 1907, mentioned in Chapter 3, that "set in motion the evolution" leading to the ICC founding (Caron 2000). International lawyers writing about the "standard of civilization" had paved the way for these events. In a wave of high-minded European internationalism, private citizens and public officials had long sought new ways to advance peace and mitigate the effects of war. Florence Nightingale's work in the Crimean War helped to spur the founding of the International Committee of the Red Cross. Coubertin wanted to revive the Olympic Games as much to promote brotherhood through peaceful competition as for the sake of sports itself. In short, at major meetings, in works of scholarship, and through new organizations, the notion that states had higher responsibilities, that sovereignty was not the ultimate value of international life, had begun to take hold, if only tentatively. The already venerable precedent for such thinking in the work of Grotius, the classic jurist of the law of war and peace, provided a further impetus for the subsequent founding of the Permanent Court of International Justice after the First World War, once again in The Hague, but this Court, like its successor, the International Court of Justice, had jurisdiction only over state disputes. At least one of the founders of the Red Cross had contemplated the possibility of a separate court to deal with misconduct in war but the idea came to naught. Well into the twentieth century, major states jealously guarded their sovereign rights; certainly none of the imperial powers would submit to an independent judicial body. Extending basic rights to all human beings required a kind of inclusiveness few Europeans could muster at the time. The very idea of genocide or a "crime against humanity" had yet to crystallize. The internationalist stirrings of the late nineteenth century thus stopped well short of creating an international criminal court. The ICC would have seemed a pipe dream to even the most starry-eyed peace activists of over a century ago.

However, they would have recognized the ICC's structure and aspirations. The state prerogatives built into the Rome Statute would not surprise them. They would appreciate the use of universal norms to define civilized behavior and the use of law to settle disputes. They would understand how the crimes under ICC jurisdiction extend older ideas (e.g., the Geneva Conventions) about proper behavior in violent conflict. They would see granting special value and protection to the individual as a bold extension of the nineteenth-century liberal revolution. Precisely because it embodies ancient hopes about international society that were familiar to many in the nineteenth century, the ICC's founding marks a "Grotian moment" (Sadat 2000: 32). In all these respects, nineteenth-century precedent has been turned into world-cultural convention. This solidifying of world culture occurred especially after the Second World War, a period of world-cultural growth symbolically marked in the legal realm by the Nuremberg Tribunal and the Universal Declaration of Human Rights. The ICC derives its legitimacy from its embrace of world-cultural standards elaborated in the decades since the war. Even its most radical innovation, the idea of universal individual accountability for grave crimes, only extends the core world-cultural idea that everyone is subject to the same standards of behavior.

The Rome conference and the Hague ceremony were quintessential world-cultural gatherings. For decades, legal experts had contemplated the possibility of an international criminal tribunal. When the political air

cleared in the early 1990s, the UN formally authorized action on their proposals. State representatives started preparatory work on a treaty, pressed
by nongovernmental organizations of many stripes to produce the most
ambitious statute possible. Experts, officials, and NGO activists then gathered in the diplomatic hothouse of the Rome conference. Though unusually intense, the negotiations followed a by-then standard model for
international agreements. Like the summits discussed in Chapter 4, they
also had a ritual quality. Once the delegations reached agreement, the
process conferred a special legitimacy on the outcome. With its ritual affirmation and idealistic rhetoric, the inauguration in The Hague further bolstered that legitimacy, creating an aura of global consensus. It called forth
a new transnational body, consisting of judges now authorized by most of
the world's states and numerous international organizations to exercise
authority independently. Such meetings, part of the scaffolding of world
culture, proved essential in building the ICC.

The Rome Statute itself is a remarkably dry document (Lee 2001; Cassese
et al. 2002). Sections on jurisdiction lead to others on procedure, rules of
evidence, and punishment. Provisions on elements of crime, negotiated separately, break down individual offenses into seven elements. It is, in short,
a proper legal document, reflecting centuries of codification of legal principles in various domestic settings. By making its very style consistent with
world-cultural expectations, the legal medium is the message. The chief
expectation it embodies is that each issue has its own experts, that those
experts bring to bear their own distinctive expertise, that they give this
expertise a particular rational form, and that they express it in their own
special language. To lawyers, no doubt, the Rome Statute reads like artful
prose, a virtuoso display of treaty writing. Given the world-cultural cult of
the expert, the involvement of people like Philippe Kirsch, experienced
attorney and diplomat, and many equally prominent colleagues from other
countries was no accident. Nor could the Court itself be left in the hands
of amateurs – hence the Statute's requirement that judges have specific legal
credentials. In this way, a once-radical idea was turned into routine world-
cultural practice.

Among the forces pushing the radical idea in the mid-1990s were a few
dozen nongovernmental organizations (Pace and Schense 2002). Within just
a few years, their numbers exploded. Mobilized by the World Federalist
Movement, several hundred groups participated in preparatory sessions.
In Rome, some 800 organizations took part. They supported understaffed
delegations from developing countries, advocated extensive jurisdiction for
the court, and offered technical advice whenever possible (Pace and Schense

2001, 2002). The Coalition for the International Criminal Court, as the loose network of NGOs came to call itself, hoped to make participation universal, a truly global effort (Pace and Schense 2002: 116–17). What excited the NGOs, above all, was the idea of "the increasing centrality of the individual in international law" (ibid.: 107). As carriers of world culture, they wanted to see this idea given concrete form in the ICC. Their fast-growing coalition replicated a pattern that had emerged in many other sectors in which voluntary associations of interested citizen-advocates have exerted influence. Evidently, "global civil society" has become an independent source of cultural authority (Anheier et al. 2001). NGO participation has itself become a regular part of world-cultural innovation. Like other ventures in global governance, the founding of the ICC was due as much to the initiative and insistence of civil society as to the actions of states.

The seemingly dry text of the Statute also contains grudging compromises that mask continuing disagreement. Its legalese splits political differences. In Rome, some states, confident of the world's shared commitment to outlawing major offenses by means of the ICC, thought broad categories of crimes were sufficient to guide the Court; others, less sanguine about a common interpretation of these categories, called for precise definitions of the elements of crimes. Some states wanted to grant the ICC prosecutor broad discretion, highlighting the ICC's independence, but others, more concerned about preserving sovereignty, sought to limit its jurisdiction by requiring approval of either the UN Security Council or the state in which an accused perpetrator held citizenship. Some states insisted on treating "aggression" as a relevant crime, if only to symbolize the ICC departure from traditional state practice, but others were concerned that a vaguely defined new kind of crime would infringe on state interests. Arguments also erupted over standards of evidence and appropriate kinds of punishment. All in all, there were ample grounds for the tumult that surrounded the negotiations. Far from a simple statement of global consensus, the ICC Statute is a complex compromise. From our standpoint, it is significant that the debate focused on a limited set of issues, that the disagreements themselves took a particular form, and that a treaty could bridge at least some of the main differences.

The ICC has all the trappings of an institution deeply embedded in world culture. It has the historical aura, the lofty principles, the rational structure, the experienced experts, the expected disagreements, and the claim to international legitimacy. So, was the founding of the ICC simply predictable, the natural outcome of world-cultural change? Yes – and no. It was predictable in that it followed a set pattern, yet something new happened in Rome and

The Hague. The ICC expands international law, transcends precedent, and marks a new commitment by the international community. It thus also displays the dynamism of world culture. The framework for constructing world culture, once available, can be applied to many problems, and the creation of the Rome Statute shows one routine process by which global governance expands. By their very generality, key tenets of world culture can be extended in new directions, as illustrated by the enhanced place of the individual in the Statute. World culture creates the presumption that any issue can in principle be brought under its canopy; its growing presence helped prompt the renewed efforts to establish an ICC in the 1990s. Applying world-cultural elements to new problems adds layers to world culture itself by creating new forms that can be mobilized in other spheres. World culture is always stretching its tentacles, as it were. The ICC helps to stretch them further.

In terms of the anthropological view of world culture, the ICC thus adds a pathway to an emerging "juriscape," to adapt a term from Appadurai, by organizing the variety of legal systems in a particular way. However, the markers on this pathway, Robertson would add, are familiar; for example, the Statute formulates the correlative rights and duties of individuals and states, considered as part of a system of states governed by common standards of humanity, and thereby relativizes individual membership in nation-states by holding individuals accountable regardless of nationality, constraining national citizenship by the principles of world citizenship. Institutionalists would reinforce this view of the fit between the ICC and world culture by emphasizing the role of experts and NGOs in writing the script of yet another rationalized institution. World-system theorists would respond more skeptically, suggesting that the content and organization of the ICC reflect the dominant influence of core powers (despite the opposition of the USA). Our four perspectives thus illuminate distinct features of governance: the anthropologists see it as the negotiation of diversity, globalization theorists stress the imprint left by an existing world-culture template, institutionalists focus on the increasingly similar script-writing in different spheres, and world-system theorists view governance as the continuation of cultural domination by other means.

The link between the ICC and world culture demonstrates that world culture is always at work in global governance, and the ongoing expansion of global governance is always adding layers to world culture. Of course, a single example cannot prove that this is "always" the case. Strictly speaking, we would have to show that world culture is similarly at work in the global campaign to combat AIDS as much as in the liberalization of world trade, in new environmental regimes as much as in the setting of technical standards. We would quickly discover that conflicts about AIDS prevention and treatment differ from those about ICC jurisdiction, that the level of consensus about engineering standards is higher than that for environmental protection, and that the principles that guide trade liberalization do not apply to international law enforcement. Global governance is not all of a piece, but the ICC model is representative in demonstrating one key pattern in the culture of governance.

America vs. World Culture?

In one of his last acts as President of the United States, Bill Clinton approved the signing of the Rome Statute on December 31, 2000. While noting that "significant flaws" remained in the Statute, even after recently completed follow-up negotiations, he argued that it was important to demonstrate America's commitment to international justice and continue America's "moral leadership" (Scheffer 2001–2). The signing was hardly a ringing affirmation of American commitment. Actual membership in the ICC would have required ratification by the Senate, and Clinton had no plans to pursue this: "I will not, and do not recommend that my successor submit the treaty to the Senate for advice and consent until our fundamental concerns are satisfied," he stated (Amann 2002: 381). An influential senator rejected even the signature as "outrageous" (ibid.). The incoming Republican administration was unlikely to be more supportive. At best, the signing preserved a role for America in further negotiations. After participating for many years in arduous talks, the Clinton administration wanted to keep the door open to eventual American membership in the ICC (Scheffer 2001–2: 58–9).

Not long after Clinton left office, that door closed. Even officials less conservative than Senator Helms shared his outrage. After several attempts to write their opposition into law, the US Congress overwhelmingly passed the American Service-members' Protection Act of 2002. Noting that Americans prosecuted by the ICC would lack the procedural protections of the American Bill of Rights, the Act insists that members of the armed forces and public officials should be free from the risk of prosecution by the ICC. It declares that "[t]he United States is not a party to the Rome Statute and will not be bound by any of its terms. The United States will not recognize the jurisdiction of the International Criminal Court over any of its nationals." As if that were not clear enough, the Act also prohibits any American cooperation with the Court, requires exemptions to ICC jurisdiction for American participants in UN peace-keeping operations, restricts military aid to parties to the ICC, and even authorizes the President to "use all means necessary and appropriate" to bring about the release of Americans detained by the ICC. President Bush reinforced this congressional action by officially abrogating Clinton's signature. To limit ICC jurisdiction still further, the USA also started negotiating bilateral agreements with various countries to exempt American personnel from ICC prosecution in any actions on their territories. America's rejection of the ICC could hardly be more complete.

What accounts for this almost viscerally negative reaction? As one American official put it shortly before Clinton signed, "[t]he Rome Statute is very much like an intricately woven oriental rug that has a hideous and conspicuous cigarette burn" (Newton 2000: 208). The main defect, Americans argued throughout the ICC negotiations, is the possibility that "the court will allow the prosecutor to trample sovereignty concerns based upon politically motivated charges" (ibid.). ICC proponents dismissed such risks as far-fetched and argued that, in any case, the USA was shielded by the principle of complementarity, which prevents the ICC from bringing cases that have been properly examined by a potential defendant's own state. Yet the USA would not give in. "[W]ithout familiar checks and balances," said one official, the Court might become "a tantalizing target for groups and governments who seek to achieve political goals. Simply put, responsible nations like the United States . . . should not have to fear the possibility of politically motivated prosecutions" (ibid.: 209). To avoid that scenario, the USA proposed to subject ICC action to Security Council approval, so that the USA might be able to wield its veto power if necessary. On this point countries supporting the Statute, especially members of the European Union, would not yield. The USA therefore began to worry about another provision in the Statute that extended ICC jurisdiction to "the nationals of states which have not ratified the treaty or even accepted the jurisdiction of the court" (ibid.: 206). Since the Statute allowed state parties to exempt themselves from new categories of crimes they might bring within the ICC's reach, after further deliberations among the signatories, the risks to non-signatories were actually greater. To the US delegation, such "legal license" constituted an "indefensible overreach of jurisdiction" (ibid.: 206). Fears that an "interventionary" court and an unaccountable prosecutor not bound by clear rules might expose potential defendants to double jeopardy led some critics to label the court "lawless" (Rosenthal 2004).

Precisely the perception of overreach riled American officials and a majority in Congress. America, they thought, occupies a special place in the international arena. It is the one superpower with responsibility for global order. By virtue of its military and economic superiority, it necessarily becomes involved in the most complex conflicts. Bearing the "substantial burdens of intervention," its representatives run special risks that demand special accommodation for the sake of "strategic stability" for the USA and the world generally (Bobbitt 2004). However, this argument about the distinct global role of America accounts for only part of the American resistance to the ICC. At bottom, it was motivated by a deep reluctance to acknowledge any external authority that would limit American sovereignty in any way. If the ICC founding marked a historic breakthrough, the US response was profoundly traditional. Though other great powers, such as Russia and China, also were reluctant to ratify the ICC treaty, the Court's founding had touched an especially sensitive political nerve in the USA. The stark result was wholesale American rejection of the project.

Our purpose is not to perform a political psychoanalysis of American decision making but to consider the implications of American resistance. We have argued that the ICC is deeply embedded in world culture. We have suggested that it shows the power of culture in global governance. Yet if America stands aside, can we really claim that world culture is at work? If there are such profound disagreements about the status of the ICC, does this not indicate an unbridgeable chasm within the international community? If the single most powerful state does not support a global institution, what does the power of culture actually amount to? As we noted above, it is a bit ironic to ask such questions in light of the ubiquitous criticism of the USA for its own "overreach" in cultural matters. Anxiety about US influence pervaded the French concern with national identity (Chapter 6); American hegemony is a prime target of the antiglobalization movement (Chapter 7); for different reasons, radical Muslims also fight against a world order they consider made in America (Chapter 9). However, here our questions imply that in world culture the USA is a deviant. How can this be?

American resistance to the ICC is far from unprecedented. After President Woodrow Wilson helped to found the League of Nations following the First World War, the US Senate refused to ratify the treaty (Link 1995). When the UN elaborated on the original Universal Declaration of Human Rights with subsequent Covenants on specific political and social rights in 1966, the USA once again declined to ratify them. At the end of the long negotiations on the law of the sea in the 1980s, which aimed to develop global rules for developing the "common heritage of mankind," the USA took an equally critical stance. In 1984 the USA also decided to leave

UNESCO (though it rejoined in 2003). In a notorious case decided by the International Court of Justice in 1986, which held the USA liable for the illegal mining of the harbor of Managua, Nicaragua, the USA decided to exempt itself from that Court's jurisdiction (Highet 1987). As we saw in Chapter 4, in recent deliberations on global problems, such as the environment and population control, the US position has often been at odds with that of many other states. In addition to opposing the ICC, the Bush administration that took office in 2001 also refused to support a number of other international agreements, such as the Kyoto Protocol on reducing global warming and the treaty to ban landmines. When the same administration, joined by Britain and Australia, decided to go to war against Iraq in 2003, justifying its actions as enforcement of previous UN resolutions even in the absence of explicit authorization from the Security Council, its opponents viewed this as yet another example of America's intransigence with regard to the international legal order. Such instances suggest that the USA would rather jealously guard its sovereignty than join high-minded multilateral efforts, rejecting the moral appeals of others rather than joining causes that might harm its interests. The record adds to skepticism about America's attachment to world culture, at least as applied to global governance.

However, this picture of American deviance is incomplete. As he signed the ICC treaty, President Clinton affirmed "our strong support for international accountability and for bringing to justice perpetrators of genocide, war crimes, and crimes against humanity" (Scheffer 2001–2: 63). This was not mere rhetoric. After all, the USA helped to lay the groundwork for the ICC. It took the initiative for the Nuremberg tribunals, a deliberate effort to replace mere victors' justice with an orderly legal process. At Nuremberg, German officials had legal representation; a prosecutor charged them with specific crimes; the court followed strict procedures and based its decisions on evidence adduced in court; some defendants were actually found not guilty. The tribunals defined new offenses, most notably "crimes against humanity." Nuremberg also established a precedent: henceforth, leaders of warring nations risked being held accountable according to universal standards. No one was exempt. In all these respects, Nuremberg led directly to Rome and The Hague. Key way stations on that road were the tribunals established by the UN in the 1990s to deal with crimes committed during the genocide in Rwanda and the conflict in the former Yugoslavia. Again, the USA was intimately involved in both, supplying both resources and personnel. Though the USA declined to join in making these courts permanent, the ICC was built on a partially American foundation.

Many of its provisions were in fact already part of America's own Uniform Code of Military Justice.

The USA has also been deeply engaged in the expansion of international law more generally. Before the First World War, it was active through the work of influential scholars, such as Henry Wheaton, and through the diplomacy of US representatives at international conferences. After the war, Woodrow Wilson's doctrine of self-determination became an integral part of international thinking about the rights of peoples and countries and the protections to which they were entitled. The Second World War greatly intensified American efforts to expand the international legal order based on universal principles. The founding of the UN was a form of legal bootstrapping, calling into existence a new body with legal personality, procedures, and authority. The International Court of Justice (ICJ), charged with applying international law to disputes between states, was an integral part of the UN's design. Most dramatically, the Universal Declaration of Human Rights of 1948, in the preparation of which Americans played a leading role, partly generalized the American Bill of Rights into a statement of global principles. In the same period, the USA participated in the drafting of additional Geneva Conventions that subjected state conduct in war to explicit legal standards. Of course, the USA always was concerned that each institution or treaty served its interest. Within the UN, it insisted on veto power in the Security Council. The ICJ's authority depended on the consent of the parties before it. However, in this institution building more was at stake than *realpolitik*. American officials deliberately aimed to create a new kind of world order rooted in universal principles that, by and large, were closely tied to the American political tradition. The new global order had to take legal form to prevent a collapse into anarchy. The resulting institutions, however, exceeded America's grasp. As international organizations proliferated and treaties covered all manner of international issues and disputes, the USA became thoroughly enmeshed in a complex legal order. Rather than a being a deviant rogue, it was a central player.

America's commitment to international law is only one sign of its enmeshment in world culture. As we have seen throughout this book, that enmeshment takes many forms. From the Olympics to Pentecostalism, Americans have been active in expanding world culture. The very content of world culture, such as principles of individual autonomy and rights, owes much to American traditions. Since the 1940s, America has helped to build institutions of governance that reflect world-cultural premises. Even in the antiglobalization movement, Americans have been vocal. In short, American society is a major source of and contributor to world culture. It has become enmeshed in many other ways as well. To mention only one example among many, its belated participation in the quintessential global game – football – enabled the US national team to win the women's World Cup. Similarly, American tastes in cars and cuisine have been influenced enormously by foreign concepts. Without reciting the vast array of links that enmeshes America in world culture, it is clear that official rejection of specific governance structures entails no cultural isolation. For a thoroughly globalized society like the USA, ranking in the top ten of an index measuring global ties in spite of being sixtieth out of 62 countries in signing international agreements (Kearney 2004), that would be an entirely implausible scenario.

A central issue here is America's stance toward the world. Clinton's reference to moral leadership touches on a long-standing American aspiration, namely to serve as a beacon to the world, a city on a hill, a force for global good. Of course, outsiders may beg to differ with America's notion of the global good. America's pursuit of its global cultural ambitions is not consistent, as twists and turns in its foreign policy indicate (Mead 2001), yet at least since the Second World War the thrust of American policy has been to shape rather than abandon world culture in those areas where culture impinges on state interests. Paradoxically, the US rejection of the ICC also affirms that world-cultural commitment, for it was based ultimately on the perceived disparity between America's own global vision and actual global reality. American leaders judged that in a still-anarchic world the sole remaining superpower could not entrust its interests to the promise and procedures of an untested institution. The USA did not reject wholesale the principles the ICC embodies or the conception of world order it symbolizes. Precisely because the ICC so closely reflects American aspirations, many American observers lamented that rejection as a costly error that harms both its interests and its values. "For the United States to position itself as the enemy of the rule of law would be a remarkable reversal of American international law enforcement policy sustained throughout the 20th century," concluded Ambassador Scheffer (2001–2: 53–4), and the consequences of its strategy could be "exceptionally negative and far-ranging." Not only does it risk eroding international law, said other prominent critics, it undermines the "prospects for realization of a coherent US vision" of global governance (Chayes and Slaughter 2000: 238–9).

In principle, we have argued, that "coherent US vision" is very much in tune with world culture, yet in crucial areas America stands apart. This stance reflects the unique military strength of the USA and America's particular historical experience. To some extent, it derives from its own democratic and constitutional tradition, which leads to a vision of world order different from the "international constitutionalism" exemplified by the ICC (Rubenfeld 2003). However, America's critical distance also reflects the new reality of world culture. Having contributed greatly to world-cultural standards, institutionalists would argue, the USA now encounters unaccustomed pressure toward conformity, as demonstrated by the lead-up to the founding of the ICC. As it confronts other global visions in the world-cultural arena, Robertson would add, the USA undergoes the ordinary relativization experienced by all societies, but from a unique vantage point that leads to extraordinary responses, such as its vigorous rejection of ICC jurisdiction. Its recent tendency to reject certain governance institutions such as the ICC, so world-system theorists claim, stems from the frustrations of declining economic supremacy, evident in America's weakening grasp on those aspects of world culture its leaders consider important to US interests. The common denominator in these interpretations is that world culture is beyond any country's control, even that of the most culturally influential, most militarily self-assured superpower. In its ideological struggle with the ICC, America is reluctantly coming to terms with that fact.

The ICC and the Future of World Culture

The ceremony in The Hague, a skeptical observer could argue, was high on pomp and circumstance in order to compensate for the ICC's modest prospects. Even as the judges took their oath of office, a prosecutor had yet to be appointed. The ICC's personnel began busily organizing the Court but lacked actual cases to prosecute. With the USA on the sidelines, enforcement of ICC rules was bound to suffer. Was the occasion, then, merely symbolic? Does world culture as instituted in the ICC lack teeth? In the final analysis, how significant is the growth of world culture we have charted in this book? We answer in two ways. On the one hand, culture by itself does little. For culture to get "teeth" – for example, in the form of prosecution of crimes against humanity – it must be institutionalized, not simply in the form of establishing a Court but also by making its work a routine feature of international affairs. That process is contingent, constrained, and conflicted. Culture alone is never enough. On the other hand, without the growth of world culture, establishing an ICC would have been unimaginable. World culture changes what it is possible to think and do. It motivates individuals, organizations, and states to do what world culture makes it possible to think.

The ICC could have been arranged differently. In the political tug-of-war, America's rivals could have given in to US demands. Amid the chaos of the Rome conference, the improvised coalition might have been less effective in its interaction with state delegations. As had happened on previous occasions, the principle of individual accountability could have been sacrificed to the primacy of state sovereignty. A formal agreement might have failed to gain the commitment of member parties to provide the necessary resources. And of course, the negotiations could have failed altogether. Bringing the ICC to life was therefore not simply a matter of acting out an already existing script. The principles and processes provided by world-cultural precedents still had to be interpreted, applied, and adapted to the task at hand. Proponents had to mobilize resources and define a concrete structure, respecting the political positions of the players and accommodating their needs. Actual institutionalization of this sort is messy and never merely symbolic. As the outcome of a complex process, institutions like the ICC do not represent elements of world culture in pure and unadulterated form. Because it depends on the confluence of many factors, instituting world culture is an inherently contingent process.

Effectively instituting world culture is also subject to many constraints. In the legal arena as in any other, culture by itself rarely commands consent. In international law this problem is all too familiar. The seemingly universal assent to principles of international conduct has rarely led to effective enforcement by the international community. If the ICC ultimately fails to stop or punish "unspeakable atrocities," it continues a long-standing pattern. By showing how governance is culturally saturated, then, we are not predicting practical success. The perspectives we employ suggest many reasons to expect that institutionalizing world culture will always be fraught with difficulty and always incomplete. For world-system theorists, the key constraint lies in the material interests of core powers. Not surprisingly, besides the USA another aspiring superpower, China, also refused to support the ICC, further hampering its eventual success. Institutionalists have stressed the decoupling between legitimated models and actual practices, which one could describe less charitably as the organized hypocrisy that is evident in the less than stellar record of at least some ICC supporters. If world culture is as contentious and locally selective as Robertson and the anthropological view suggest, then institutionalization is bound to be uneven, leading to selective prosecution by the ICC in particular regions. As these arguments imply, making culture work is never the work of culture alone.

Whether the ICC could do that work was not clear at the time of the Hague ceremony. Judging by the record of the previous century, the ICC potentially would have a lot to do. Its work would necessarily flow from the cruelties of continued conflict. Historically, the resolution of major conflicts has involved political, military, diplomatic, and economic struggles and negotiations. The mere presence of a legal body, a skeptic might argue, will not override such processes. After all, even within the most stable countries that enjoy broad cultural consensus about standards of crime and punishment, the unquestioned authority of judicial bodies hardly ensures their effectiveness in preventing crime or punishing the guilty. In the far more contentious and divided international arena, the impact of a new, still-evolving judicial authority in dealing with the most disturbing atrocities is likely to be much more tenuous. The ICC's capacity to do its intended work depends on the outcome of conflicts it cannot control.

This skeptical view of the ICC introduces a healthy dose of realism. That realism applies to many forms of governance rooted in world culture, even if they are more securely institutionalized than the ICC. In this realistic vein, any sociological account of world culture in action has to take seriously contingencies, constraints, and conflicts such as those that affect the ICC. Instituting world culture is often fraught with difficulty. In making the case "for" world culture, and "for" America as deeply embedded in world culture, we therefore do not celebrate world culture as a source of harmony and bliss. Yet the skeptic also underestimates the significance of institutions like the ICC, as imperfect as they may be.

While noncultural contingencies shape the form of institutions, in the case of the ICC these contingencies affected a process that could only be initiated because world culture provided a template. Without shared assumptions about the importance of legal procedures, the sacred worth of the individual, and the common interests of humanity, the negotiators could hardly have begun negotiating. As this process illustrates, world culture enables more people to think more broadly about global problems. It gives form to otherwise diffuse experiences and varied interests. Similarly, among the constraints that affect institutions like the ICC we must also count culture itself. World-cultural precedents constrained the kind of judicial body that could emerge, the kinds of crimes it could judge, and the procedures it should follow. Precedents leave room for argument, but the argument itself moves within definite parameters. To adapt a famous phrase from Max Weber, world culture lays the tracks along which parties pursue their global interests. Finally, though the ICC certainly lacks control over the outcomes of future conflicts, it is also the case that those outcomes henceforth will be shaped to some extent by the standards and authority of the ICC. Concretely, world leaders must calculate the legal risks of their actions. Individual victims increasingly will know that they have legal recourse. Both in actual battles and in efforts to settle disputes, the ICC will lurk in the background. Once it successfully prosecutes a few notorious cases, a global sense that "justice is being done" by the Court will add to its importance. By instituting world culture, to vary a line from Emile Durkheim, it becomes one of the nonconflictual elements in conflict. Even if it never actually convicts anyone, the ICC's redefinition of the global situation will be real in its consequences.

The record of the UN's war crimes tribunals gives us a more tangible basis for refuting the skeptics' objections. In the mid-1990s, any collective legal response to the atrocities of the war in Bosnia would have seemed far-fetched. Perhaps the single most appalling act in that war was committed in 1994 by Bosnian-Serb forces. Overwhelming the Muslims who had fled to Srebenica, the Serbs separated the men from the women and children and massacred them by the thousands. Dutch peacekeepers, sent to create a "safe area" for Muslims, passively stood by. The Netherlands' world-cultural commitment to the peaceful settlement of disputes and protection of human rights lacked teeth, but the disaster in fact helped to galvanize a more vigorous response: within a short period, the USA led NATO in a bombing campaign directed at the Serbs. The UN established its tribunals and Serb leaders were arrested and convicted. Some even confessed to planning the operations that led to the Srebenica massacre. Thus, after failing the Muslims of Srebenica, the international community regrouped to give its professed commitment some muscle. In implementing world culture in this way, complex political and military considerations were surely at work – yet what skeptics of the mid-1990s might have derided as a merely symbolic possibility had become a surprisingly effective institution.

Chapter 11

Epilogue: Reflections on World Culture

Our tour through the landscape of world culture has passed by many notable landmarks: the Olympic Games, UN conferences, antiglobalization critiques, the International Criminal Court, amongst others. These examples reveal some of the processes by which world culture shapes the way the world works and how the world deals with its problems. Without covering the full extent and complexity of world culture, we have tried to show that world culture is indeed growing inexorably. World culture is the symbolic kudzu of our era. As people in the American South know all too well, once kudzu, a hardy and invasive plant, has taken root, it is difficult to get rid of. Once a social arena has been defined in world-cultural terms, it cannot easily be "undefined." Losing global consciousness would require a truly traumatic global catastrophe. Given that many social arenas are already defined in world-cultural terms, others are sure to follow. World culture, in short, is here to stay and hard to stop.

In this concluding chapter, we will review a number of themes that we have developed throughout the book. The first is elementary but, we think, worth emphasizing up front because it is so often overlooked in discussions of globalization and world-cultural development. As explained in Chapter 1, world culture is not simply a set of disembodied, free-floating ideas and principles disconnected from everyday life. We have stressed the structuration of world culture in organizations and institutions, particularly in those organizations and institutions that operate at the transnational level. International nongovernmental organizations are especially important in this regard because they explicitly take the world as their arena of discourse and action, debating and revising and advocating – and often resisting – particular elements or segments of world culture. They also embody a wide array of world-cultural elements in their own structures, activities, and goals. Many other global actors – intergovernmental organizations, transnational corporations, states, and individuals such as scientists, policy advisors, technical experts, organizational consultants, activists, and so on – are important world-culture developers and embodiments as well. Of greater importance for the operations and effects of world culture, however, are the national and local organizations and institutions in which world-cultural elements are embedded. An example we have alluded to in previous chapters is the worldwide institutionalization of modern schooling (Meyer, Ramirez, and Soysal 1992; Meyer, Kamens, and Benavot 1992), directed by states and built on principles of individual performance, rationalized socialization, formal knowledge, abstract learning, occupational credentialing, and the like. Schooling incorporates a substantial majority of the world's children and in most places it is ever more effective in orienting those children not only to the local and national but to the world as a whole.

We could multiply the schooling example many times over – e.g., with respect to business models, social insurance, health care systems, advertising, scientific training, agricultural techniques, civil society associations, and much, much more. We cannot, however, emphasize the point too much: to understand world culture, we need to understand the local, the regional, and the national as they are affected by, and more or less fully embody, cultural influences from the global level. World culture is all around us, if only we know how to recognize it.

Some of the examples we have presented, like the International Criminal Court (Chapter 10) and the anti-slavery movement of the nineteenth century (Chapter 3), may seem very distant from most people. Much of world culture, however, concerns the routine realities of everyday life. Most directly involved are people of the relatively affluent countries and social classes but increasingly we find world culture influencing the lives of even the most remote places and poorest people. It is obviously at work in such global practices as watching the Olympics, flying long distances, using a credit card abroad, taking a course of antibiotics against an infectious disease, or communicating with friends and colleagues via the Internet. For these kinds of activities, it is easy to identify the global organizations at work and to specify the many elements of shared knowledge they spread around the world (Chapter 5). For many other routine practices, however, world culture is less obvious. When a rice farmer in Mali attends a village workshop to learn about a new disease-resistant strain of rice, or a Mexican construction worker in Houston first picks up a pneumatic nail gun, or an Indian villager adds her mark to a petition opposing the construction of a new dam that will flood her valley, world culture may seem less present – but the rice strain is a result of scientific research of global applicability, the nail gun an application of engineering and machine production techniques used around the world, and the petition an instance of the worldwide movement against large dams (Khagram 2003). World culture is at work in many more places much more of the time than is commonly recognized.

From this vantage point, perhaps paradoxically, acting globally does not always entail thinking globally. Global thinking is deliberate and routine among the organizations and types of individuals mentioned above. It is the daily practice of INGOs, IGOs, states, and transnational corporations. It is commonplace among business and political elites, the well educated, professionals, academics, transnational activists, and the like. These are the organizations and people that debate, structure, and spread world culture, and they do so habitually, as a matter of course. However, for the ordinary construction worker or small-scale rice farmer, acting globally may involve thinking only locally. The construction worker sees the nail gun as a tool that allows him to earn enough to pay rent on a shared apartment, support a simple diet, and send money each month to his family in Guadalajara (his other local context). The rice farmer may see the rice strain as something foreign but his concern is its potential to increase his crop yield so he can better feed his family or send another child to school. People acting globally need not be particularly well informed about the world-cultural knowledge and global systems that affect their local lives. Much of world culture is embedded in national and local structures to such an extent that it is simply taken for granted, yet the reach of world culture is so great that global awareness is often routine even for the construction worker and rice farmer. It is hardly restricted to the explicitly global actors that we have discussed at length in this book.

The interplay between the local and the global is complex and not easily disentangled. At the heart of the matter is the ongoing debate regarding homogenization and diversity. As we showed in Chapter 2, the arguments and analyses offered by the global institutionalist approach associated with John Meyer point to extensive homogenization (isomorphism) as states, organizations, and individuals adopt world-cultural identities, structures, and goals in largely uniform ways. World-system theory also posits extensive homogenization in the form of economic and cultural imperialism, as the capitalist core imposes its institutions and modes of life on the rest of the world. However, the globalization perspective of Roland Robertson and the anthropological views exemplified by Ulf Hannerz and Arjun Appadurai temper this view of a world-cultural juggernaut leveling everything in its path. Robertson's process of the particularization of the universal emphasizes the variable adaptation of world-cultural principles, institutions, and ideas at the local level. Every place has its own unique history, traditions, constellations of political and cultural interests, and so on. How world-cultural elements take concrete form and how they relate to existing world-views and modes of living are thus determined by national and local circumstances. The anthropological view adds to this the important point that world culture is not the only type of "external" cultural influence on local and national cultures. Influences come from near and far, including the local and national levels, and different types of cultural exchange and pressure affect particular locales to varying degrees. World culture thus contributes to the ongoing hybridization or creolization of national and local cultures but it is not the sole or even the most important creolizing influence in many places.

Another of Robertson's processes, the universalization of the particular, also increases diversity. Cultural elements associated with particular locales are increasingly likely to spread throughout the world and become part of the menu of choices available to large numbers of people in a great many places. Think of the range of literal menu options – that is, types of restaurants – available in urban areas. To take our own locale as an example, just in the past two decades Atlanta has witnessed a veritable explosion of gastronomic diversity. We can choose from not only long-familiar cultural options – Italian, French, Cantonese, Mandarin, Japanese, Indian, and so on – but also from such "exotic" kinds as Moroccan, Ethiopian, Malaysian, Costa Rican, Korean, Vietnamese, Brazilian, and many more. Behind many of these are growing numbers of immigrants with their own neighborhoods, grocery stores, economic niches, artifacts, and religions, and some of their unique cultural elements are well on the way to becoming part of "standard" American culture. The average American – and Venezuelan, Nigerian, Iranian, Filipina, and Aussie – thereby experiences far more diversity in everyday life than her grandparents could have imagined. The same thing is happening in world culture as a whole: particular local and national elements are lifted up by universalizing processes and structures such that they become part of the global cultural repertoire available to everyone who is plugged in to world culture. Ironically enough, the increasing local diversity that follows from this process produces an ultimate sameness in the world's cities. Everywhere is more diverse but that diversity is composed of many common ethnicities and cultural elements, so the devotee of sushi or mah jong or West African street drummers can find these universalized particulars almost anywhere.

We do not want to exaggerate the diversifying and creolizing effects of world culture, however. Much of the local diversity we encounter in daily life is rather superficial, a matter only of consumption styles and taste options. Similarly, much of the ethnocultural diversity so mightily championed by advocates of multiculturalism, local authenticity, and indigenous uniqueness, has little depth. This is evident at American universities that are wont to sponsor "Celebration of Diversity" events, at which students of different ethnocultural backgrounds display their unique foods, dance, and styles of dress. In terms of world-views, life goals, daily routines, and personal styles, the students are often quite alike regardless of their ethnicity. Their celebrated distinctiveness is often a kind of façade diversity that masks deeper homogenization, and we observe a similar process at work at the regional and national levels throughout world society. The cultures of the world are far from entirely homogenized and standardized, but homogenization is more fundamental and extensive among a much larger proportion of the world's population than was the case a century ago.

Many of our examples of world-cultural processes illustrate the tensions and contradictions of world culture. An especially good case is the International Criminal Court, which lies at the intersection of the principle of state sovereignty and the set of responsibilities attached to individual world citizenship. State sovereignty is a principal pillar of international law and interstate relations. States are uniquely empowered to exercise formal authority backed by coercive means that can be employed to regulate and manage their respective societies. Yet the ICC transcends state sovereignty, relying instead on a principle of individual responsibility for one's actions and the presumed capacity of individuals to follow their consciences in choosing good over evil. Political and military leaders who commit crimes against humanity can no longer cloak themselves in the mantle of state sovereignty to protect them from justice. Neither can they use state sovereignty to shield the underlings who do their bidding. They are obligated to behave as responsible world citizens, meeting the standards of acceptable behavior that are embedded in world culture. This clash of principles will generate much domestic and international political debate and maneuvering in coming years, adding yet another dynamic element to world-cultural development.

World culture is replete with such tensions and contradictions. The commitment to rationalized progress clashes with the concern for cultural authenticity, since the former calls for adoption of modern rationalized institutions that threaten the unique and distinctive features of local cultures. The insistence on equality of opportunity and concomitant abhorrence of discrimination collide with the drive for greater individual autonomy and freedom, since measures to promote equality and inhibit discrimination usually entail restrictions on the economic, social, or behavioral choices available to individuals. The principle of freedom of religion runs head-on into the spiritual certainty of a single and indivisible reality given by the one true faith – whether that faith is constituted by Christianity, Islam, or a secular ideology. Like all cultural formations – but even more so – world culture's internal tensions and contradictions create an enormous amount of misunderstanding, uncertainty, strategic mobilization, and struggle. The resulting dynamism is bound to grow all the more intense as world culture incorporates ever more elements from ever more cultural sources.

Critics of neoliberalism (Chapter 7), opponents of radical Islamism (Chapter 9), and defenders of national identity (Chapter 6) deal with these built-in tensions in many and varied ways. On specific occasions, such as the UN summits described in Chapter 4, such tensions come to a head. In many cases, even individuals are torn, caught on the horns of world-cultural dilemmas. Such dilemmas are not just the stuff of individual contemplation or abstract discourse. They affect the way many global institutions work, as our example of the Olympic Games in Chapter 1 showed. While providing routine answers to some questions, world culture also raises new questions about how to address common global problems and unique national and local issues. Viewed in this way, world culture is an ongoing, expanding argument among many parties about many issues.

In this book we do not sing the praises of world culture. Since it constitutes a complex amalgam of ideas and a messy arena of contention, we could not possibly embrace world culture in its entirety. Though we might like to have a bumper sticker reading, "I ♥ World Culture," reality, alas, is too complex for such a catchy summary. Each of us appreciates various dimensions of world culture, enjoys some of the activities it makes possible, and welcomes the benefits of many globally available opportunities. As students of world culture, we are fascinated by the debates it frames and the consciousness it fosters. Life would be the poorer without it. However, we are acutely aware that, considered from the vantage point of our own or any other particular set of values, the effects of world culture are radically ambiguous. Technical and infrastructural standardization makes it easier to travel and adapt to new locales but it also diminishes the sense of unfamiliarity that is one of the great attractions of foreign travel for many people. Pentecostalism provides a sense of community and spiritual comfort to many of its adherents but also generates tension and hostility on the part of established religions that feel threatened by its rapid growth. Revitalizing national or religious identities can make life more meaningful for many and foster tolerance among different groups, but also risks provoking aggression and even terrorism.

We are thus not unabashedly enthusiastic about world culture. We recognize its complexities, contradictions, and unintended consequences. Some new features of world culture and new steps in global governance promote values we endorse; others we find problematic. In the usual case, however, such either/or judgments are simplistic, and they will become even more inadequate as world culture continues to become more complex. Assessing world culture on normative or moral grounds is no easy matter but this only strengthens our commitment to scholarly analyses that grapple with the range of world culture's effects on the peoples of the world.

In the twenty-first century, world culture will be a fact of life. Its content will change; its influence may rise or decline. But in many respects, the world works the way it does because world culture has grown as it has. For better and for worse, it envelops us all. If it is not to become a straitjacket, we must first of all try to understand it. We hope this book has taken a few steps toward that goal. We invite others to continue on the path we have tried to clear.

References

Abou El Fadl, Khaled. 2001. *Rebellion and Violence in Islamic Law*. Cambridge: Cambridge University Press.

Abrahamian, Ervand. 1993. *Khomeinism: Essays on the Islamic Republic*. Berkeley: University of California Press.

Adshead, S. A. M. 2000. *China in World History*. Basingstoke: Macmillan Press.

Aguiton, Christophe, Riccardo Petrella, and Charles-André Udry. 2001. "A Very Different Globalization," in *The Other Davos: The Globalisation of Resistance to the World Economic System*, ed. François Houtart and François Polet. London: Zed Books, pp. 63–8.

Ajami, Fouad. 1993. "The Summoning," *Foreign Affairs* 72:2–9.

Algar, Hamid. 2001. *Wahhabism: A Critical Essay*. Oneonta, NY: Islamic Publications International.

Alker, Hayward R., and Peter M. Haas. 1993. "The Rise of Global Ecopolitics," in *Global Accord: Environmental Challenges and International Responses*, ed. Nazli Choucri. Cambridge, MA: MIT Press, pp. 133–71.

Amann, Diane Marie. 2002. "The United States of America and the International Criminal Court," *American Journal of Comparative Law* 50:381.

An-Naim, Abdullahi Ahmed. 1990. *Toward an Islamic Reformation: Civil Liberties, Human Rights, and International Law*. Syracuse, NY: Syracuse University Press.

Ancelovici, Marcos. 2002. "Organizing Against Globalization: The Case of ATTAC in France," *Politics and Society* 30:427–63.

Anderson, Allan H. 1999a. "Introduction: World Pentecostalism at a Crossroads," in *Pentecostals after a Century: Global Perspectives on a Movement in Transition*, ed. Allan H. Anderson and Walter J. Hollenweger. Sheffield: Sheffield Academic Press, pp. 19–31.

Anderson, Allan H. 1999b. "African Pentecostals in Mission," *Swedish Missiological Themes* 87:389–404.

Anderson, Allan H. 2004. "The Contextual Pentecostal Theology of David Yonggi Cho," *Asian Journal of Pentecostal Studies* 7:101–23.

Anderson, Allan H., and Walter J. Hollenweger (eds.). 1999. *Pentecostals after a Century: Global Perspectives on a Movement in Transition*. Sheffield: Sheffield Academic Press.

Anderson, Benedict. 1991. *Imagined Communities: Reflections on the Origin and Spread of Nationalism*. London: Verso.

Angell, Norman. 1913. *The Great Illusion: A Study of the Relation of Military Power to National Advantage*. New York: G. P. Putnam's Sons.

Anheier, Helmut, Marlies Glasius, and Mary Kaldor (eds.). 2002. *Global Civil Society 2001*. Oxford: Oxford University Press.

Anti-Slavery, International. 2003. "The History of Anti-Slavery International," Anti-Slavery International (http://www.antislavery.org/homepage/antislavery/history.pdf).

Appadurai, Arjun. 1996. *Modernity at Large: Cultural Dimensions of Globalization*. Minneapolis, MN: University of Minnesota Press.

Appiah, Anthony, and Henry Louis Gates (eds.). 1997. *The Dictionary of Global Culture*. New York: Alfred A. Knopf.

Arjomand, Said Amir. 1988. *The Turban for the Crown: The Islamic Revolution in Iran*. New York: Oxford University Press.

Arjomand, Said Amir. 1993. *The Political Dimensions of Religion*. Albany: State University of New York Press.

Asamoah-Gyadu, Kwabena. 1998. "The Church in the African State: The Pentecostal/Charismatic Experience in Ghana," *Journal of African Christian Thought* 1:51–7.

Banks, Arthur S. 1976. *Cross-National Time Series, 1815–1973*. Ann Arbor, MI: Inter-university Consortium for Political and Social Research.

Barber, Benjamin R. 1995. *Jihad vs. McWorld*. New York: Times Books.

Barrett, David B., George Thomas Kurian, and Todd M. Johnson. 2001. *World Christian Encyclopedia: A Comparative Survey of Churches and Religions in the Modern World*. Oxford: Oxford University Press.

Barrett, Deborah, and David John Frank. 1999. "Population Control for National Development: From World Discourse to National Policies," in *Constructing World Culture: International Nongovernmental Organizations since 1875*, ed. John Boli and George M. Thomas. Stanford, CA: Stanford University Press, pp. 198–221.

Bastian, Jean-Pierre. 1994. *Le Protestantisme en Amérique Latine: Une Approche Socio-historique*. Genève: Labor et Fides.

Bederman, David J. 2002. *The Spirit of International Law*. Athens, GA: University of Georgia Press.

Bello, Walden. 2001. *The Future in the Balance: Essays on Globalization and Resistance*. Oakland, CA: Food First Books.

Bello, Walden. 2004. "The Global South," in *A Movement of Movements: Is Another World Really Possible?*, ed. Tom Mertes. London: Verso, pp. 49–69.

Berger, Peter L. 1997. "Four Faces of Global Culture," *National Interest* 49:23–9.

Berger, Peter L. 2002. "Introduction: The Cultural Dynamics of Globalization," in *Many Globalizations: Cultural Diversity in the Contemporary World*, ed. Peter L. Berger and Samuel P. Huntington. Oxford: Oxford University Press, pp. 1–16.

Berger, Peter L., and Thomas Luckmann. 1966. *The Social Construction of Reality: A Treatise in the Sociology of Knowledge*. Garden City, NY: Doubleday.

Berger, Peter L., and Samuel P. Huntington (eds.). 2002. *Many Globalizations: Cultural Diversity in the Contemporary World*. Oxford: Oxford University Press.

Berkovitch, Nitza. 1999a. *From Motherhood to Citizenship: Women's Rights and International Organizations*. Baltimore, MD: Johns Hopkins University Press.

Berkovitch, Nitza. 1999b. "The Emergence and Transformation of the International Women's Movement," in *Constructing World Culture: International Nongovernmental Organizations since 1875*, ed. John Boli and George M. Thomas. Stanford, CA: Stanford University Press, pp. 100–26.

Berman, Harold J. 1988. "The Law of International Commercial Transactions," *Emory Journal of International Dispute Resolution* 2:235–310.

Berman, Harold J. 1995. "World Law," *Fordham International Law Journal* 18:1617–22.

Berman, Paul. 2003. *Terror and Liberalism*. New York: W. W. Norton.

Bernard, François de. 2003. "The New Nero," in www.haaretzdaily.com.

Bertinotti, Fausto. 2003. "Reformist Social Democracy is No Longer on the Agenda," *Guardian* (August 11).

Bestor, Theodore C. 2000. "How Sushi Went Global," *Foreign Policy* (November/December):54–63.

Bin Laden, Osama. 1998. "Interview," PBS Frontline 2003.

Bobbitt, Philip C. 2004. "Better Than Empire," *Financial Times* (March 12).

Boli, John. 1999. "World Authority Structures and Legitimations," in *Constructing World Culture: International Nongovernmental Organizations since 1875*, ed. John Boli and George M. Thomas. Stanford, CA: Stanford University Press, pp. 267–300.

Boli, John. Forthcoming. "International Nongovernmental Organizations," in *The Nonprofit Sector*, ed. Walter W. Powell and Richard Steinberg. New Haven, CT: Yale University Press.

Boli, John, and George M. Thomas. 1997. "World Culture in the World Polity: A Century of International Non-governmental Organization," *American Sociological Review* 62:171–90.

Boli, John, and George M. Thomas (eds.). 1999. *Constructing World Culture: International Nongovernmental Organizations since 1875*. Stanford, CA: Stanford University Press.

Bond, Michael. 2000. "The Backlash Against NGOs," in *Prospect Magazine*.

Boswell, Terry, and Christopher Chase-Dunn. 2000. *The Spiral of Capitalism and Socialism: Toward Global Democracy*. Boulder, CO: Lynne Rienner Publishers.

Bourdieu, Pierre. 2001. *Contre-Feux 2: Pour un Mouvement Social Européen*. Paris: Éditions Raisons d'Agir.

Bové, José, and François Dufour. 2001. *The World is Not for Sale: Farmers Against Junk Food*. London: Verso.

Brand, Ronald A. 2002. "Sovereignty: The State, the Individual, and the International Legal System in the Twenty-First Century," *Hastings International and Comparative Law Review* 25:279.

Brecher, Jeremy, Tim Costello, and Brendan Smith. 2002. *Globalization from Below: The Power of Solidarity*. Cambridge, MA: South End Press.

Breidenbach, Joana, and Ina Zukrigl. 2000. *Tanz der Kulturen: Kulturelle Identität in einer Globalisierten Welt*. Reinbek bei Hamburg: Rowohlt Taschenbuch Verlag.

Briggs, Asa, and Daniel Snowman. 1996. *Fins de Siècle: How Centuries End, 1400–2000*. New Haven, CT: Yale University Press.

Bright, Edward Brailsford, and Charles Bright. 1899. *The Life Story of the Late Sir Charles Tilston Bright*. Westminster: Constable.

Broad, Robin (ed.). 2002. *Global Backlash: Citizen Initiatives for a Just World Economy*. Lanham, MD: Rowman & Littlefield.

Brouwer, Steve, Paul Gifford, and Susan D. Rose. 1996. *Exporting the American Gospel: Global Christian Fundamentalism*. New York: Routledge.

Brusco, Elizabeth. 1993. "The Reformation of Machismo: Asceticism and Masculinity among Colombian Evangelicals," in *Rethinking Protestantism in Latin America*, ed. Virginia Garrard-Burnett and David Stoll. Philadelphia, PA: Temple University Press, pp. 143–58.

Bulliet, Richard W. 2002. "The Crisis within Islam," *The Wilson Quarterly* 26 (Winter).

Burgess, Stanley M., Gary B. McGee, and Patrick H. Alexander (eds.) 1988. *Dictionary of Pentecostal and Charismatic Movements*. Grand Rapids, MI: Regency Reference Library.

Caldwell, Christopher. 2003. "The Decline of France and the Rise of an Islamist-Leftist Alliance," *The Weekly Standard* (December 8).

Caron, David D. 2000. "War and International Adjudication: Reflections on the 1899 Peace Conference," *The American Journal of International Law* 94:4–30.

Carrigan, Ana. 2001. "Afterword: Chiapas, the First Postmodern Revolution," in *Our Word is Our Weapon: Selected Writings of Subcomandante Marcos*, ed. Juana Ponce de Leon. New York: Seven Stories Press, pp. 417–43.

Cassen, Bernard. 2004. "Inventing ATTAC," in *A Movement of Movements: Is Another World Really Possible?*, ed. Tom Mertes. London: Verso, pp. 152–74.

Cassese, Antonio, Paola Gaeta, and John R. W. D. Jones (eds.) 2002. *The Rome Statute of the International Criminal Court: A Commentary* (3 volumes). Oxford: Oxford University Press.

Ceaser, James W. 1997. *Reconstructing America: The Symbol of America in Modern Thought*. New Haven, CT: Yale University Press.

César, Waldo. 2001. "From Babel to Pentecost: A Socio-Historical Study of the Growth of Pentecostalism," in *Between Babel and Pentecost: Transnational*

Pentecostalism in Africa and Latin America, ed. André Corten and Ruth Marshall-Fratani. Bloomington: Indiana University Press, pp. 22–40.

Chayes, Abram, and Anne-Marie Slaughter. 2000. "The ICC and the Future of the Global Legal System," in *The United States and the International Criminal Court*, ed. Sarah B. Sewall and Carl Kaysen. Lanham, MD: Rowman & Littlefield, pp. 237–48.

Codding, George A. 1964. *The Universal Postal Union: Coordinator of the International Mails*. New York: New York University Press.

Coleman, Simon. 2000. *The Globalisation of Charismatic Christianity: Spreading the Gospel of Prosperity*. Cambridge: Cambridge University Press.

Coleman, Simon. 2002. "The Faith Movement: A Global Religious Culture?" *Culture and Religion* 3:3–19.

Conca, Ken. 1996. "Greening the UN: Environmental Organisations and the UN System," in *NGOs, the UN, and Global Governance*, ed. Thomas G. Weiss and Leon Gordenker. Boulder, CO: Lynne Riener Publishers, pp. 103–19.

Cornwell, Grant H., and Eve Walsh Stoddard (eds.). 2001. *Global Multiculturalism: Comparative Perspectives on Ethnicity, Race, and Nation*. Lanham, MD: Rowman & Littlefield.

Cowen, Tyler. 2002. *Creative Destruction: How Globalization is Changing the World's Cultures*. Princeton, NJ: Princeton University Press.

Cox, Harvey. 1995. *Fire from Heaven: The Rise of Pentecostal Spirituality and the Reshaping of Religion in the Twenty-first Century*. Reading, MA: Addison-Wesley.

Cox, Harvey. 1999. "'Pentecostalism and Global Market Culture': A Response to Issues Facing Pentecostalism in a Postmodern World," in *The Globalization of Pentecostalism: A Religion Made to Travel*, ed. Murray W. Dempster, Byron D. Klaus, and Douglas Petersen. Oxford: Regnum Books International, pp. 389–95.

Cranmer-Byng, J. L. (ed.). 1962. *An Embassy to China: Being the Journal Kept by Lord Macartney During His Embassy to the Emperor Chien-lung, 1793–1794*. London: Longmans.

Crawford, Elisabeth, Terry Shin, and Sverker Sörlin. 1993. "The Nationalization and Denationalization of the Sciences: An Introductory Essay," in *Denationalizing Science: The Contexts of International Scientific Practice*, ed. Elisabeth Crawford, Terry Shin, and Sverker Sörlin. Dordrecht: Kluwer Academic Publishers, pp. 1–42.

Crowley, John. 2000. "France: The Archetype of a Nation-State," in *European Nations and Nationalism: Theoretical and Historical Perspectives*, ed. Louk Hagendoorn, György Csepeli, Henk Dekker, and Russell Farnen. Aldershot: Ashgate, pp. 67–106.

Demeny, Paul. 1985. "Bucharest, Mexico City, and Beyond," *Population and Development Review* 11:99–106.

Dempster, Murray W., Byron D. Klaus, and Douglas Petersen (eds.). 1999. *The Globalization of Pentecostalism: A Religion Made to Travel*. Oxford: Regnum International Books.

Dias, Clarence J. 2001. "The United Nations World Conference on Human Rights: Evaluation, Monitoring, and Review," in *United Nations-sponsored World Conferences: Focus on Impact and Follow-up*, ed. Michael G. Schechter. Tokyo: United Nations University Press, pp. 29–62.

Doran, Michael Scott. 2004. "The Saudi Paradox," *Foreign Affairs* 83:35–51.

Douglas, Mary. 1986. *How Institutions Think*. Syracuse, NY: Syracuse University Press.

Droogers, André. 1994. "The Normalization of Religious Experience: Healing, Prophecy, Dreams, and Visions," in *Charismatic Christianity as Global Culture*, ed. Karla Poewe. Columbia, SC: University of South Carolina Press, pp. 33–49.

Droogers, André. 1998. "Paradoxical Views on a Paradoxical Religion: Models for the Explanation of Pentecostal Expansion in Brazil and Chile," in *More than Opium: An Anthropological Approach to Latin American and Caribbean Pentecostal Praxis*, ed. Barbara Boudewijnse, André Droogers, and Frans Kamsteeg. Lanham, MD: The Scarecrow Press, pp. 1–34.

Droogers, André. 2001. "Globalisation and Pentecostal Success," in *Between Babel and Pentecost: Transnational Pentecostalism in Africa and Latin America*, ed. André Corten and Ruth Marshall-Fratani. Bloomington: Indiana University Press, pp. 41–61.

Drori, Gili S., John W. Meyer, Francisco O. Ramirez, and Evan Schofer (eds.). 2003. *Science in the Modern World Polity: Institutionalization and Globalization*. Stanford, CA: Stanford University Press.

Dryzek, John S. 1997. *The Politics of the Earth: Environmental Discourses*. Oxford: Oxford University Press.

Eisenstadt, S. N. 1999. *Fundamentalism, Sectarianism, and Revolution: The Jacobin Dimension of Modernity*. Cambridge: Cambridge University Press.

Eley, Geoff, and Ronald Grigor Suny (eds.). 1996. *Becoming National: A Reader*. New York: Oxford University Press.

Erdogan, Recep Tayyip. 2004. "Conservative Democracy and the Globalization of Freedom," Washington, DC: AEI.

Esposito, John L. 1990. "The Iranian Revolution: A Ten-Year Perspective," in *The Iranian Revolution: Its Global Impact*, ed. John L. Esposito. Miami: Florida International University Press, pp. 17–39.

Esteva, Gustavo, and Madhu Suri Prakash. 1998. *Grassroots Post-modernism: Remaking the Soil of Cultures*. London: Zed Books.

Evans, Peter. 2000. "Fighting Marginalization with Transnational Networks: Counter-Hegemonic Globalization," *Contemporary Sociology* 29:230–41.

Evans, Peter. 2005. "Counter-Hegemonic Globalization: Transnational Social Movements in the Contemporary Global Political Economy," in *Handbook of Political Sociology*, ed. Thomas Janoski, Alexander M. Hicks, and Mildred Schwartz. Cambridge: Cambridge University Press.

Fairbank, John King (ed.). 1968. *The Chinese World Order: Traditional China's Foreign Relations*. Cambridge, MA: Harvard University Press.

Falk, Richard. 1999. *Predatory Globalization: A Critique*. Malden, MA: Polity Press.

Feldman, Noah. 2003. *After Jihad: America and the Struggle for Islamic Democracy*. New York: Farrar, Straus and Giroux.

Ferguson, Niall. 2003. *Empire: The Rise and Demise of the British World Order and the Lessons for Global Power*. New York: Basic Books.

Finger, Matthias. 1994. "Environmental NGOs in the UNCED Process," in *Environmental NGOs in World Politics*, ed. Thomas Princen and Matthias Finger. London: Routledge, pp. 186–213.

Finkle, Jason L., and Barbara B. Crane. 1975. "The Politics of Bucharest: Population, Development and the New International Economic Order," *Population and Development Review* 1:87–114.

Fisher, William F., and Thomas Ponniah (eds.). 2003. *Another World is Possible: Popular Alternatives to Globalization at the World Social Forum*. London: Zed Books.

Fitzgerald, C. P. 1964. *The Chinese View of Their Place in the World*. London: Oxford University Press.

Francophonie, La. 2001. "Dossier de Presse 'Diversité Culturelle: un Combat Francophone'," Agence Intergouvernementale de la Francophonie (http://confculture.francophone.org/dossierpresse/doc0.cfm).

Frank, David John. 1997. "Science, Nature, and the Globalization of the Environment, 1870–1990," *Social Forces* 75:411–37.

Frank, David John, Ann Hironika, John W. Meyer, Evan Schofer, and Nancy Brandon Tuma. 1999. "The Rationalization and Organization of Nature in World Culture," in *Constructing World Culture: International Nongovernmental Organizations since 1875*, ed. John Boli and George M. Thomas. Stanford, CA: Stanford University Press, pp. 81–99.

Frank, David John, and John W. Meyer. 2002. "The Profusion of Individual Roles and Identities in the Postwar Period," *Sociological Theory* 20:86–105.

Freston, Paul. 1993. "Brother Votes for Brother: the New Politics of Protestantism in Brazil," in *Rethinking Protestantism in Latin America*, ed. Virginia Garrard-Burnett and David Stoll. Philadelphia, PA: Temple University Press, pp. 66–110.

Freston, Paul. 1997. "Charismatic Evangelicals: Mission and Politics on the Frontiers of Protestant Growth," in *Charismatic Christianity: Sociological Perspectives*, ed. Stephen Hunt, Malcolm Hamilton, and Tony Walter. New York: St. Martin's Press, pp. 184–204.

Friedman, Thomas L. 1999. *The Lexus and the Olive Tree: Understanding Globalization*. New York: Farrar, Straus and Giroux.

Friedman, Thomas L. 2002. "An Islamic Reformation," *New York Times*, December 4.

Fukuyama, Francis. 1992. *The End of History and the Last Man*. New York: Free Press.

Fuller, Bruce. 1991. *Growing Up Modern: The Western State Builds Third World Schools*. New York: Routledge.

Gabel, Medard, and Henry Bruner. 2003. *Global Inc.: An Atlas of the Multinational Corporation*. New York: New Press.

Geertz, Clifford. 1983. *Local Knowledge: Further Essays in Interpretive Anthropology*. New York: Basic Books.

Geith, Suleiman Abu. 2002. "Why We Fight America," Middle East Media Research Institute (June 18).

Gellner, Ernest. 1983. *Nations and Nationalism*. Ithaca, NY: Cornell University Press.

Gifford, Paul. 1994. "Ghana's Charismatic Churches," *Journal of African Religion* 24:241–65.

Giulianotti, Richard. 1999. *Football: A Sociology of the Global Game*. Oxford: Polity Press.

Glover, Bill. 2004. "History of the Atlantic Cable & Submarine Telegraphy. Cable Timeline: 1850–2004," http://atlantic-cable.com/cbles/CableTimeLine/index.htm

Gong, Gerrit W. 1984. *The Standard of "Civilization" in International Society*. Oxford: Clarendon Press.

Goodman, David. 1991. "Conclusion," in *The Rise of Scientific Europe, 1500–1800*, ed. David Goodman and Colin A. Russell. Sevenoaks, Kent: Hodder & Stoughton, pp. 415–23.

Goodman, David C., and Colin A. Russell (eds.). 1991. *The Rise of Scientific Europe, 1500–1800*. Sevenoaks, Kent: Hodder & Stoughton.

Gordon, John Steele. 2002. *A Thread across the Ocean: The Heroic Story of the Transatlantic Cable*. New York: Walker.

Gordon, Philip H., and Sophie Meunier. 2001. *The French Challenge: Adapting to Globalization*. Washington, DC: Brookings Institution Press.

Gray, John. 1998. *False Dawn: The Delusions of Global Capitalism*. New York: The New Press.

Gray, John. 2002. *Straw Dogs: Thoughts on Humans and Other Animals*. London: Granta.

Greenfeld, Liah. 1992. *Nationalism: Five Roads to Modernity*. Cambridge, MA: Harvard University Press.

Grubb, Michael, Francis Sullivan, and Kay Thompson. 1993. *The "Earth Summit" Agreements: A Guide and Assessment*. London: Earthscan Publications.

Guéhenno, Jean-Marie. 2000. *The End of the Nation-State*. Minneapolis: University of Minnesota Press.

Gunn, Geoffrey C. 2003. *First Globalization: The Eurasian Exchange, 1500 to 1800*. Lanham, MD: Rowman & Littlefield.

Guttmann, Allen. 1984. *The Games Must Go On: Avery Brundage and the Olympic Movement*. New York: Columbia University Press.

Hackett, Rosalind. 1998. "Charismatic/Pentecostal Appropriation of Media Technologies in Nigeria and Ghana," *Journal of Religion in Africa* 28:258–77.

Hall, John A. 1996. *International Orders*. Cambridge: Polity Press.

Hannerz, Ulf. 1992. *Cultural Complexity: Studies in the Social Organization of Meaning*. New York: Columbia University Press.

Hannerz, Ulf. 1996. *Transnational Connections: Culture, People, Places*. London: Routledge.

Hansen, Tom, and Enlace Civil. 2001. "Zapatista Timeline," in *Our Word is Our Weapon: Selected Writings of Subcomandante Marcos*, ed. Juana Ponce de Leon. New York: Seven Stories Press, pp. 445–51.

Hardt, Michael. 2004. "Today's Bandung?" in *A Movement of Movements: Is Another World Really Possible?*, ed. Tom Mertes. London: Verso, pp. 230–6.

Hardt, Michael, and Antonio Negri. 2003. "Foreword," in *Another World is Possible: Popular Alternatives to Globalization at the World Social Forum*, ed. William F. Fisher and Thomas Ponniah. London: Zed Books, pp. xvi–xix.

Harvey, David. 1989. *The Condition of Postmodernity: An Enquiry into the Origins of Cultural Change*. Oxford: Basil Blackwell.

Hecht, Jeff. 1999. *City of Light: The Story of Fiber Optics*. New York: Oxford University Press.

Held, David, Anthony McGrew, David Goldblatt, and Jonathan Perraton. 1999. *Global Transformations: Politics, Economics and Culture*. Stanford, CA: Stanford University Press.

Held, David, and Anthony McGrew (eds.). 2002. *Governing Globalization: Power, Authority and Global Governance*. Cambridge: Polity.

Highet, Keith. 1987. "Evidence, the Court, and the Nicaragua Case," *The American Journal of International Law* 81:1–52.

Hoberman, John. 1995. "Toward a Theory of Olympic Internationalism," *Journal of Sport History* 22:1–37.

Hobsbawm, E. J. 1975. *The Age of Capital, 1848–1875*. London: Weidenfeld and Nicolson.

Hobsbawm, E. J. 1990. *Nations and Nationalism since 1780: Programme, Myth, Reality*. Cambridge: Cambridge University Press.

Hollenweger, Walter J. 1999. "The Black Roots of Pentecostalism," in *Pentecostals after a Century: Global Perspectives on a Movement*, ed. Allan H. Anderson and Walter J. Hollenweger. Sheffield: Sheffield Academic Press, pp. 33–44.

Houtart, François. 2001. "Alternatives to the Neoliberal Model," in *The Other Davos: The Globalisation of Resistance to the World Economic System*, ed. François Houtart and François Polet. London: Zed Books, pp. 47–59.

Houtart, François, and François Polet (eds.). 2001. *The Other Davos: The Globalisation of Resistance to the World Economic System*. London: Zed Books.

Hunter, James Davison, and Joshua Yates. 2002. "In the Vanguard of Globalization: The World of American Globalizers," in *Many Globalizations: Cultural Diversity in the Contemporary World*, ed. Peter L. Berger and Samuel P. Huntington. Oxford: Oxford University Press, pp. 323–57.

Huntington, Samuel P. 1993. "The Clash of Civilizations?" *Foreign Affairs* 72:22–49.

Huntington, Samuel P. 1997. *The Clash of Civilizations and the Remaking of World Order*. New York: Touchstone.

Huntington, Samuel P. 2004. "The Hispanic Challenge," *Foreign Policy* (March/April):30–45.

IFG (International Forum on Globalization). 2001. *Does Globalization Help the Poor?* San Francisco: IFG.

IFG. 2002. *Alternatives to Economic Globalization: A Better World is Possible.* San Francisco: Berrett-Koehler Publishers.

Imber, Mark F. 1996. "The Environment and the United Nations," in *The Environment and International Relations*, ed. John Vogler and Mark F. Imber. London: Routledge, pp. 138–54.

International Cable Protection Committee. 2003. "About the IPC," http://www.ispc.org/

International Law Association. 2003. "About Us," http://www.ila-hq.org/html/layout_about.htm

International Telecommunications Union. 1991. *Yearbook of Common Carrier Telecommunications Statistics.* Geneva: ITU.

International Telecommunications Union. 2003. "ITU World Telecommunication Indicators 2003" (CD-ROM Infobase). Geneva: ITU.

Internet Systems Consortium. 2003. "Domain Survey Information," http://www.isc.org/

Iraq Interim Governing Council. 2004. "Law of Administration for the State of Iraq for the Transitional Period." Baghdad: IIGC.

Ireland, Rowan. 1991. *Kingdoms Come: Religion and Politics in Brazil.* Pittsburgh, PA: University of Pittsburgh Press.

ISO. 2004. "Technical Committee 68, Sub-Committee 4, 'Securities and Related Financial Instruments,'" http://www.iso.org/iso/en/stdsdevelopment/tc/tclist/Technical CommitteeDetailPage.TechnicalCommitteeDetail?COMMID=2203

Iyer, Pico. 2000. *The Global Soul: Jet Lag, Shopping Malls, and the Search for Home.* New York: Alfred A. Knopf.

Jejeebhoy, Shireen J. 1990. "FamPlan: The Great Debate Abates," *International Family Planning Perspectives* 16:139–42.

Jones, Geoffrey. 1996. *The Evolution of International Business.* New York: Routledge.

Karliner, Joshua. 1997. *The Corporate Planet: Ecology and Politics in the Age of Globalization.* San Francisco: Sierra Club Books.

Kearney, A. T. 2004. "Measuring Globalization: Economic Reversals, Forward Momentum." *Foreign Policy* 141 (March/April):54–69.

Keddie, Nikki R. (ed.). 1968. *An Islamic Response to Imperialism: Political and Religious Writings of Sayyid Jamal ad-Din "al-Afghani."* Berkeley: University of California Press.

Kedourie, Elie. 1993. *Nationalism.* Oxford: Blackwell.

Kepel, Gilles. 2002. *Jihad: The Trail of Political Islam.* Cambridge, MA: The Belknap Press of Harvard University Press.

Kern, Stephen. 1983. *The Culture of Time and Space, 1880–1918.* Cambridge, MA: Harvard University Press.

Khagram, Sanjeev. 2003. "Neither Temples Nor Tombs: A Global Analysis of Large Dams," *Environment* 45:28–36.

Khatami, Mohammad (with Hans Küng and Josef van Ess). 2001. "Symposium: Islam, Iran and the Dialogue of Civilisations," *Global Dialogue* 3:1–13.

Khomeini, Ruhollah, and Hamid Algar. 1985. *Islam and Revolution: Writings and Declarations of Imam Khomeini*. London: KPI.

Kimmelman, Michael. 2002. "Global Art Show with an Agenda: The Biggest Documenta Ever," *New York Times* (June 18).

Kinzer, Stephen. 2003. "The Quiet Revolution," *The American Prospect* 14 (December).

Klein, Naomi. 2001. "A Fete for the End of the End of History," *The Nation* (March 19).

Kohn, Hans. 1967. *Prelude to Nation-States: The French and German Experience, 1789–1815*. Princeton, NJ: Van Nostrand.

Kramer, Eric. 2002. "Making Global Faith Universal: Media and a Brazilian Prosperity Movement," *Culture and Religion* 3:21–47.

Kurzman, Charles. 2002. "The Globalization of Rights in Islamic Discourse," in *Islam Encountering Globalization*, ed. Ali Mohammadi. London: RoutledgeCurzon, pp. 131–55.

Kurzman, Charles. 2003. "Bin Laden and Other Thoroughly Modern Muslims," *Contexts* (Fall/Winter):8–20.

Kurzman, Charles. 2004. *The Unthinkable Revolution in Iran*. Cambridge, MA: Harvard University Press.

Kurzman, Charles (ed.). 1998. *Liberal Islam: A Sourcebook*. New York: Oxford University Press.

Küng, Hans. 1998. *A Global Ethic for Global Politics and Economics*. Oxford: Oxford University Press.

Lawrence, Bruce B. 1989. *Defenders of God: The Fundamentalist Revolt against the Modern Age*. San Francisco: Harper & Row.

Lechner, Frank J. 2005. "Religious Rejections of Globalization," in *Religion and Global Civil Society*, ed. Mark Juergensmeyer. Oxford: Oxford University Press.

Leclerc, Gérard. 2000. *La Mondialisation Culturelle: Les Civilisations à l'Épreuve*. Paris: Presses Universitaires de France.

Lee, Roy S. (ed.). 2001. *The International Criminal Court: Elements of Crimes and Rules of Procedure and Evidence*. Ardsley, NY: Transnational Publishers.

Lehmann, David. 1996. *Struggle for the Spirit: Religious Transformation and Popular Culture in Brazil and Latin America*. Cambridge: Polity Press.

Lewis, Bernard. 1990. "The Roots of Muslim Rage," *Atlantic Monthly* 266:47–60.

Link, Arthur S. 1995. "Woodrow Wilson: A Cautionary Tale," *Wake Forest Law Review* 30:585–92.

Livingstone, David N. 1993. *The Geographical Tradition: Episodes in the History of a Contested Enterprise*. Oxford: Blackwell.

Lloyd, John. 2001. "Attack on Planet Davos," *Financial Times* (February 24).

Löwy, Michael, and Frei. Betto. 2003. "Values of a New Civilization," in *Another World is Possible: Popular Alternatives to Globalization at the World Social Forum*, ed. William F. Fisher and Thomas Ponniah. London: Zed Books, pp. 329–37.

Lubeck, Paul. 2000. "The Islamic Revival: Antinomies of Islamic Movements under Globalization," in *Global Social Movements*, ed. Robin Cohen and Shirin M. Rai. New Brunswick, NJ: Athlone Press, pp. 146–64.

Lyons, F. S. L. 1963. *Internationalism in Europe, 1815–1914*. Leiden: A. W. Sythoff.

MacAloon, John J. 1981. *This Great Symbol: Pierre de Coubertin and the Origins of the Modern Olympic Games*. Chicago, IL: University of Chicago Press.

Marcos, Subcomandante. 2001. *Our Word is Our Weapon: Selected Writings*. New York: Seven Stories Press.

Marshall-Fratani, Ruth. 1998. "Mediating the Global and the Local in Nigerian Pentecostalism," *Journal of Religion in Africa* 28:278–315.

Martin, David. 1990. *Tongues of Fire: The Explosion of Protestantism in Latin America*. Oxford: Blackwell.

Martin, David. 2002. *Pentecostalism: The World Their Parish*. Oxford: Blackwell.

Maudoodi, Syed Abul Ala. 1984. *The Islamic Movement: Dynamics of Values, Power, and Change*. Leicester, UK: Islamic Foundation.

Maudoodi, Syed Abul Ala. 1991. *West versus Islam*. New Delhi: International Islamic Publishers.

Mayer, Ann Elizabeth. 1993. "The Fundamentalist Impact on Law, Politics, and Constitutions in Iran, Pakistan, and the Sudan," in *Fundamentalisms and the State: Remaking Polities, Economies, and Militance*, ed. Martin E. Marty and R. Scott Appleby. Chicago, IL: University of Chicago Press, pp. 110–51.

McClellan, James E. 1985. *Science Reorganized: Scientific Societies in the Eighteenth Century*. New York: Columbia University Press.

McCormick, John. 1995. *The Global Environmental Movement*. New York: Wiley.

McIntosh, C. Alison, and Jason L. Finkle. 1995. "The Cairo Conference on Population and Development: A New Paradigm?" *Population and Development Review* 21:223–60.

Mead, Walter Russell. 2001. *Special Providence: American Foreign Policy and How It Changed the World*. New York: Alfred A. Knopf.

Mertes, Tom (ed.). 2004. *A Movement of Movements: Is Another World Really Possible?* London: Verso.

Meunier, Sophie. 2000. "The French Exception," *Foreign Affairs* (July–August):104–16.

Meyer, Birgit. 1998. "'Make a Complete Break with the Past.' Memory and Post-colonial Modernity in Ghanaian Pentecostalist Discourse," *Journal of African Religion* 28:316–49.

Meyer, Birgit, and Peter Geschiere (eds.). 1999. *Globalization and Identity: Dialectics of Flow and Closure*. Malden, MA: Blackwell.

Meyer, John W. 1980. "The World Polity and the Authority of the Nation-State," in *Studies of the Modern World-System*, ed. Albert Bergesen. New York: Academic Press, pp. 109–37.

Meyer, John W. 1983. "Institutionalization and the Rationality of Formal Organizational Structure," in *Organizational Environments: Ritual and Rationality*, ed. John W. Meyer and W. Richard Scott. Beverly Hills, CA: Sage, pp. 261–82.

Meyer, John W. 1986. "Myths of Socialization and Personality," in *Reconstructing Individualism: Autonomy, Individuality, and the Self in the Western Cultural Account*, ed. Thomas C. Heller. Stanford, CA: Stanford University Press, pp. 208–21.

Meyer, John W. 1996. "Otherhood: The Promulgation and Transmission of Ideas in the Modern Organizational Environment," in *Translating Organizational Change*, ed. Barbara Czarniawska and Guje Sevón. Berlin: Walter de Gruyter, pp. 241–52.

Meyer, John W., John Boli, and George M. Thomas. 1987. "Ontology and Rationalization in the Western Cultural Account," in *Institutional Structure: Constituting State, Society, and the Individual*, ed. George M. Thomas, John W. Meyer, Francisco O. Ramirez, and John Boli. Newbury Park, CA: Sage, pp. 12–37.

Meyer, John W., John Boli, George M. Thomas, and Francisco O. Ramirez. 1997. "World Society and the Nation-State," *American Journal of Sociology* 103:144–81.

Meyer, John W., David Kamens, and Aaron Benavot. 1992. *School Knowledge for the Masses: World Models and National Curricula in the Twentieth Century*. London: Falmer.

Meyer, John W., Francisco O. Ramirez, and Yasemin Soysal. 1992. "World Expansion of Mass Education, 1870–1970," *Sociology of Education* 65:128–49.

Meyer, John W., and Brian Rowan. 1991. "Institutionalized Organizations: Formal Structure as Myth and Ceremony," in *The New Institutionalism in Organizational Analysis*, ed. Walter Powell and Paul DiMaggio. Chicago, IL: University of Chicago Press, pp. 41–62.

Micklethwait, John, and Adrian Wooldridge. 2000. *A Future Perfect: The Essentials of Globalization*. New York: Crown Business.

Mitchell, B. R. 1992–98. *International Historical Statistics: Europe, 1750–1993*. London: Stockton Press.

Mittelman, James H. 2000. *The Globalization Syndrome: Transformation and Resistance*. Princeton, NJ: Princeton University Press.

Moore, Sally Falk, and Barbara G. Myerhoff. 1977. "Introduction. Secular Ritual: Forms and Meanings," in *Secular Ritual*, ed. Sally Falk Moore and Barbara G. Myerhoff. Assen: Van Gorcum, pp. 3–24.

Moussalli, Ahmad S. 1999. *Moderate and Radical Islamic Fundamentalism: The Quest for Modernity, Legitimacy, and the Islamic State*. Gainesville, FL: University Press of Florida.

Murad, Khurram. 1984. "Introduction," in *The Islamic Movement: Dynamics of Values, Power and Change (by Sayyid Abul Ala Maudoodi)*, ed. Khurram Murad. Leicester: The Islamic Foundation, pp. 5–69.

Murphy, Craig. 1994. *International Organization and Industrial Change: Global Governance since 1850*. New York: Oxford University Press.

Muzaffar, Chandra. 2002. *Rights, Religion and Reform: Enhancing Human Dignity Through Spiritual and Moral Transformation*. London: RoutledgeCurzon.

Needham, Joseph. 1954. *Science and Civilization in China*. Cambridge: Cambridge University Press.

Nettl, J. P., and Roland Robertson. 1968. *International Systems and the Modernization of Societies: The Formation of National Goals and Attitudes*. New York: Basic Books.

Newton, Michael A. 2000. "The International Criminal Court Preparatory Commission: The Way it is and the Way Ahead," *Virgina Journal of International Law* 41:204.

Notes from Nowhere. 2003. *We Are Everywhere: The Irresistible Rise of Global Anticapitalism*. London: Verso.

Nye, Joseph S., and John D. Donahue (eds.). 2000. *Governance in a Globalizing World*. Washington, DC: Brookings Institution Press.

O'Brien, Conor Cruise. 1968. *United Nations, Sacred Drama*. London: Hutchinson.

Oakes, Leigh. 2001. *Language and National Identity: Comparing France and Sweden*. Amsterdam: John Benjamins.

Okuma, Shigenobu (ed.). 1909. *Fifty Years of New Japan*. London: Smith Elder.

Pace, William, and Jennifer Schense. 2001. "NGOs Contribution to the International Criminal Court," in *The International Criminal Court: Elements of Crimes and Rules of Procedure and Evidence*, ed. Roy S. Lee. Ardsley, NY: Transnational Publishers, pp. 705–34.

Pace, William, and Jennifer Schense. 2002. "The Role of Non-Governmental Organizations," in *The Rome Statute of the International Criminal Court* (Vol. II), ed. Antonio Cassese, Paola Gaeta, and John R. W. D. Jones. Oxford: Oxford University Press, pp. 105–44.

Panjabi, Ranee K. L. 1997. *The Earth Summit at Rio: Politics, Economics, and the Environment*. Boston, MA: Northeastern University Press.

Parker, John. 2003. "Preparing for the Future of SWIFT Messaging," Sunnyvale, CA: Vitria Technology (http://www.eubfn.com/arts/Vitriapaper_2003.htm)

Pasha, Mustapha Kamal. 2000. "Globalization, Islam and Resistance," in *Globalization and the Politics of Resistance*, ed. Barry K. Gills. Basingstoke: Macmillan Press, pp. 241–54.

Passet, René. 2000. *L'Illusion Néo-Libérale*. Paris: Fayard.

Pecora, Vincent P. 2001. "Introduction," in *Nations and Identities*, ed. Vincent P. Pecora. Malden, MA: Blackwell, pp. 1–42.

Pei, Minxin. 2003. "The Paradoxes of American Nationalism," *Foreign Policy* (May–June):31–7.

Pianta, Mario. 2001. "Parallel Summits of Global Civil Society," in *Global Civil Society 2001*, ed. Helmut Anheier, Marlies Glasius, and Mary Kaldor. Oxford: Oxford University Press, pp. 169–94.

Poewe, Karla O. 1994. *Charismatic Christianity as a Global Culture*. Columbia, SC: University of South Carolina Press.

Polanyi, Karl. 1985 [1944]. *The Great Transformation*. Boston, MA: Beacon Press.

Ponniah, Thomas, and William F. Fisher. 2003. "Overview: Key Questions, Critical Issues," in *Another World is Possible: Popular Alternatives to Globalization at the World Social Forum*, ed. William F. Fisher and Thomas Ponniah. London: Zed Books, pp. 23–9.

Prakash, Aseem, and Jeffrey A. Hart (eds.). 1999. *Globalization and Governance*. London: Routledge.

Qutb, Sayyid. 1981. *Milestones*. Cedar Rapids, IA: The Mother Mosque Foundation.

Qutb, Sayyid. 1983. *Islam and Universal Peace*. Indianapolis: American Trust Publications.

Qutb, Sayyid. 2000. *Social Justice in Islam*. Oneonta, NY: Islamic Publications International.

Renan, Ernest. 1996. "What is a Nation?" in *Becoming National: A Reader*, ed. Geoff Eley and Ronald Grigor Suny. New York: Oxford University Press, pp. 42–55.

Revel, Jean-François. 2003. *Anti-Americanism*. San Francisco: Encounter Books.

Richter, Philip. 1997. "The Toronto Blessing: Charismatic Global Warming," in *Charismatic Christianity: Sociological Perspectives*, ed. Stephen Hunt, Malcolm Hamilton, and Tony Walter. New York: St. Martin's Press, pp. 97–119.

Ritzer, George. 1993. *The McDonaldization of Society: The Changing Character of Contemporary Social Life*. Newbury Park, CA: Pine Forge Press.

Robertson, Roland. 1991. "The Globalization Paradigm: Thinking Globally," in *Religion and the Social Order*, vol. I: *New Developments in Theory and Research*, ed. David Bromley. Greenwich, CT: JAI Press, pp. 207–24.

Robertson, Roland. 1992. *Globalization: Social Theory and Global Culture*. London: Sage.

Robertson, Roland. 1995. "Glocalization: Time–Space and Homogeneity–Heterogeneity," in *Global Modernities*, ed. Mike Featherstone, Scott Lash, and Roland Robertson. London: Sage, pp. 25–44.

Robertson, Roland. 1998. "The New Global History: History in a Global Age," in *Time and Value*, ed. Scott Lash, Andrew Quick, and Richard Roberts. Oxford: Blackwell, pp. 210–26.

Robertson, Roland, and JoAnn Chirico. 1985. "Humanity, Globalization and Worldwide Religious Resurgence: A Theoretical Exploration," *Sociological Analysis* 46:219–42.

Rodrik, Dani. 1997. *Has Globalization Gone Too Far?* Washington, DC: Institute of International Economics.

Rosenau, James N. 1997. *Along the Domestic–Foreign Frontier: Exploring Governance in a Turbulent World*. Cambridge: Cambridge University Press.

Rosenthal, John. 2004. "A Lawless Global Court," *Policy Review* (February).

Rothenbuhler, Eric W. 1989. "Values and Symbols in Orientations to the Olympics," *Critical Studies in Mass Communication* 6:138–57.

Rubenfeld, Jed. 2003. "The Two World Orders," *The Wilson Quarterly* (Autumn).

Sadat, Leila Nadya. 2000. "The Evolution of the ICC: From the Hague to Rome and Back Again," in *The United States and the International Criminal Court*, ed. Sarah B. Sewall and Carl Kaysen. Lanham, MD: Rowman & Littlefield, pp. 31–50.

Sader, Emir. 2004. "Beyond Civil Society: The Left after Porto Alegre," in *A Movement of Movements: Is Another World Really Possible?*, ed. Tom Mertes. London: Verso, pp. 248–61.

Sahlins, Marshall D. 2000. *Culture in Practice: Selected Essays*. New York: Zone Books.

Sanadjian, Manuchehr. 2002. "The World Cup and Iranians' 'Home-Coming': A Global Game in a Local Islamicized Context," in *Islam Encountering Globalization*, ed. Ali Mohammadi. London: RoutledgeCurzon, pp. 156–77.

Scandinavian Association for Dental Research. 2004. "A Short History of the NOF," http://www.helsinki.fi/~hkl.hamm/Nof/history.htm

Schama, Simon. 2002. *A History of Britain*, vol. III: *The Fate of Empire*. New York: Miramax Books.

Schechter, Michael G. (ed.). 2001. *United Nations-sponsored World Conferences: Focus on Impact and Follow-up*. Tokyo: United Nations University Press.

Scheffer, David J. 2001–2. "Staying the Course with the International Criminal Court," *Cornell International Law Journal* 35:47–100.

Schnapper, Dominique. 1991. *La France de l'Intégration: Sociologie de la Nation en 1990*. Paris: Gallimard.

Scholte, Jan Aart. 2000. *Globalization: A Critical Introduction*. New York: St. Martin's Press.

Scruton, Roger. 2002. *The West and the Rest: Globalization and the Terrorist Threat*. Wilmington, DE: ISI Books.

Shatz, Adam. 2002. "His Really Big Show," *New York Times Magazine* (June 2).

Simmel, Georg. 1971. *On Individuality and Social Forms: Selected Writings*. Chicago, IL: University of Chicago Press.

Singh, Jyoti S. 1998. *Creating a New Consensus on Population: The International Conference on Population and Development*. London: Earthscan.

Sivan, Emmanuel. 1985. *Radical Islam: Medieval Theology and Modern Politics.* New Haven, CT: Yale University Press.

Sklair, Leslie. 1995. *Sociology of the Global System* (2nd edition). London: Prentice Hall.

Smith, Jackie. 2002. "Globalizing Resistance: The Battle of Seattle and the Future of Social Movements," in *Transnational Dimensions of Social Movements*, ed. Jackie Smith and Hank Johnston. Lanham, MD: Rowman & Littlefield, pp. 207–28.

Smith, Willoughby. 1974. *The Rise and Extension of Submarine Telegraphy.* New York: Arno Press.

Solheim, James. 2000. "Parliament of the World's Religions in South Africa Presses for Interfaith Cooperation," *Episcopal News Service* (January 13).

Stewart-Gambino, Hannah W., and Everett Wilson. 1997. "Latin American Pentecostals: Old Stereotypes and New Challenges," in *Power, Politics, and Pentecostals in Latin America*, ed. Edward L. Cleary and Hannah W. Stewart-Gambino. Boulder, CO: Westview Press, pp. 227–46.

Stiglitz, Joseph E. 2002. *Globalization and Its Discontents.* New York: W. W. Norton.

Stone, Norman. 1984. *Europe Transformed, 1878–1919.* Cambridge, MA: Harvard University Press.

SWIFT (Society for Worldwide Interbank Financial Telecommunication). 2004. La Hulpe, Belgium (http://www.swift.com/index)

Taheri, Amir. 1986. *The Spirit of Allah: Khomeini and the Islamic Revolution.* Bethesda, MD: Adler & Adler.

Taylor, Peter J. 1996. *The Way the Modern World Works: World Hegemony to World Impasse.* Chichester: Wiley.

Taylor, Peter J. 1999. *Modernities: A Geohistorical Interpretation.* Minneapolis: University of Minnesota Press.

Taylor, Timothy D. 1997. *Global Pop: World Music, World Markets.* New York: Routledge.

Tehranian, Majid. 1993. "Fundamentalist Impact on Education and the Media," in *Fundamentalisms and Society: Reclaiming the Sciences, the Family, and Education*, ed. Martin E. Marty and R. Scott Appleby. Chicago, IL: University of Chicago Press, pp. 313–40.

Tibi, Bassam. 2002. *The Challenge of Fundamentalism: Political Islam and the New World Disorder.* Berkeley, CA: University of California Press.

Tomlinson, Alan. 1996. "Olympic Spectacle: Opening Ceremonies and Some Paradoxes of Globalization," *Media, Culture & Society* 18:583–602.

Tomlinson, John. 1991. *Cultural Imperialism: A Critical Introduction.* London: Pinter Publishers.

Tomlinson, John. 1999. *Globalization and Culture.* Chicago, IL: University of Chicago Press.

Touraine, Alain. 1999. *Comment Sortir du Libéralisme?* Paris: Fayard.

Tyrrell, Heather. 1999. "Bollywood versus Hollywood: Battle of the Dream Factories," in *Culture and Global Change*, ed. Tracey Skelton and Tim Allen. London: Routledge, pp. 260–73.

UN. 1948–98. *Statistical Yearbook*. New York: United Nations.

UN. 1968. *Yearbook of the United Nations 1968*. New York: United Nations.

UN. 1972. *Yearbook of the United Nations 1972*. New York: United Nations.

UN. 1995. *The United Nations and Human Rights, 1945–1995*. New York: United Nations.

UN. 1996. *The United Nations and the Advancement of Women, 1945–1996*. New York: United Nations.

UN. 1997. *The World Conferences: Developing Priorities for the 21st Century*. New York: United Nations.

UN. 1999. "United Nations Conferences: What Have They Accomplished?" New York: United Nations (www.un.org)

UNDP. 2002. *The Arab Human Development Report 2002: Creating Opportunities for Future Generations*. New York: United Nations Development Programme.

UNDP. 2003. *The Arab Human Development Report 2003: Building a Knowledge Society*. New York: United Nations Development Programme.

UNESCO. 2000. *World Culture Report 2000*. Paris: UNESCO Publishing.

UNESCO. 2003. *Global Education Digest 2003: Comparing Education Statistics across the World*. Paris: UNESCO (http://www.uis.unesco.org/TEMPLATE/pdf/ged/GED_EN.pdf)

Union of International Associations. 2000. "Citations between International Organizations by Relationship Type (Table 3.2)," in *Yearbook of International Organizations by Relationship Type 1999/2000 Edition*. Brussels: UIA.

Union of International Associations. 2001. *Yearbook Plus, International Organizations, v. 7.0* (CD-ROM Infobase). Brussels: UIA.

Van Bottenburg, Maarten. 2001. *Global Games*. Urbana: University of Illinois Press.

Van Dijk, Rijk. 1997. "From Camp to Encompassment: Discourses of Transsubjectivity in the Ghanaian Pentecostal Diaspora," *Journal of Religion in Africa* 27:135–59.

Van Dijk, Rijk. 2001. "Time and Transcultural Technologies of the Self in the Ghanaian Pentecostal Diaspora," in *Between Babel and Pentecost: Transnational Pentecostalism in Africa and Latin America*, ed. André Corten and Ruth Marshall-Fratani. Bloomington: Indiana University Press, pp. 216–34.

Védrine, Hubert. 2001. *France in an Age of Globalization*. Washington, DC: Brookings Institution Press.

Von Weizsäcker, Ernst U. 1994. *Earth Politics*. London: Zed Books.

Wallerstein, Immanuel. 1974. *The Modern World-System: Capitalist Agriculture and the Origins of the European World-Economy in the Sixteenth Century*. New York: Academic Press.

Wallerstein, Immanuel. 1980. *The Modern World-System II: Mercantilism and the Consolidation of the European World-Economy, 1600–1750*. New York: Academic Press.

Wallerstein, Immanuel. 1991a. "The National and the Universal: Can There Be Such a Thing as World Culture?" in *Culture, Globalization and the World-System*, ed. Anthony D. King. Binghamton: State University of New York.

Wallerstein, Immanuel. 1991b. *Geopolitics and Geoculture: Essays on the Changing World-System*. Cambridge: Cambridge University Press.

Wallerstein, Immanuel. 1995. *After Liberalism*. New York: New Press.

Wallerstein, Immanuel. 1998a. *Utopistics, or, Historical Choices of the Twenty-First Century*. New York: New Press.

Wallerstein, Immanuel. 1998b. *Historical Capitalism with Capitalist Civilization*. London: Verso.

Wallerstein, Immanuel. 2000. "Where Should Sociologists Be Heading?" *Contemporary Sociology* 29:306–8.

Wallerstein, Immanuel. 2001. "Davos vs. Porto Alegre: The World Soccer Cup?" Binghamton, NY: Fernand Braudel Center.

Wallerstein, Immanuel. 2004. "New Revolts Against the System," in *A Movement of Movements: Is Another World Really Possible?*, ed. Tom Mertes. London: Verso, pp. 262–73.

Waltz, Kenneth N. 1979. *Theory of International Politics*. New York: McGraw-Hill.

Watson, James L. 1997. "McDonald's in Hong Kong: Consumerism, Dietary Change, and the Rise of a Children's Culture," in *Golden Arches East: McDonald's in East Asia*, ed. James L. Watson. Stanford, CA: Stanford University Press, pp. 77–109.

Weber, Eugen. 1976. *Peasants into Frenchmen: The Modernization of Rural France, 1870–1914*. Stanford, CA: Stanford University Press.

Wendt, Alexander. 1999. *Social Theory of International Politics*. Cambridge: Cambridge University Press.

Weschler, Lawrence. 2000. "Exceptional Cases in Rome: The United States and the Struggle for an ICC," in *The United States and the International Criminal Court*, ed. Sarah B. Sewall and Carl Kaysen. Lanham, MD: Rowman & Littlefield, pp. 85–113.

Westney, D. Eleanor. 1987. *Imitation and Innovation: The Transfer of Western Organizational Patterns to Meiji Japan*. Cambridge, MA: Harvard University Press.

Wills, John E. 2001. *1688: A Global History*. New York: W. W. Norton.

World, Bank. 2002. *World Development Indicators 2002*. Washington, DC: World Bank.

WSF (World Social Forum). 2001a. "Porto Alegre Call for Mobilisation," Porto Alegre: World Social Forum.

WSF. 2001b. "World Social Forum Charter of Principles," São Paolo: World Social Forum (http://www.forumsocialmundial.org.br/main.asp?id_menu=4&cd_language=2)

Wuthnow, Robert. 1987. *Meaning and Moral Order: Explorations in Cultural Analysis*. Berkeley, CA: University of California Press.

Yergin, Daniel, and Joseph Stanislaw. 1998. *The Commanding Heights: The Battle between Government and the Marketplace that is Remaking the Modern World.* New York: Simon & Schuster.

Young, Oran R. 1994. *International Governance: Protecting the Environment in a Stateless Society.* Ithaca, NY: Cornell University Press.

Zoavi, Fawzia. 2001. "Synthèse des Rapports et des Contributions," Agence Intergouvernementale de la Francophonie.

Index